THE GOOD CALORIE DIET

THE GOOD CALORIE DIET

THE REVOLUTIONARY NEW
DIET PROGRAM BASED ON
INHIBITING FAT FORMATION

PHILIP LIPETZ, Ph.D.

HarperCollins*Publishers*

Author's Note

The Good Calorie Diet, like any diet or health program, should be followed only after consulting with your own physician. While my own research has led me to conclude that following the Good Calorie Diet will inhibit fat formation and create a state of metabolic normalcy that will result in weight loss, each person is different, and decisions affecting your health should be made by you and your personal physician or other health professional. You may want to share the information in this book with your doctor so that the two of you can determine the best and safest diet for you to follow. In particular, if you suffer from diabetes, hypoglycemia, gall bladder, liver, kidney, digestive or other chronic disease, you should not follow the Good Calorie Diet under any circumstances other than a doctor's close supervision.

Cathy cartoons on pages viii, 2, 4, 5, 6, 12, 22, 23, 27, 31, 51, 64, 75, 81, 82, 119, 161, and 191 copyright by Cathy Guisewite. Reprinted with permission of Universal Press Syndicate. All rights reserved.

HarperCollins books may be purchased for educational, business, or sales promotional use. For information please write: Special Markets Department, HarperCollins Publishers, Inc., 10 East 53rd Street, New York, NY 10022.

FIRST EDITION

Designed by Nancy Singer

Library of Congress Cataloging-in-Publication Data

Lipetz, Philip.
    The good calorie diet / Philip Lipetz.
       p.   cm.
    Includes index.
    ISBN 0-06-017112-X
    1. Reducing diets.   I. Title.
    RM222.2.L534   1994   93-44202
    613.2'5—dc20

94 95 96 97 98 PS/RRD 10 9 8 7 6 5 4 3 2 1

CONTENTS

ACKNOWLEDGMENTS   vii

CHAPTER ONE
GOOD CALORIES LOWER FAT FORMATION   1

CHAPTER TWO
THE STARVATION RESPONSE CREATES EXCESS FAT   11

CHAPTER THREE
AVOIDING THE PROBLEMS OF THE MODERN DIET   26

CHAPTER FOUR
GOOD AND BAD CALORIES   45

CHAPTER FIVE
HOW TO USE GOOD CALORIES   58

CHAPTER SIX
WHAT TO DO IF YOU DO NOT LOSE WEIGHT   80

CHAPTER SEVEN
THE GOOD CALORIE SOLUTION   88

INTRODUCTION TO THE APPENDIXES   99

Contents

APPENDIX A
SAMPLE DAILY MENUS   101

APPENDIX B
GOOD CALORIE RECIPES   118

APPENDIX C
EATING IN RESTAURANTS   160

APPENDIX D
GLYCEMIC INDEXES OF COMMON FOODS   185

APPENDIXES 1–30
GOOD AND BAD CALORIES BY CATEGORY   191

1 Bakery Items   16 Meat, Luncheon
2 Beverages   17 Meat Substitutes
3 Cereals   18 Nuts
4 Chili   19 Pasta and Pasta Sauces
5 Condiments   20 Pasta, Frozen
6 Dairy Products   21 Pizza, Frozen
7 Dinners, Frozen   22 Poultry
8 Entrées, Canned   23 Rice Dishes
9 Entrées, Frozen and   24 Rice Dishes, Frozen
   Refrigerated   25 Snacks
10 Fish   26 Soups, Canned
11 Fruit, Fresh   27 Sugars
12 Fruit, Canned   28 Vegetables, Fresh
13 Fruit, Frozen   29 Vegetables, Canned
14 Legumes   30 Vegetables, Frozen
15 Meat

SOURCE NOTES   235
INDEX   241
THE GOOD CALORIE DIET: AN OVERVIEW

ACKNOWLEDGMENTS

I would like to thank the teachers who made this book possible: Ellis D. Lutz, high school literature; Mr. Calvin, high school chemistry; Nolan Miller, college creative writing; and Ronald Hart and Karl Kornacker, graduate studies in science. All too often we ignore these people who shape our lives.

My daughter, Rebekah Devi Lipetz, helped compile the lists of Good and Bad Calories. She said that it would be one of the thrills of her young life if she could see her name in print. I just wish I had a quarter of her writing talent.

Dorothea Lipetz, my mother, helped with the daily menus. There is something pleasing about involving three generations of a family in a single project.

Larry Ashmead and Charlotte Abbott at HarperCollins furnished invaluable help in shaping this project. They missed many dinners so this book could move forward on an accelerated schedule. It was the enthusiasm they shared with Lynn Franklin, my super agent, that made it all possible. I also would like to thank Adrienne Bosworth and Sheela Tarbi for their editorial assistance, Barbara Miller for her library research assistance and generalized support, and Linda Jardine for the recipes.

Everyone who helped is a great teacher. Thank you all.

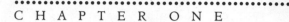

GOOD CALORIES LOWER FAT FORMATION

MY PROMISE TO YOU

...

If there is one thing that the world has in abundance, it is diet plans. The Good Calorie Diet is *not* a diet plan. It is a program that allows you to reshape your body while enjoying full meals; pounds disappear once you're on it because you stop making the new fat it takes to maintain your weight. Therefore, you can eat fully and still lose weight. Isn't such a program better than a restrictive diet that starves or exercises you into submission?

To understand how the Good Calorie Diet works, you have to recognize

that our bodies constantly make new fat and constantly burn old fat. *The balance between these two processes determines our weight.*

Thus, there are two ways to lose weight: burn more fat or make less fat. Of these two approaches, lowering the level of fat created produces much better results. Overweight people may burn 30 or 40 percent less fat than may thin people, but, in extreme cases, they may also *create* three or four times more fat from the same quantity of certain foods. So why do conventional diets attack the lesser problem?

The Good Calorie Diet works by overcoming a metabolic condition called the Starvation Response, which stimulates the creation of fat. Even though you may eat only 1,000 calories a day, the Starvation Response makes you create the same fat as a "thin" person does after eating 3,000 or 4,000 calories. Thus, the problem is not that you eat too much, but that you *make too much fat from what you do eat.*

Once you subdue the Starvation Response and fat-creation returns to normal, weight loss occurs painlessly, without hunger or excessive exercise. Normal quantities of food will produce the low level of fat formation you may have previously achieved only with starvation diets. Without the burden of excessive fat formation, "resting" levels of fat burning are enough to stimulate weight loss. Caloric restriction and excessive exercise are no longer needed. Your body will behave as though you were eating less even though you consume normal portions. The only thing that changes is that you make less fat.

Many modern foods and food combinations can evoke the Starvation Response in those people who are genetically susceptible to it. Fortunately, there are also some foods that inhibit the fat-creation and thereby overcome the Starvation Response. I call these miracle foods "Good Calories." The Good Calorie Diet is as simple as eating Good Calories and avoiding the "Bad Calorie" foods and food combinations that create excess fat.

The weight-loss portion of the Good Calorie Diet offers so few restrictions that some people have trouble believing that something so painless can be so powerful. We all feel pretty awful on conventional diets. They make us irritable, grumpy, and hungry. The reason for such discomfort is that those diets make the Starvation Response grow strong enough to alter our brain biochemistry, producing the food cravings that can trigger eating binges.

In contrast, you feel good on the Good Calorie Diet because your brain biochemistry returns to normal, and you'll no longer be irritable because of hunger or cravings. You eat less because you have less of an appetite.

Conventional diets do nothing to overcome the Starvation Response. Even after you lose weight, you still form excess fat, so the moment you resume your normal eating patterns, you regain every pound of lost weight. *More than 95 percent of dieters regain every pound.*

The dieters of the world should rise up in anger against ineffective diets that ignore the Starvation Response. Instead, dieters blame themselves. They say that their metabolisms burn less fat and that they are the exceptions to the rules of calorie counting. These dieters, and their metabolisms, are *not* exceptions to the rules. Instead, they form the overwhelming majority that proves a new rule: *The problem is not that you burn too little fat, but that you make too much fat.* You cannot permanently lose weight until you deal with this reality.

So, after the Starvation Response subsides, how fast will you lose weight? I lost over two pounds a week. Some of my friends lost less than a pound during some weeks. Still others lost four or five pounds during a week. The

more overweight you are, the more quickly you'll lose weight on the Good Calorie Diet. Losing twenty or thirty pounds can be simple.

I promise.

CONVENTIONAL DIETS FAIL ME
···

As long as you follow conventional diet programs, it is not your fault that you remain overweight. I know because I was fat, and it wasn't because I was lazy. I counted calories until I had a constant ache in my belly—and my head. I joined the Columbus World Gym and pumped iron three days a week.

Even though I worked hard, it was a flabby body that sweated with effort. Whenever I looked at my jelly belly, I felt the horrible disappointment that comes from dieting without success. I even tried liposuction. Nothing worked.

If anyone should have known how to lose weight, it should have been me. I had been an assistant professor at The Ohio State University School of Medicine. I had coauthored several scientific books and dozens of articles

4

and certainly had a sound medical background. The national press had spotlighted my work as a biotechnologist and entrepreneur. Yet, I still could not lose weight.

Even though I carried only forty extra pounds, fellow scientists would comment on my weight and offer helpful suggestions. Although they meant well, this barrage of constant advice simply made me feel fatter and more inadequate.

Just as a drowning person grabs at anything that floats, I leaped at every possible clue to achieving weight loss. When anyone I knew went on a diet, I closely followed his or her progress, or lack of it.

Many championship bodybuilders—people who seemed to have perfect bodies—went to my gym. I wondered if they had the answer to my problem. After all, championship bodybuilders have less than 10 percent body fat, compared to the typical American man with over 30 percent body fat.

Since bodybuilders carefully note the caloric content of every morsel that passes between their lips, they seemed to be the perfect group to study, since they would quickly note the effect of any change in diet. I expected to watch them and find a simple solution, though that was not to be.

It turned out that there was no relationship between caloric intake and the amount of weight they lost. Some bodybuilders ate only 600 calories a day and could not lose the last bit of fat. Other bodybuilders ate 3,000 to 4,000 calories a day and had bodies without an ounce of extra fat. All these people exercised for four to six hours per day. All were in good health. What accounted for the difference in their loss of fat?

CARBOHYDRATES VARY IN FAT-FORMING ABILITY

•••

When I analyzed what these bodybuilders ate, it became apparent that carbohydrates were responsible for the greatest disparities: Some carbohydrates allow weight loss and others create fat. I had trouble accepting this observation, since I, too, was raised on the myth that weight loss is automatic as long as you eat fewer calories than you burn and that all calories are equal.

It took a while before I realized the flaw in this reasoning. A calorie measures the heat released when food is "digested" in test tubes, not in people. The originators of the caloric theory of dieting assumed that our bodies use every bit of excess calories to make fat. However, scientists now know that different foods convert different percentages of calories into fat. Even when the limitations of calorie counting became obvious, nobody paid attention. The calorie theory was already the basis of a growing industry, one that ignored the Starvation Response and the realities of Good and Bad Calories.

Clearly, I had seen things that contradicted conventional diet theory. My bookshelves contained dozens of diet books, but none of these books could tell me why there was such a difference in the fat-forming potential of different carbohydrates.

From my days as a medical researcher, I knew that carbohydrates become blood sugar as they enter the bloodstream. In overweight people— and only in them—excess blood sugar becomes fat.[1] This means that a food that creates a lot of blood sugar will produce more fat in overweight people than it will in thin people.

Conventional diets say nothing about this fact. One of the central tenets of calorie counting is that one calorie of one food creates the same amount of fat as does one calorie of another food. I saw something different. I saw that the fat-forming ability of carbohydrates can vary even when they have the same caloric content.

Excited by this new understanding, I returned to The Ohio State University School of Medicine and used the school's computers to search over a million scientific articles. The data I found amazed me and taught me the diet lesson of my life: The best way for overweight people to lose weight is to inhibit the formation of fat by eating the proper foods.

Hallelujah!

THE GLYCEMIC INDEX
•••

So how do you figure out what foods are Good Calories and create less fat? Obviously, you have to know how much blood sugar is created by each food.

Physicians use the word *glycemic* whenever they talk about anything to do with blood sugar. When people have too much blood sugar, they are hyperglycemic. When they have too little blood sugar, they are hypoglycemic. When physicians measure the amount of blood sugar a food induces, they use the glycemic index.

A high number on the glycemic index means that a food creates more blood sugar, whereas a low number means that it causes only a small rise in blood sugar. A food with a glycemic index of 96 (such as ripe bananas) will create almost twice the blood sugar as a food with a glycemic index of 50 (say, protein-enriched spaghetti). Hence, eating two portions of spaghetti creates the same amount of blood sugar as does eating one portion of ripe bananas. Therefore, eating low glycemic-index foods allows us to eat fully while maintaining a low level of fat formation.

Hundreds of scientific reports support the notion that eating low glycemic-index foods results in weight loss. Almost none of these reports is on weight loss, but they all are still relevant. Almost every report indicates that altering the glycemic index of foods changes some part of the fat-forming metabolism.

Scientists have published the glycemic indexes of fewer than 200 foods (see Appendix D), representing a wide spectrum of common carbohydrates. Although this may seem a small number, its impact has been revolutionary.

There can be more than a sixfold difference between high- and low glycemic-index foods (see Figure 1–1). Why is this difference important for people who suffer from the Starvation Response? High glycemic-index foods plunge you deeper into the Starvation Response and thus make you grow fatter and make it impossible for you to lose weight permanently.

One look at Figure 1–1 told me why I was fat. I had been dieting with two meals of low-calorie rice cakes, baked potatoes, unbuttered bread, followed by a low-fat dinner. I would have lost more weight with meals of common table sugar. The rice cakes created twice the blood sugar, calorie for calorie, as would table sugar, and the unbuttered potato created one-third more blood sugar. I could have eaten 3,000 calories of lentils, plums, grapes, or soybeans and made less fat than I would have if I'd eaten 1,000 calories of French bread and rice cakes.

I found it difficult to believe these results, yet I saw them in study after study. Foods with both a low glycemic index and a low-to-moderate fat content represent the pot of gold at the end of the rainbow. With these foods, we can eat thousands of calories and still lose weight, by making less fat.

FIGURE 1–1

Glycemic Index of Common Foods
(Smaller Is Better)

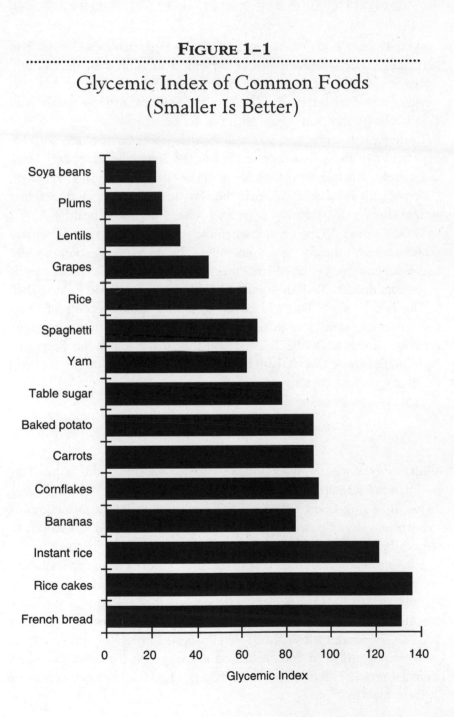

GOOD CALORIES AND BAD CALORIES

···

I gave the name Good Calories to these miracle foods that create less fat. Not surprisingly, foods that are high in fat-forming ability are called Bad Calories.

Forget about the caloric value of the food; all you have to know is whether a food is composed of Good or Bad Calories. You lose weight with Good Calories and gain weight with Bad Calories.

In the next few chapters you will see that Good Calories are not only beneficial diet foods, but they also defeat the Starvation Response. Thus, one simple principle is the foundation of the Good Calorie Diet: Eat Good Calories until you safely overcome the Starvation Response and then lose weight effortlessly because you live in a state of improved health.

Good Calories do their magic when they are combined with a program that removes the dietary signals that induce the Starvation Response. There are also special tricks that enhance the medicinal value of Good Calories. It is the combination of all these elements that forms the Good Calorie Diet.

The Good Calorie Diet allows you to eat an endless variety of Good Calorie foods, while recognizing that it is only human nature to enjoy forbidden foods occasionally. After you thwart the Starvation Response, Bad Calories create less fat than they otherwise would, so you can eat them every day without creating excess fat.

IT WORKED FOR ME

···

With Good Calories as my foundation, I put aside all my calorie books. I ate as much as I wanted to and still lost weight.

Just by eating Good Calories, I lowered my level of fat formation. At every meal I would push away a plate still loaded with food. It was easy to stop eating. I was full and could not eat any more.

I was no fanatic. I learned how to eat Good Calories in such a way that I could safely enjoy the occasional junk-food treat.

Even though my clothes seemed to be much looser, I refused to believe that I was losing weight. As a fat person, I associated weight loss with pain and hunger. Since I felt neither, I never weighed myself.

When my girlfriend commented on my sexy new look, I immediately weighed myself, and the results amazed me. I had lost twenty-five pounds in three months.

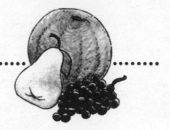

CHAPTER TWO

THE STARVATION RESPONSE CREATES EXCESS FAT

DO YOU SUFFER FROM THE STARVATION RESPONSE?

•••

Obviously, you suffer from the Starvation Response if you gain weight easily and regain it even more easily after dieting. There are several other specific symptoms. All of them stem from the way the Starvation Response alters your brain biochemistry so that you eat too many of the wrong foods and then make too much fat from them. Not all sufferers show the same symptoms. For example, I experienced only three or four of these symptoms.

Symptoms of the Starvation Response

1. Regular overeating.
2. Eating rapidly.
3. Difficulty knowing when one's stomach is full.
4. Strong or persistent hunger.
5. Craving high-fat or high-sugar food.
6. Occasional binge eating.
7. Snacking at night.
8. Gaining weight on less food.
9. Regaining weight easily.
10. Gaining weight after a pregnancy or while taking either birth control or estrogen-replacement pills.

1. The Starvation Response makes us overeat regularly. Ravenous hunger guarantees that our bodies will stockpile enough blood sugar to create excess fat.

2. The Starvation Response makes us eat rapidly. We all have seen hungry people wolf down a meal. That's the Starvation Response at work. Even though our minds know that our refrigerator is full of food and the grocery store is open all night, our bodies act as though this may be our last meal. It takes a while—generally about twenty minutes—before our brains realize that our stomachs are full. By eating rapidly, we consume extra food before we lose our ravenous hunger.

3. The Starvation Response prevents us from knowing when our stomachs are full. Two different hormones signal when our stomachs are full. However, the Starvation Response makes our brain ignore one of the hormones while it prevents the other from being released. The result is predictable. We don't feel full, so there is no way that we can stop eating before we overeat.

4. The Starvation Response makes us experience strong hunger. Ordinarily, a neurotransmitter in our brain controls hunger. For sufferers of the Starvation Response, that vital chemical is altered. The result is an appetite that leads to obesity.

5. The Starvation Response makes us crave fattening foods. Next to obesity, the symptom most commonly shared by victims of the Starvation Response is a craving for fat and sugar. Ice cream and potato chips. Cookies and colas. The problem is that the same neurotransmitter that controls our appetite also determines our cravings. If we make less of that neuro-transmitter, there is no escape from the craving for fattening foods because our brain automatically enters into a program that makes fattening foods taste good.

6. The Starvation Response makes us go on eating binges. Once our brain loses control of our eating habits, there is nothing to stop us from overindulging. We eat more of the wrong foods without being aware that we are eating to excess.

7. The Starvation Response makes us eat late at night, when our bodies create extra fat. How about that great American Tradition—to sit in front of the television set and snack the night away? Late-night hunger is a sure sign that blood sugar is out of control. The Starvation Response can cause blood-sugar levels to be so low at night that there is nothing to feed our bodies. The only thing we can do is to eat an additional meal.

8. The Starvation Response makes us create more fat from what we do eat. The Starvation Response changes our body's biochemistry, so even if we eat only a small amount of food, we create more fat than would a normal person who was eating larger portions of food.

9. The Starvation Response makes us regain weight after dieting. Ordinarily, we burn or excrete excess fat rather than store it in fat cells. Now, fat moves directly into fat cells.

10. The hormonal flows within women make it harder for them to lose weight. Everyone knows that it is easier for women to gain weight and harder for them to lose it. A woman's natural hormones can unleash the Starvation Response, creating these problems after pregnancy or after taking medications that contain estrogen.

THE GENETIC PROGRAM
THAT CREATES FAT
...

To understand why we carry the genetic program that readily creates excess fat, we have to go back in time to when our ancestors first evolved the Starvation Response.

Once, humans were rarely fat. Before the rise of the Starvation Response, the people who evolved to become modern humans lived in peace with their bodies. They ate what they found: roots, berries, vegetables and carrion. The earth was abundant. It was the world humans evolved to enjoy.

Our ancestors didn't worry about dieting or counting calories. They digested food into blood sugar and used it for short-term energy. Since food was plentiful, their bodies had more blood sugar than was needed, so they evolved hormones to keep their blood sugar low.

Then great sheets of ice descended from the polar regions of the planet.

The plants that fed our ancestors vanished, along with easy days of eating food as they gathered it. The only way to eat was to hunt, and it could be days or weeks between kills. As a result, our ancestors evolved ways to maximize the conversion of excess blood sugar into stored energy in the form of body fat. Camels can live for months by digesting the fat stored in their humps. Hibernating bears live off fat during their winter sleep. Our fat can feed us for weeks and weeks. In the ice ages, it saved our ancestors' lives. Whenever they starved, they lived off stored fat.

Today our bodies still behave this way. When food intake is low, everything takes second place to the creation of fat from excess blood sugar. Having enough energy to live until the next meal is all that matters.

These ancient patterns cause the yo-yo cycle of dieting. We temporarily lose weight while we starve ourselves, but the moment we return to normal eating, we become fatter than we were before we started to diet. The reason we create extra fat is simple: Caloric restriction resembles starvation and evokes the Starvation Response.

This is a radically new viewpoint about the origin of obesity. The conventional explanation is that obesity is a direct result of overeating. I believe that obesity has more in common with something completely opposite—starvation.

My theory makes sense if you consider one question: When does the body most need to store excess food energy for later use—when one is eating too much food or when one faces starvation?

FATTENING FOODS AND STARVATION HAVE THE SAME EFFECT

...

Jack was a recent immigrant from Russia. Under the Communist regime, he was a dissident and lived under house arrest. He ate only what neighbors brought him. When he arrived in the United States, he was thirty or forty pounds underweight. However, within a year, he had gained so much weight that he was thirty pounds overweight. He asked me to help him lose weight.

I analyzed his food intake and found that he was eating about 2,000 calories per day, three-quarters of which were from beef. He said that such meat was unknown in Russia, so he wanted to enjoy as much of it now as he could. Although 2,000 calories a day is not a weight-loss diet, it certainly could not account for the amount of weight he gained. Somehow his previous experience with prolonged starvation had altered his body, so he made abnormal amounts of fat from a relatively normal diet.

I asked Jack what sort of food he ate when he was in Russia. When he said that he ate potatoes, beets, cabbage, rye bread, beans, and very little meat, I was intrigued because his new way of eating was a classic case of evoking the Starvation Response by experiencing the excess of the modern diet. So, I suggested that he return to his old diet of carbohydrates, but not at the old starvation levels. Instead, he should continue to eat 2,000 calories a day.

He lost weight on the carbohydrate diet, which proved that the caloric content of his food was irrelevant. It was clear that his previous starvation had changed his response to foods, but how? Why did he continue to make excess fat and gain weight with meat but not with carbohydrates?

The answer to these questions was first discovered in 1927, by Dr. J. Shirley Sweeney, who fed different diets to healthy medical students (see Figure 2-1).[1] One diet was high in saturated fats, one was high in protein, and one was high in carbohydrates. The caloric content of all three diets was the same. Another group of students starved themselves. Each student followed a special diet for two days and then drank a glass of glucose. Physicians then compared the students' blood-sugar levels to see if the students' previous meals, or a starvation diet, changed their reaction.

Sweeney found that two days of starvation induces four times more blood sugar in a future meal than does a carbohydrate diet, a fatty diet creates almost as much blood sugar, and a protein diet causes a threefold increase. Later studies confirmed Sweeney's discovery.[2]

Sweeney's results explain why Americans are overweight even though they may not experience starvation. The classic American meals, which are high in protein and fat, mimic the long-term consequences of starvation by pushing the body to create extra fat from all subsequent meals.

Why do fat and protein induce the same response as starvation? To answer this question, we have to go back to the time when our ancestors switched from food gathering to hunting.

Our ancestors ate flesh meat and fat only when starvation forced them to deviate from their normal vegetable- and fruit-eating patterns. It was simply too difficult to hunt with the primitive weapons available in those

16

FIGURE 2-1

Blood Sugar After Different Diets
(Smaller Is Better)

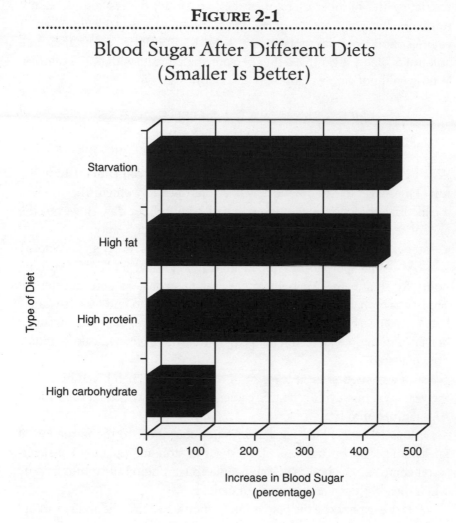

times, and there were days or weeks between kills. Our ancestors' bodies adapted to conditions during which days or weeks of hunger always followed meals of meat and fat. Deep within our DNA is the genetic memory of these times. In some people, this memory still actively drives their behavior. Even today, the bodies of susceptible people respond to meat, fat, and high blood sugar by gearing up for the starvation that may follow, by making more fat.

This starvation response is also why caloric-restriction diets fail. After restricting the number of calories they consume, dieters resume eating normally, but they are doomed. Even eating a reasonable number of calories, 1,500 per day, is fattening if the 1,500 calories create the same amount of blood sugar that a thin person would create with 6,000 calories. Who would not gain weight on 6,000 calories a day?

CREATING FAT FROM EXCESS BLOOD SUGAR

...

When I was in college, I dated a woman who I shall call Laura. Laura was full of fire, eager to explore the new horizons open to women. She also had a chocolate addiction and ate nearly half a pound per day. However, the chocolate never affected her weight. Laura was a slim beauty.

After graduation, we went our separate ways. It was nearly a year before I saw her again. She had developed high blood sugar and was returning home for treatment. We both knew that her constant consumption of candy was probably the cause. What I did not expect to find was that Laura had gained nearly thirty pounds. When she lost control of her blood sugar, her fat forming metabolism changed, so that her excessive caloric intake now mattered.

Laura was my first great love, and I have always remembered her. Over the years, as I pursued a scientific career, I wondered why her excess blood sugar turned into fat.

Ordinarily, excess blood sugar does not contribute to the formation of fat.[3] Lean people burn excess blood sugar or store it as glycogen, a sugar-water complex. The bodies of lean people convert blood sugar into fat only when their glycogen stores are saturated.[4]

When we experience the Starvation Response, we lose the ability to store or burn excess blood sugar.[5] Blood sugar cannot be stored as glycogen because the enzyme needed to convert blood sugar into glycogen is 50 percent to 85 percent less active.[6] Furthermore, we create so much more blood sugar that we would exceed the capacity of our glycogen stores even if that pathway was fully active.

The resulting excess blood sugar becomes fat.[7] People who suffer from the Starvation Response convert up to three to four times *more* blood sugar to triglyceride fats (the fats that pass into fat cells), creating more permanent body weight than do thin people.[8]

In 1988 a group of Swiss researchers deliberately induced the Starvation Response in their subjects with a four-day high-fat diet and then induced excess blood sugar by feeding the subjects a high carbohydrate diet.[9] Their experiment (see Figure 2-2) shows that people who experience the Starvation Response have a vastly increased capacity to convert excess blood sugar into fat. After the high carbohydrate diet, the subjects exhibited more than a tenfold increase in triglyceride fats.

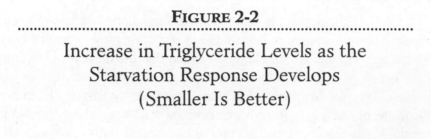

FIGURE 2-2

Increase in Triglyceride Levels as the Starvation Response Develops (Smaller Is Better)

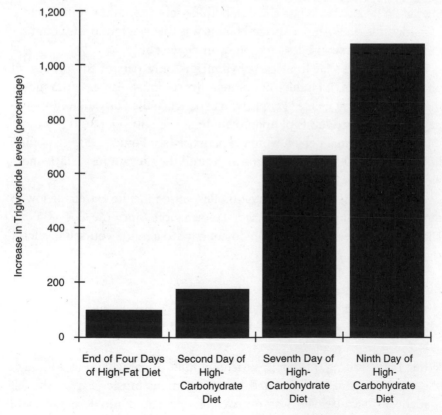

This is why you must avoid the Starvation Response: It makes you create more fat from carbohydrates, as happened to Laura. When Laura began to suffer from the Starvation Response, excessive consumption of chocolate caused her body to create more fat.

PUTTING FAT INTO FAT CELLS

•••

Ann lost over thirty pounds using conventional caloric restriction. Then, she ate a meager amount of food and exercised constantly to maintain her weight loss. Despite all this effort, she found that the only way she could keep her ideal weight was by eating a diet that was extremely low in fat.

I told Ann that her dieting had altered her body, so that any fat in her bloodstream was moved directly into permanent fat stores. I suggested that she go on the Good Calorie Diet, not to lose weight but to overcome the Starvation Response. When she did, both her cravings and her intolerance of fat disappeared. An unexpected bonus was that she found she could eat more food and exercise less without gaining weight.

Creating excess fat from carbohydrates is only part of the process of obesity. Enzymes, including lipoprotein lipase, must also ease the movement of fat into fat cells.[10] People who experience the Starvation Response have supercharged levels of lipoprotein lipase activity—up to thirty times more than a normal person would experience (see Figure 2-3),[11] and their lipoprotein lipase activity remains high until they regain just a little more weight than they lost.[12]

Any diet that ignores the Starvation Response must be extremely low in dietary fat to compensate for excess fat formation. Since the Good Calorie Diet thwarts these problems, you do not have to confine yourself to such a rigorous regime. Moderate fat is fine.

MAKING US EAT MORE

•••

While I was writing this book, a friend of mine approached me. Although she is a successful musician and directs a famous music festival, she felt inadequate because she was overweight and could not lose the extra

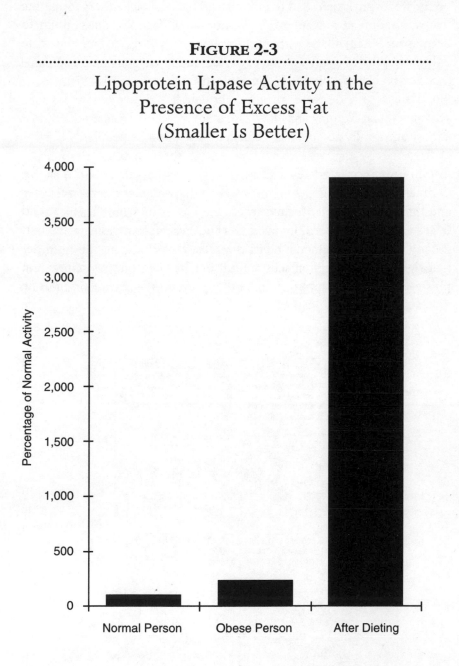

FIGURE 2-3

Lipoprotein Lipase Activity in the Presence of Excess Fat (Smaller Is Better)

pounds. Her physicians and friends all said that she lacked willpower, but that was not my impression of this wonderful woman. No one could have been as successful as she without discipline.

I told her that she was a victim of the Starvation Response and explained that her body was selectively ignoring insulin's normal ability to lower blood sugar and decrease appetite, though it did not ignore insulin's activation of fat-forming enzymes. This state, known as *insulin resistance*, is almost universally accepted as a characteristic of obese people.[13]

Triggered by the *same things* that evoke the Starvation Response,[14] insulin resistance interferes with three of the systems that control eating. Ordinarily, eating produces an insulin rush that enters the nervous system and limits our appetite. Insulin resistance makes us ignore this signal.[15] Instead, high levels of insulin make fats and sweets seem more desirable.[16] Second, insulin resistance inhibits the release of glucagon, the hormone that signals when our stomachs are full.[17] Finally, insulin resistance suppresses serotonin, a neurotransmitter that prevents the craving of carbohydrates and excessive appetites.[18]

As I told my friend, you can stop feeling guilty about your inability to control your appetite. You are a good person with sufficient willpower. You eat the wrong foods, and more of them, because you suffer from the Starvation Response.

THE STARVATION RESPONSE AND WOMEN
•••

Since the nutrients that enter a woman's body can be diverted to support her fetus or nursing child, women have evolved the equivalent of periods of starvation that can induce the Starvation Response. Women carry this program even if they are not pregnant.

The signal that induces this type of Starvation Response appears to be related to estrogen, a sex hormone. When extra levels of estrogen are present, a woman's fat cells become enlarged. It is the estrogen released during adolescence that causes women to accumulate fat on their hips and thighs.

When women take birth control pills or estrogen-replacement pills for menopause, they may trigger the Starvation Response. If they cannot lose weight, then they should consult a physician about the possibility of lowering their dosage of estrogen.

For women, consuming animal fats can be extra fat-forming because these Bad Calories increase the production of estrogen.[19]

Despite these problems, women need not assume that they cannot lose weight just because they are female. No matter what the inducing factor, the Good Calorie Diet treats the ultimate problem—the Starvation Response.

THE STARVATION RESPONSE IS A COLLECTION OF MANY DIFFERENT CONDITIONS
...

I will conclude this chapter by emphasizing that the Starvation Response is made up of a wide variety of metabolic variations that all cause the formation of excessive fat. These differences arose because each racial group evolved its own solution to the problem of creating excess fat. Any of the following can result in the increased formation of fat:

1. high blood sugar
2. high insulin levels
3. high triglyceride levels
4. high lipid levels
5. high lipoprotein lipase levels
6. impaired fat burning
7. insulin resistance
8. decreased excretion of fat
9. variations in female hormones
10. other enzyme functions

Clearly, this is an open-ended description of a wide variety of clinical symptoms. That is why the Good Calorie Diet includes a program of controlled experimentation that allows you to tailor a program for yourself that overcomes your version of the Starvation Response. Such a program guarantees that each person will enjoy the freedom to choose foods and to achieve the maximum results.

I should mention that thin people can also suffer from the Starvation Response, remaining thin until the wrong diet exposes them to high amounts of fat or protein or the restriction of calories.[20] Thus, the Starvation Response can be a hidden time bomb, waiting for the wrong diet to detonate it.

That was my experience. I had always thought of myself as a person who could eat without worrying about gaining weight. I always ate second and third helpings and yet maintained a constant weight in the low 180s. Then I got divorced and wanted to look more attractive as I began to develop a new social life. When I was about to go snorkeling in Florida, I went on a high protein–low carbohydrate diet and lost five or six pounds. Within the next two months, I gained fifteen pounds. Within a year, I had ballooned to nearly 216 pounds. Clearly, my diet had unleashed the Starvation Response.

CHAPTER THREE

AVOIDING THE PROBLEMS OF THE MODERN DIET

MODERN FOODS EVOKE THE STARVATION RESPONSE

•••

Think of the irony. We live in a land of plenty and eat foods whose richness and sweetness would have dazzled ancient kings. Yet, in the midst of all this abundance, our bodies can behave as though we face starvation.

The problem is simple. We eat an abundance of high-energy foods that resemble the foods our ancestors ate when starvation forced them to hunt.

Following genetically programmed patterns of survival, our bodies interpret this diet to mean that we face starvation. So our bodies make extra blood sugar and convert that food energy into fat.

Not only do we eat more Bad Calories now, but the modern diet is low in the Good Calories that can prevent the Starvation Response. In 1860 Good

Calories accounted for over half the food we Americans ate (see Figure 3-1). In the 1920s they made up just under 40 percent of our diet. Twenty years ago, they constituted no more than one quarter of our diet. Who knows what today's figure is?

If we understand what elements of the modern diet evoke or perpetuate the Starvation Response, we can then take the first step toward curing it. Just by avoiding a few foods and food combinations, we can decrease our formation of fat. We will still eat fully. There will be no difference in our caloric intake.

FIGURE 3-1

Decreasing Amount of Calories from Good Calorie Carbohydrates in the American Diet

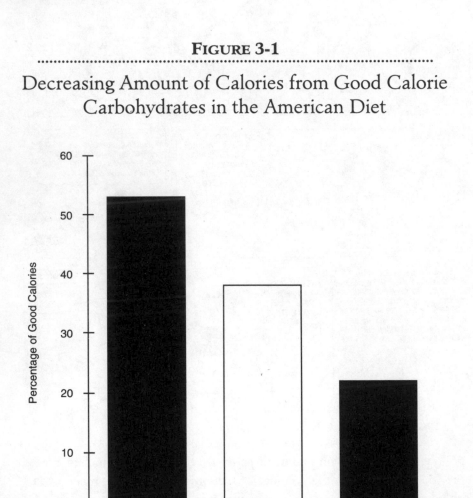

Foods that induce the Starvation Response all have one thing in common: None was part of our ancestors' normal diet. So why are we surprised that our bodies panic when they are exposed to foods that signal the absence of "normal foods"?

This understanding means that we must adopt a new mind-set when we use the Good Calorie Diet. A conventional diet allows us to eat any low-fat food, but in lesser amounts than we otherwise might. The Good Calorie Diet says we are better off choosing the proper foods and then eating as much of them as we want.

So which is more restrictive: starving on an infinite variety of foods or eating as much as we want of the proper foods? I prefer that my stomach is full and that my body is disease free. My mind no longer misses unhealthy foods or combinations of foods; instead it looks on them as a form of poison that I have finally learned to avoid. How can I miss eating something that made me grow fat?

AN EASY WAY TO LOSE WEIGHT
...

"I'm a good friend of yours, why won't you give me a copy of your manuscript?"

I heard this request constantly while writing this book, and it always presented me with a dilemma. Should I give out only a portion of the manuscript or make my friends wait for the entire book? One friend, Marianne, was twenty pounds overweight and was going on a vacation, where she intended to meet the man of her dreams. She didn't care that I had written only a few chapters. She believed she could make herself more attractive if only I would give them to her. I gave in, not because I think that the Good Calorie Diet can be split into small pieces, but because I wanted to boost Marianne's self-confidence. I gave her this chapter.

To my complete amazement, Marianne lost ten pounds in a month. She did less than the complete program and thus never lost the last ten pounds, but Marianne did not care. She was slimmer and felt more beautiful.

It thrilled me that the tricks contained in this chapter were so powerful. I know that without the benefit of my full Good Calorie program, these tricks are not enough to overcome the Starvation Response. So Marianne still stands a good chance of regaining all the weight she lost. Furthermore, she did not lose all the weight that she wanted to lose and would have lost had she used the entire program.

You will apply these tricks throughout the entire Good Calorie Diet. Remember that the foods that evoke the Starvation Response must be considered a special class of Bad Calories and that one of the cornerstones of the program is to avoid Bad Calories.

This rule brings up the question of practicality. Bad Calories may be difficult to avoid altogether in the modern diet. Must you be fanatical about avoiding them? Obviously, to do so would be prohibitively inconvenient. Therefore, the Good Calorie Diet is a two-stage program. Until the first stage tames the Starvation Response, you should be particularly vigilant about observing the suggestions of the program. After you stop making excess fat, you will enter a period when you can experiment to see if your genetics will allow you to violate some of these rules occasionally.

Eventually you will find your limits. You will know how many Bad Calories you can tolerate without provoking the formation of excess fat. Then you can stay thin by merely staying within those limits.

The Good Calorie Diet could have been designed arbitrarily to eliminate all Bad Calories. Certainly that method is guaranteed to work. However, because the Starvation Response is a collection of different genetic programs, there is no need to avoid food and combinations of foods that are harmful only to someone else.

Now we will consider the tricks that eliminate adverse physiological signals of the modern diet. They do not constitute the entire Good Calorie Diet, but only those problems that induce the Starvation Response.

In brief, this is the list of tricks:

Avoid foods that are high in fat.
Avoid saturated fats; substitute unsaturated fats.
Avoid overcooked carbohydrates.
Avoid overly ripe fruit.
Avoid processed foods.
Avoid canned starches and legumes.
Avoid fructose.
Avoid alcohol before a meal.
Avoid smoking before a meal.
Avoid Bad Calories before and during exercise.

AVOID FOODS THAT ARE HIGH IN FAT
•••

Over the past 100 years, the percentage of calories that the average person derives from fat has increased (see Table 3-1).[1] This is a disaster. The ingestion of large amounts of fat decreases the rate at which we burn energy, making it harder to lose weight.[2] It also ignites the Starvation Response, making it easy to manufacture more fat.[3]

How much fat is too much? Many governmental agencies recommend that no more than 30 percent of our daily calories should be from fat. I accept this recommendation. Therefore, any food that derives more than 30 percent of its calories from fat is a Bad Calorie.

Why do I *not* recommend that you follow an extremely low-fat diet? Because it alters your physiology, so you will create more fat from blood sugar.[4] Your appetite will also increase.[5] Even more important, there is no need for an extremely low-fat diet when you substitute unsaturated fats for animal fats.

People with extremely high levels of cholesterol, atherosclerosis, or heart

TABLE 3-1

....

Percentage of Calories in the American Diet from Three Sources

	1860	1920	1975
Protein	12	12	14
Fat	25	32	43
Carbohydrates	63	56	43

disease should not take this recommendation to mean that an extremely low-fat diet won't help treat their diseases. For these people, an extremely low-fat diet can be a lifesaver. I recommend that they follow the Good Calorie Diet while watching their fat intake, though they should consult with their physicians first.

PRACTICAL SUGGESTIONS: As I will explain in the next section, sometimes, a low-fat food that is high on the glycemic index can produce more fat than can a high glycemic-index food combined with the proper amount of vegetable fat; therefore, you should not automatically consume any food that is advertised as being low in fat.

AVOID SATURATED FATS; SUBSTITUTE UNSATURATED FATS

...

Dietary studies that recommend a low-fat diet usually refer to the elimination of saturated animal fats. I agree that saturated fats should make up less than 10 percent of your caloric intake. However, diets that are extraordinarily low in fat seem unnecessary when the beneficial effects of unsaturated fats are considered.

Unsaturated (vegetable) fats, but not saturated (animal) fats, inhibit the creation of fat from carbohydrates (see Figure 3-2).[6] Butter, a saturated fat, increases the glycemic index of bread by over 20 percent, whereas olive oil and corn oil, both unsaturated fats, reduce the glycemic index of bread by over 70 percent. Olive oil is better than corn oil for reducing blood sugar.[7]

Thus, eating a little unsaturated fat may actually reduce the total fat you

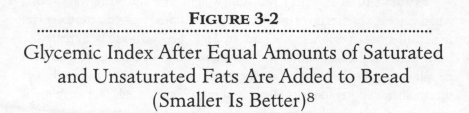

FIGURE 3-2

Glycemic Index After Equal Amounts of Saturated and Unsaturated Fats Are Added to Bread (Smaller Is Better)[8]

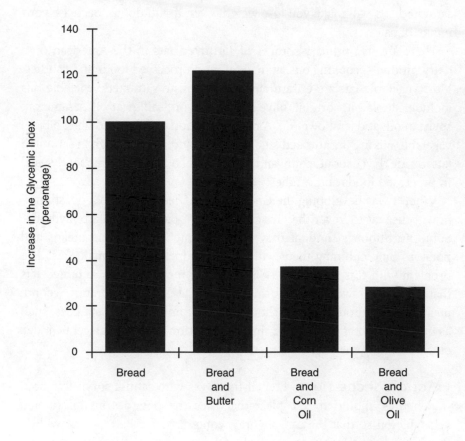

create when you are faced with meals of Bad Calorie carbohydrates. Say that you *have* to eat garlic bread. Since there is a lot of bread and it will make a lot of fat, you will get ahead of the game by adding a *small* amount of unsaturated corn oil margarine, which lowers the amount of fat created from the bread. However, the *best* solution would be to avoid the garlic bread altogether.

Unsaturated fats also help you lose weight in three other ways. First, when you eat a high ratio of unsaturated to saturated fats, you create less fat than if all those fat calories were saturated fat.[9] Second, your body *prefers* to burn unsaturated fats, rather than to place them in fat cells.[10] Third, in people who suffer from the Starvation Response, but not in lean people, the metabolism of other foods is 50 percent higher after meals that are high in unsaturated fats.[11] All this means that substituting unsaturated fats for saturated fats will make you lose weight even if you do not decrease your intake of calories.

There are five primary sources of saturated fats in the American diet: dairy products, cooking oils, animal fat, and processed foods and candies. Most vegetable fats are unsaturated. Common unsaturated vegetable oils include canola oil, corn oil, olive oil, peanut oil, safflower oil, sesame oil, soybean oil, and sunflower oil. A note of caution is warranted here: Not all vegetable oils are unsaturated fats. Avocados and nuts are high in saturated fats. So are the coconut, palm, and palm kernel oils that are frequently used in processed foods and candies.

When I was developing the Good Calorie Diet, there was a question of how to use fat to lower the glycemic index of Bad Calorie carbohydrates. Some nutritionists thought they could counter Bad Calorie breads and potatoes by combining them with butter or meats that contain fats. The problem with this solution is twofold. First, meat contains saturated fats that raise, not lower, the fat-forming potential of carbohydrates. Second, meat contains protein, which should not be combined with starches, such as bread and potatoes, because this combination raises the glycemic index of the resulting meal (see Chapter 5).

PRACTICAL SUGGESTIONS: French-fry lovers who cannot survive without french fries should find a place that fries the potatoes in unsaturated vegetable oil so that the carbohydrate content of the Bad Calorie will do them less harm. However, remember that you cannot lose weight on a constant diet of french fries, even those that are cooked in unsaturated fat.

You shall see that in the early part of the Good Calorie Diet, you are asked to decrease your consumption of animal products. You do so to avoid not only the protein that evokes the Starvation Response, but the saturated fats that accompany animal products.

You can enjoy the benefits of unsaturated fats only when a small percentage of your fat intake consists of saturated fats, so you should remove most saturated animal fats from your diet.[12] Almost all red meats and dairy products are high in saturated fats. Chicken and turkey also have more saturated than unsaturated fats, but they have a better ratio of unsaturated to saturated fats than does red meat.

Fish often have a better ratio of unsaturated to saturated fats than does red meat, but not all fish are high in unsaturated fat (see Table 3-2). You can cut your consumption of saturated fat by up to 75 percent by switching from red meat to the proper fish. Therefore, you can improve your creation of fat simply by substituting fish for meat.

Although I recommend eating unsaturated fats, do not take it as a license to consume excess fat. No one should use too much fat of any type. If you

TABLE 3-2

....

Unsaturated Fat in Fish

Fish with More Unsaturated Fat	Fish with Less Unsaturated Fat
Bass, striped	Abalone
Clams	Catfish
Cod	Gefilte fish
Crab	Herring
Haddock	Lobster
Halibut	Mussels
Perch	Oyster
Pike, northern	Pompano
Salmon, Atlantic, coho, pink	Roughy
Scallops	Sablefish
Shrimp	Salmon, chinook, chum
Sea bass	Sea trout
Snapper	Sturgeon
Trout	Swordfish
Tuna	
Whitefish	
Whiting	

are suffering from the Starvation Response, most fat calories go directly into fat cells. However, when you do consume fat, just make sure that it is unsaturated fat.

AVOID OVERCOOKED CARBOHYDRATES
...

Eating overcooked foods can double the blood sugar available for conversion into fat. Why does overcooking do so? Because it destroys the fibers needed to prevent carbohydrates from being converted into blood sugar.

You can lower a carbohydrate's fat-forming potential by slightly undercooking it. This rule applies to almost all sources of carbohydrates—rice, potatoes, and vegetables. All pastas, except canned pasta, appear to be an exception to this rule. It is one of the simplest weight-loss tricks.

You should also avoid instant oatmeal. Substitute "slow-cooked" varieties which, surprisingly, can also be microwave cooked.

Figure 3-3 shows what happens with rice. Instant rice cooked for six minutes produces double the blood sugar of instant rice cooked for one minute. Without changing the caloric content, overcooking doubles the rice's fat-forming ability.

PRACTICAL SUGGESTIONS: Some Chinese restaurants overcook rice or use glutenous rice because it helps the rice kernels stick together, so they can be easily eaten with chopsticks. The glycemic index of glutenous rice is nearly 100, or almost double that of properly cooked rice.

If you order a potato or another starch, slightly underdone, you may halve the fat it creates.

Stews and soups tend to feature overcooked carbohydrates, so be careful when ordering these items.

AVOID OVERLY RIPE FRUIT
...

As a fruit ripens, its sugars break down into simple, and better-tasting, sugars that have higher glycemic indexes. Therefore, avoid excessively ripe fruits; they create excess fat.

Bananas are a perfect example of how the ripeness of a fruit influences its glycemic index. Starch is the principal ingredient in an underripe banana, a

FIGURE 3-3

Blood Sugar Created by Equal Portions of Rice by Type of Rice and Different Cooking Times (Smaller Is Better)

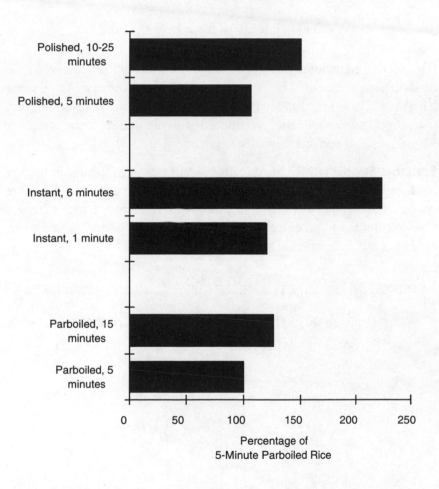

Percentage of
5-Minute Parboiled Rice

low glycemic-index carbohydrate. As the banana ripens its starch turns into free sugars, and the glycemic index increases by 70 percent, changing the fruit from a Good Calorie one to a Bad Calorie one.[13] Although there have been are no scientific studies, the same process is likely to occur with other fruits, such as pears and peaches.

PRACTICAL SUGGESTIONS: You do not have to eat green, unripe fruit. Rather, choose firm yellow bananas and avoid mushy, brown-spotted ones. Other fruits do not have to be hard, choose soft but not mushy or obviously juicy ones.

Many health bars sell fruit drinks that are freshly prepared in a blender. Frequently, they use overly ripe fruit (because no one will see the condition of the fruit). It's probably best to avoid those that do.

AVOID PROCESSED FOODS
...

Food processing includes many of manufacturing techniques that make food easier to handle or to use. The more processed the food, the more blood sugar it makes. Dr. Janet Brand and her colleagues at the University of Sidney found that processing increased the glycemic index of corn by 60 percent; of rice, by 90 percent; and of potatoes, by 50 percent (see Table 3-3).[14]

PRCTICAL SUGGESTIONS: Most ready-to-eat foods—including almost any food on the shelf in a grocery store—that are packaged in a bag or a box are processed foods. Foods have been precooked or altered so they take less time to cook are all processed food. All are bad calories and can be eaten only in accordance with the rules in Chapter 5.

TABLE 3-3
....

Food Processing Increases the Glycemic Indexes of Foods

Food	Glycemic Index
Potatoes	100
Instant potatoes	156
Corn	100
Corn chips	152
Cornflakes	163
Rice	100
Instant rice	178
Puffed rice	190

AVOID CANNED STARCHES
AND LEGUMES
...

Canning drastically increases the glycemic index of starches. Canned pasta, for example, has twice the glycemic index of home-cooked pasta.[15] It also stimulates the body to release nearly 50 percent more insulin, thereby activating fat-forming enzymes.

Canning also doubles the glycemic index of legumes, such as kidney beans and lentils. Thus it raises them from the best Good Calories to foods with barely acceptable levels on the glycemic index.

PRACTICAL SUGGESTIONS: Canned pasta lies hidden within minestrone, chicken noodle, and many other canned soups; watch out for it. Those canned soups that do not contain canned pasta usually contain beans or other legumes. whose glycemic index is raised by canning. Therefore, try to avoid canned soups, dehydrated soups are no better.

Most canned children's foods contain pasta. Even if your children are not generally overweight, it is not a good idea to feed them foods that induce the Starvation Response. Remember, the Starvation Response is a genetically programmed response and hence the children of sufferers have a higher probability of being susceptible.

AVOID FRUCTOSE
...

The most commonly used sweetener in manufactured foods is corn syrup. Fructose, the active ingredient, is a greater part of the American diet than is table sugar. The average American consumes 15 percent of his or her calories as fructose.[16]

Of the many forms of sugar in our diet, fructose is the easiest for the body to convert into fat.[17] When it is combined with fat, such as in a candy bar, fructose is capable of producing more new fat than common table sugar.[18]

What is most remarkable about fructose sweetener is that it may be harmless for normal people and fattening for those who suffer from the Starvation Response. Fructose sweetener increases insulin levels and insulin resistance in people who are predisposed to high levels of insulin or blood sugar (see Figure 3-4)[19] Although it has no effect on normal men, fructose sweetener increases the synthesis of triglycerides by more than 50 percent in men who suffer from the Starvation Response (see Figure 3-5).[20]

FIGURE 3-4

Insulin Levels in Men After Five Weeks
of Consuming Different Amounts
of Fructose Sweetener
(tested one-half hour after test
carbohydrates were ingested)
(Smaller Is Better)[21]

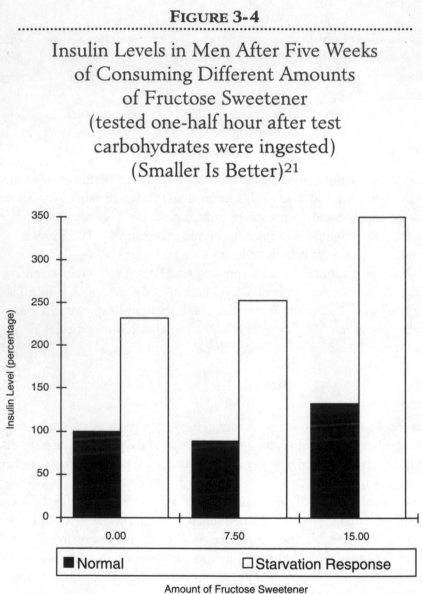

Amount of Fructose Sweetener
(percentage)

FIGURE 3-5

Triglyceride Levels in Men After Five Weeks of Consuming Different Amounts of Fructose Sweetener (Smaller Is Better)[22]

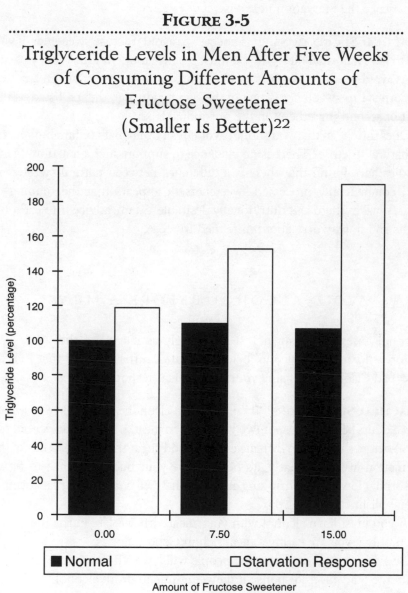

Triglyceride Level (percentage)

Amount of Fructose Sweetener
(percentage)

■ Normal　　　□ Starvation Response

Strangely, it does not affect normal women in the same way. I do not know of any studies showing what effect fructose sweetener has on women who experience the Starvation Response.

PRACTICAL SUGGESTIONS: It is not easy to avoid fructose sweetener. If you are to have a normal lifestyle, you must practice moderation. What you can do is avoid products, such as candies, jams, and sweets, in which fructose or corn syrup sweetener is one of the two major ingredients, listed as the first or second ingredient on the nutritional label.

Does this mean that you should avoid fresh fruits that contain high levels of natural fructose? There is no evidence to support such an action. Many studies have found that there is a difference between natural sweeteners and commercially processed sweeteners. It appears that the refining of sugars makes them less nutritionally desirable. So my advice is to eat fresh fruits and don't worry about unrefined fructose.

AVOID ALCOHOL BEFORE A MEAL
•••

Alcohol raises blood sugar just as strongly as if it were the worst Bad Calorie. If you drink alcohol before a meal, it turns the food that follows into Bad Calories by raising your blood-sugar response.[23]

PRACTICAL SUGGESTIONS: If you want an alcoholic drink, have it two or three hours before a meal or two hours after a meal. If you drink alcohol too soon before a meal, you'll create excess blood sugar that is diverted into the formation of fat. Similarly, it's best to give your body a chance to finish absorbing food before drinking anything that will change your fat-forming metabolism.

If you must have alcohol with your meal, drink it late in the meal, and then only if you are eating a meal rich in Good Calories.

Be aware, however, that some people will have a difficult time escaping from the Starvation Response if they continue to drink alcohol.

AVOID SMOKING BEFORE OR DURING MEALS

...

Swedish physicians reported that aside from its other harmful effects, smoking produces a sudden rise in blood sugar, followed by a sharp decrease immediately after the nicotine high vanishes.[24] This reaction can increase the formation of fat. When you can possibly do so, you should let more than an hour pass between smoking and eating.

AVOID BAD CALORIES BEFORE AND DURING EXERCISE

...

Exercise helps you to lose weight by lowering blood-sugar levels, reversing insulin resistance, and lowering triglycerides.[25] However, ingesting Bad Calorie carbohydrates before or during aerobic and anaerobic exercise make you burn glycogen instead of blood sugar and promotes insulin resistance, thus increasing the availability of blood sugar for the formation of fat.[26] This problem is particularly relevant because most exercise drinks, including many that are designed to replace electrolytes, are Bad Calories. When you consume these drinks while exercising, you negate the benefits of exercise.

PRACTICAL SUGGESTIONS: If you exercise, eat Good Calorie meals or exercise moderately so that Bad Calories will have less of a negative impact. The U.S. Centers for Disease Control recently announced that people do not need to exercise vigorously to experience the benefits of aerobic exercise. Rather, thirty minutes of moderate exercise, four times a week, is enough.[27] The president of the American College of Sports Medicine suggested that "people can climb stairs instead of riding elevators and escalators. They can garden. They can rake leaves, they can dance. They can walk part or all of the way to work." "We made a mistake by insisting that it must be sustained aerobic activity," said the director of epidemiology at the Cooper Institute for Aerobics Research.

What about anaerobic exercises, such as those found in the slow movements of hatha yoga, tai chi, weight lifting, and isometrics? These exercises now qualify as moderate aerobic exercises, and, according to the new guidelines, are as helpful as are strenuous aerobic exercises.

One quick note for my bodybuilding friends. Anabolic steroids increase insulin resistance and decrease the ability to regulate blood sugar.[28] Clearly, they contribute to the Starvation Response.

CHAPTER FOUR

GOOD AND BAD CALORIES

WHAT MAKES A FOOD INTO A GOOD CALORIE?

•••

Good Calories represent the pot of gold at the end of the rainbow. With them, you can eat thousands of calories and still lose weight because you make less fat.

Creating a list of Good Calorie foods is more complicated than simply selecting every food with a low glycemic index because the glycemic index of a food can be lowered by its fat content. Thus, some low glycemic-index foods are high in fat, and none of us wants a diet of high-fat foods. Candy bars, pâté, and high-fat ice cream all have low glycemic indexes but a high-fat content. We should not eat them. Although at least two books have

45

proposed weight-loss diets that include high-fat foods with low glycemic indexes, no one can lose weight on such diets. Such an idea may sell books, but it is absurd. Good Calories must derive 30 percent or less of their calories from fat.

Where is the dividing line between Good Calories and Bad Calories? Clearly, table sugar is fat inducing, so let's use it as the dividing point. Any food that derives less than 31 percent of its calories from fat and has a glycemic index lower than table sugar is a Good Calorie, and any food with more fat or a higher glycemic index is a Bad Calorie. Among the Good Calories are rice, spaghetti, yams, grapes, lentils, and plums.[1] Among the Bad Calories are almost all types of bread, carrots, rice cakes, processed breakfast cereals, and white potatoes.

If you use the list of Good and Bad Calories in Appendixes 1–30, you do not have to calculate the percentage of calories from fat. If you still want to calculate the percentage of calories that are derived from fat, multiply the grams of fat in a portion (9 calories in a gram of fat, and 4 calories in a gram of carbohydrate) by 9 and divide that figure by the total number of calories in the portion. For example, if one portion of a food has 140 calories and 6 grams of fat, then that portion contains 54 calories of fat ($6 \times 9 = 54$), and 38.6 percent of the calories are from fat ($54 \div 140 = .386$). So the next time some product advertises that it contains only a few grams of fat, you should realize that that number may still be more than the 30 percent maximum allowed for a Good Calorie food. In fact, listing the grams of fat instead of the calories of fat is a deceptive labeling practice.

GOOD CALORIES
...

The following sections present an overview of the wide variety of Good Calorie foods found in Appendixes 1–30.

Rye bread. Unlike breads made from wheat flour, rye bread has a low glycemic index. Therefore, pumpernickel and rye breads are good substitutes for modern white breads.

Be careful though. Many pumpernickel and rye breads have more wheat flour than rye and thus have a greater fat-forming potential. The easiest way to tell which flour predominates is to examine the list of ingredients. If wheat flour is listed before rye flour, it means that there is more wheat flour in the bread.

Until this century, pumpernickel formed the basis of many European diets. Perhaps that is the reason why obesity is a modern phenomenon in those countries.

Whole-grain breads. Substituting whole or cracked grains for milled flour lowers the glycemic index of bread[2] and can turn wheat bread from a Bad Calorie into a Good Calorie. However, just the addition of kernels of whole grain does not guarantee that a wheat bread will have a low glycemic index. The bread may have to consist of at least 50 percent to 75 percent whole kernels.

Many breads are marketed as whole-grain breads but are not composed of intact kernels. Rather, they contain milled flour made from the whole kernel. Although this type of flour increases the availability of certain nutrients, it does nothing to lower the glycemic index of the bread.

I have included a list of acceptable breads in Appendix 1.[3] These are breads that list whole- or sprouted-wheat grains as the first, and primary, ingredient. Although they are good enough to be listed as Good Calories, they are just barely good enough. They still have much higher glycemic indexes than does whole rye flour bread. Eat wheat bread sparingly.

There are two other ways to make wheat bread or other bakery products so they will be extremely low on the glycemic index: by increasing the size of the wheat particles[4] or by adding viscous fiber, such as guar gum.[5] Unfortunately, I do not know any nationally distributed breads that are prepared this way. However, the coarsely ground wheat breads in India are reported to have a glycemic index that is only one-third that of modern bread. So it is not impossible to prepare such breads commercially.

If you cannot find Good Calorie bread, you may have to make the difficult decision to give up bread. Bad Calorie breads are one of the prime contributors to the Starvation Response.

Pasta. Since it is made from wheat flour, scientists expected pasta to have a high glycemic index, similar to bread, but it does not. Pasta is a Good Calorie.

It appears that the process of extruding dough through a cold press changes the fibers of pasta and lowers its glycemic index. Perhaps scientists will soon learn how to apply this same technique to other wheat products. It would be a pleasure to see bread with a low glycemic index.

When you eat pasta, it is important to avoid mixing it with large quantities of animal protein (see Chapter 6). A small amount of animal protein in the sauce is fine, but a large amount transforms the meal into a Bad Calorie disaster.

Drinks. The best drinks are decaffeinated and lack natural sweeteners. They include water, diet soda, decaffeinated coffee and tea, herbal tea, fruit juice, and vegetable juice.

It is important to drink sufficient quantities of liquid in between meals rather than only with meals. Doing so avoids diluting your digestive enzymes by excessive drinking during meals.

Oatmeal. Old-fashioned slow-cooked oatmeal (cooked for six or more minutes) is the perfect breakfast food. Many Scandinavians eat breakfasts laden with fatty meats, yet they avoid obesity because they combine meats with oatmeal. Although this is not a recommended practice, it does show the power of oatmeal.

Be sure to avoid instant varieties of oatmeal. They have a much higher glycemic index.

Chicken and turkey. After you overcome the Starvation Response, low-fat chicken or turkey is a Good Calorie food. You should avoid combining either with starch or fruit (see Chapter 6). Eat chicken or turkey during the noon meal.

All white meats, except wings, are acceptable. Skinless dark meats, except thighs, are also Good Calories. When possible, avoid the skin.

The major problem with poultry is that it has a high ratio of saturated to unsaturated fats. Therefore, you must be careful about combining poultry with starches.

Chili. Although meat chili is almost universally high in fat, products made with chicken or vegetarian substitutes are Good Calories.

Low-fat dairy products. Diet cheese, nonfat milk, nonfat cottage cheese, and nonfat ice cream are all Good Calories.

Some people are unable to digest lactose, the sugar in milk. For them, lactose creates digestive problems that can turn dairy products into Bad Calories. The symptoms are bloating, gas, diarrhea, and discomfort. The solution is to use reduced-lactose products or to take lactase enzyme pills.

Fish. Good Calorie fish include bass, cod, clams, crab, flounder, haddock, halibut, perch, scrod, scallops, shrimp, snapper, trout, and tuna canned in water.

It is best to eat fish that are high in unsaturated fats (see Chapter 3). This fish can be more safely combined with starches, but only in small quantities.

Some types of fish are high in fat and should be avoided. These include some forms of farm-bred salmon. Check the source of your salmon.

As with other protein products, consume fish after curing the Starvation Response and, when possible, at the noon meal. Avoid back-to-back fish meals.

Frozen dinners and entrées: Not all convenience food is junk. At the same time, few convenience foods are nutritionally equal to freshly prepared meals.

Good Calories predominate among these brands of frozen dinners: Armour Classics, Armour Dinner Classics Light, Banquet Gourmet Light & Healthy, Budget Gourmet Slim Selects, Healthy Choice, Kraft Eating Right, Lean Cuisine, Le Menu Healthy, Le Menu Light Style, Stouffer's Right Course, Tyson Loony Tunes, Ultra Slim Fast, and Weight Watchers (see Appendixes 7 and 9).

To determine if frozen dinners are Good Calories, judge them as a whole. A Good Calorie dinner may contain foods that would be Bad Calories if they were eaten individually (see Chapter 6). Be careful to eat the entire meal or at least an equal percentage of each food. The most common error is to eat a Bad Calorie entrée and ignore the vegetables.

Another common error is to eat a Bad Calorie dessert or entrée before you eat the Good Calories. This practice is almost as bad as eating only Bad Calories because it will flood your body with blood sugar and insulin *before* you take your first mouthful of Good Calories.

Fruit. Almost all fruits are Good Calories. Avoid dried fruits, fruits packaged in syrup, and overly ripe fruit, since these have high glycemic indexes.

Pizza. Pizza is made from wheat and cheese, each of which is a Bad Calorie. Taken together, wheat and cheese can form a Good Calorie because the fat in the cheese lowers the glycemic index of the bread crust. Just make sure that less than 30 percent of the calories in the pizza come from fat. Generally, a pizza with slightly less than a single portion of cheese and no meat topping fulfills this requirement.

Deep-dish pizzas typically have a greater fat content than do thin-crust pizzas.

The same principle applies to cheese sandwiches.

Legumes (beans). Legumes are the lowest glycemic-index food. Combining them with other foods is one of the most powerful principles of the Good Calorie Diet. Legumes will drastically reduce the amount of blood sugar produced by the resulting meal.

Though the Hindu diet is composed of many Bad Calories, many meals are preceded by dal soups, composed of lentils. Lentils are so low on the glycemic index that you can eat eight times more lentils than rice cakes and still make less fat. Eating lentils protects Indians against their genetic tendency to become obese.[6] Perhaps it is no coincidence that lentils form such an important part of the Indian diet that Indian newspapers list the prices of over 300 varieties.

It is easy for Americans to do the same thing: Start meals with bean soup and serve peas or beans with entrées. There are many ways to prepare legumes. You should use them to accelerate your weight loss. Time and time again, I have seen people kick their diets into high gear with legumes.

You can create a perfect substitute for animal protein by combining 1 part legume with 2½ parts of grains, such as rice. This combination produces a mixture of amino acids that is optimal for creating muscle. One of the greatest bodybuilders of all time, Bill Pearl, used legumes and grains to build and maintain his Mr. Universe body on a vegetarian diet. Mexicans do the same thing when they combine beans and corn in burritos, as do Indians when they eat dal lentils with native breads.

A note of caution: Soybeans are very low on the glycemic index, but tofu is made with fermented soybeans and should be avoided because its fat content may be as high as 70 percent of its caloric content. Canning also increases the glycemic index of legumes.

Mexican food. Authentic Mexican food is generally a Good Calorie unless it has a high fat content, usually because of excess cheese. It is a classic example of a cuisine in which legumes protect a genetically susceptible population from obesity. Beans form an integral part of many dishes, from burritos to tacos.

Unfortunately, you must be careful in Mexican restaurants because they often add excessive amounts of animal fat to their dishes.

Breakfast cereals. Most breakfast cereals are Bad Calories; however, a few national brands may be Good Calories. Kellogg's adds psyllium, a fiber that lowers the glycemic index, to its Heartwise and Fiberwise cereals. Kellogg's Extra Fiber All Bran and General Mills's Fiber One are also Good Calories, although not all bran cereals are.

Vegetables. Most vegetables are Good Calories, which is not surprising since they closely resemble our ancestors' preferred diet. The most notable exceptions are carrots and potatoes, which induce high blood sugar.

The greatest problem with vegetables is that many people eat them with added fats, such as margarine or butter. By consuming too much fat, you will turn Good Calories into Bad Calories. Try powdered butter substitutes, such as Molly McButter, or low-fat sauces. If you use fat-based spreads, they should be high in unsaturated fats, such as corn oil margarines. Olive oil is *much* better than butter.

BAD CALORIES

...

The Good Calorie Diet is fundamentally different from conventional diets that limit your caloric intake but allow you to continue to eat your normal selection of low-fat foods. In the Good Calorie Diet, you avoid a few key foods and food combinations, but do not limit calories.

Bad Calories *can* form part of your diet, but only if you combine them with Good Calories. For example, carrots are Bad Calories, but they can

safely be part of a mixed-vegetable dish. The rules for combining foods are given in Chapter 5.

Many of the foods you were brought up with are Bad Calories. That is why nutritional diseases are so prevalent in our society. According to Dr. Walter C. Willet, chairman of the Department of Nutrition at Harvard School of Public Health, the American eating pattern is "probably one the unhealthiest diets ever to exist on the face of the earth."[7]

Wheat bread. Common wheat bread is one of the worst Bad Calories. French bread can have twice the fat-forming capacity of table sugar. Yet, what is immediately brought to the table when we dine out? A basket of bread. And what do we do? We eat it. By the time our meal arrives, the bread has already raised our blood sugar and insulin, diverting all subsequent food, even Good Calories, into the synthesis of fat. Our appetite also increases. Eliminating bread before meals seems to be one of the easiest paths to quick weight loss.

It does not matter whether it is white-wheat or dark-wheat bread. It is the refining process that makes wheat so fattening. Even whole wheat flour and health-food wheat breads are Bad Calories if they are finely ground or do not contain the majority of their weight in whole kernels.

If a bread dissolves in your mouth, then it is certainly a Bad Calorie. Oat bread and most barley breads should also be avoided.[8]

One more caution, many bakeries proclaim that their goods are diet products solely because the items are low in fat. Don't be fooled; these baked goods are not acceptable on the Good Calorie Diet. Lowering their fat content does not lower the potential of these products to raise blood sugar; in fact, it can raise their glycemic index.

Cookies, cakes, and pastries. These products are made with wheat flour and create the same problems as does bread. And, of course, they have large amounts of sugar.

White potatoes. White potatoes have one-third more fat-forming capacity than does table sugar. Dieters sabotage themselves whenever they eat white potatoes without combining them with Good Calories.

Occasionally, I enjoy a white potato by adding a little olive oil to reduce the glycemic index. But be careful to do so only when the rest of the meal is low in fat. You do not want to make a high-fat meal even higher in fat.

White potatoes make even more fat when they are processed into instant mashed potatoes. You may think you are avoiding instant potatoes because a product is not labeled as such. However, many restaurants use instant potatoes, and several fast-food chains manufacture their french fries from instant potatoes.

And, of course, white potatoes are usually served as a side dish with animal protein, such as meat, fish, and poultry. That combination increases the formation of fat and suppresses appetite controls (see Chapter 5).

Yams and sweet potatoes are Good Calorie alternatives to potatoes, with two-thirds less the fat-forming capacity of white potatoes.

Instant and overcooked rice. Rice is a Good Calorie, but instant rice is a Bad Calorie. Instant rice has twice the fat-forming potential of regular rice. If there is any question as to whether a rice is instant, examine the uncooked grains. If the grains are smooth, they are probably regular rice; if they are rough, they are probably instant.

Overcooking rice can double its fat-forming potential, creating a Bad Calorie. The glutenous rice found in many Chinese restaurants is over-cooked, as is the rice found in many convenience foods, frozen and packaged. These rice dishes are easily identified because the rice grains are not firm and they instantly coagulate into lumpy masses.

When you encounter convenience foods based on rice, it sometimes helps to cook them for less than the recommended time. Then you should examine the cooked product. If the rice grains do not coagulate, your cooking methods have helped it become a Good Calorie.

Rice cakes. Rice cakes are a favorite of dieters, yet they have one of the highest known glycemic indexes. They form twice the blood sugar of table sugar.

Rice drinks. Rice drinks are becoming increasingly popular in health food stores. In California, they are found in convenience stores and gas stations. These drinks are popular because they provide one of the strong-est known sugar rushes.

In these drinks processed rice, which already has a high glycemic index, is broken down further. The result is a drink that may be one of the worst Bad Calories.

Corn. Modern corn was developed to fatten cattle for market. Therefore, it should be no surprise that corn creates high amounts of blood sugar and fat. Both fresh corn and corn products, such as corn chips and corn flakes, should be avoided.

Just as with white potatoes, I occasionally enjoy corn on the cob with a light coating of olive oil. However, I eat it only when the rest of the meal is low in fat.

Breakfast cereals. A morning bowl of cereal is one of the principal causes of obesity. Most breakfast cereals are made from wheat or corn flour and exhibit the high glycemic indexes common to these products. Likewise, puffed rice has the same high glycemic index as do rice cakes. Cereals with high glycemic indexes are why many of us feel so bad in the morning.

Frequently, we follow cereal with an order of eggs, another source of protein. This combination of protein and starch is extremely fattening.

Starting the day with cereal evokes high levels of insulin and ensures that lunch and supper will create extra fat since breakfast has activated your fat-forming enzymes.

Slow-cooked oatmeal appears to be a safe breakfast cereal. However, this does not mean that other oat cereals are Good Calories. The food processing involved in converting oats into instant oatmeal, flakes, or other forms of dry cereals raises their glycemic index to that of table sugar. The oats in granola, Muesli, and even oat-bran cereals are equally bad; all these cereals have high glycemic indexes.

In Chapter 5, you will see that without a Good Calorie breakfast, it is nearly impossible to lose weight.

Bananas. Ripe bananas create excess blood sugar and should be avoided.

Canned pasta. Canned pasta has twice the glycemic index of home-cooked pasta, ranking it among the worst Bad Calorie foods.

Canned soups. You must be careful to choose low-fat soups that do not fall into the following traps. The greatest problem is a high-fat content, so read the label. Also, many companies add food starch, a Bad Calorie, to make their soups thicker. If a canned soup has a substantial pasta or bean content, it probably counts as a Bad Calorie because canning increases the glycemic index of starches and legumes. Similar problems apply to dehydrated soups.

I have not included an extensive appendix on canned or dehydrated soups, simply because a careful analysis of the glycemic index of soups is frequently impossible without expensive laboratory measurements. That is why so many soup recipes are given in Appendix B.

Dried fruits. Drying fruits concentrates their natural sugars and raises their glycemic indexes. For example, the glycemic index of raisins is triple that of grapes. Therefore, you should avoid raisins, dates, dried apples, dried apricots, and dried peaches. Soaking dried fruits or nuts does *not* substantially change their glycemic indexes.

Carrots. Carrots and carrot juice have an extremely high fat-forming potential. They should be avoided in all forms, including raw.

Sugar and honey. Obviously, you should avoid table sugar. What is not so obvious is that honey has a greater fat-forming capacity than does table sugar.

I wish I could tell you just to substitute artificial sweeteners. Unfortunately, some people have the same insulin reaction to artificial sweeteners as they do to natural ones. To determine if you are susceptible to artificial sweeteners, see if you have the same reactions (lightheadedness, increased appetite, delayed lethargy) to both artificial and naturally sweetened drinks.

When I must use a sweetener, I use table sugar. Since I cannot use artificial sweeteners, there is no alternative for me.

Fructose. Fructose is a sugar extracted from fruit. Although it has a low glycemic index, it can raise the activity of fat-forming enzymes. Therefore, fructose sweetener is a Bad Calorie. Naturally occurring fructose, as found in fruits, is not a Bad Calorie.

Red meat. What is unique about the Good Calorie Diet is that you eat protein and starches or fruit in separate meals. Eat protein early in the day rather than late in the evening. Separate meals containing protein from the next food by several hours. Avoid successive meals that feature protein.

Remember to limit your intake of protein and saturated fat. Since red meats are uniquely high in both protein and saturated fats, you should eat red meat sparingly, not in successive meals. Eat only low-fat meats (see Appendix 15). Most types of beef derive more than 30 percent of their calories from fat, although some types fall between 31 percent and 40 percent and so can be eaten occasionally, according to the diet's guidelines.

Fast foods. Fat, not fast foods, is the enemy. Resist french fries and similar goodies. Many fast foods, especially sandwiches, combine protein and starch, which causes them to create extra fat, even if they are low in fat (see Chapter 6). Furthermore, the saturated fat in fast-food meats and deep-fried fish increases the glycemic index of the bread in sandwiches.

Tofu. Although soybeans are low on the glycemic index, the soybean product tofu is high in fat and should be avoided.

Salads with high-fat salad dressings. High-fat salad dressing is enough to ruin your entire meal. The common ingredients in a green salad—lettuce and tomatoes—have almost no calories. Therefore, the salad dressing determines the majority of the caloric content of the salad. Because most salad dressings are high in fat, they make the entire salad into a Bad Calorie choice.

High-fat salad dressings pose an additional problem—and opportunity. Since they usually are eaten at the beginning of a meal, the fats in salads will affect how you digest the carbohydrates contained in the main courses. If your salad is high in saturated fats, then it is likely to increase the formation of fat. If it is high in unsaturated fats, then it will decrease the fat-forming ability of the rest of the meal. Thus, an olive-oil dressing may actually reduce the fat-forming capacity of the food that follows. Remember that the total fat content of your entire meal must be less than 30 percent. Therefore, if you start with a fatty salad dressing, then the rest of the meal must be correspondingly low in fat.

Many dieters eat lunches that consist only of salads because salads are low in calories. This is a prime example of how calorie counting can lead you to choose the wrong foods.

Snacks: Most snack foods are high in fat or sugar. Most chips are Bad Calories because they have both high glycemic indexes and a high fat content.

Most diets feature in-between-meal snacks in an attempt to prevent the insulin surges common to the Starvation Response. When you need a snack, you should make it a low glycemic-index fruit.

Alcohol. Preliminary evidence suggests that alcohol will make all other foods behave as if they are Bad Calories. Thus, consuming alcohol before a meal will raise the effective glycemic index of the whole meal.

Consume all alcohol two to three hours after or before a meal. Avoid drinking alcohol on an empty stomach.

Beer. Beer offers a double whammy. Its caloric content comes from two sources, alcohol and maltose sugar. Maltose has a higher glycemic index than does table sugar. The rules for consuming beer are the same as for consuming any other alcoholic beverage.

Sugared soft drinks and juices. Not only do these drinks create high blood sugar levels, but they have far-reaching effects on the other foods you eat, making them more fat forming.

Fresh-squeezed juices. Juicing a fruit can raise its glycemic index. In general, the more pulp left in the juice, the lower the glycemic index will be. Some juices, such as carrot, beet, and celery, are almost always Bad Calories.

Juicers create drinks that give you the same sugar rush that you used to get from soda pop.

High-fat foods. You know these foods. They include salad dressings, many animal products (red meat, dark meat in poultry, most dairy products, and many candies). Don't eat them.

Overcooked foods. Overcooking can double the fat-forming potential of carbohydrates. But not all carbohydrates have an increased glycemic index after overcooking. Potatoes and rice do, but the thicker forms of spaghetti do not.[9] Avoid overcooking any starchy carbohydrate, since it is not known which ones will have an increased glycemic index after overcooking.

Just by ordering a food lightly cooked or lightly steamed, you can decrease its fat-forming potential.

Instant or processed foods. Remember, the more processed the food, the more blood sugar it makes. Forms of food processing that increase the glycemic response are precooking and enzymatic digesting to make instant foods, grinding, extruding, flaking, and popping.

A good general rule is to avoid any form of processed starchy food.

Popcorn. Popcorn has traditionally been used as an appetite suppressant. However, it has a high glycemic index and will actually increase your appetite.

Buttering popcorn just increases its glycemic index. However, adding a little corn-oil spread or olive oil will lower the glycemic index to acceptable levels. Then your only problem is that you are eating a high-fat snack.

Do not think that this is all the help you will get in selecting Good Calories. To make it easy to choose Good Calories, this book divides over 2,000 foods into Good and Bad Calories (see Appendixes 1–30). The lists include foods from all food groups: meats, poultry, fish, fruit, vegetables, grains, and nuts. Appendixes A, B, and C also present daily menus, recipes, and restaurant menus. Altogether, over 3,000 items are listed, making it easy to follow the Good Calorie Diet. Chapter 5 is also important because it presents the Golden Dozen, rules that are essential for using Good Calories.

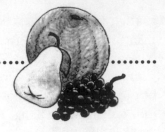

CHAPTER FIVE

HOW TO USE GOOD CALORIES

HOW TO USE GOOD CALORIES: THE GOLDEN DOZEN

···

The Golden Dozen are the rules that define the Good Calorie Diet. They are much simpler than constantly consulting handbooks to determine calories or grams of fat. Everyone who tries the Good Calorie Diet tells me that these principles soon become second nature.

The Good Calorie Diet is divided into two stages, before and after curing the Starvation Response. The first ten rules serve a dual purpose; they help you counter the Starvation Response and help you lose weight. The last two rules help you eat a wider range of food, but do nothing to help you lose weight. Therefore, it is important to postpone experimenting with the freedoms of the last two rules until you have cured the Starvation Response.

THE GOLDEN DOZEN

· ·

The Rules Everyone Must Initially Follow

1. Eat primarily Good Calories.
2. Combine Good and Bad Calories using the four-to-one ratio.
3. Eat Good Calorie breakfasts.
4. Eat the most fat-forming foods for lunch, not for dinner.
5. Eat Good Calorie snacks.
6. Don't miss a meal.
7. Avoid combining excessive amounts of animal protein with starchy carbohydrates or fruit.
8. Avoid excessive amounts of animal products while curing the Starvation Response.
9. Avoid the Starvation Response triggers.
10. Avoid vitamin and mineral deficiencies.

Rules to Follow after Overcoming the Starvation Response

11. Good Calorie meals should precede and follow Bad Calorie meals.
12. Find your personal limits of freedom.

Your first task, as you embark on the Good Calorie Diet, is to embrace the first ten rules. During the first few weeks, you will discover that your body will fight to maintain the Starvation Response. Therefore, during your first few days on the diet, you may experience a suddenly strengthened Starvation Response. Food cravings will grow worse. A few people may experience temporary fluctuations in blood sugar that manifest as minor headaches or lethargy. Do not be alarmed and continue to follow the rules, especially the rule about never missing a meal. Eat frequent snacks. Only by reassuring your body that it does not face starvation can you overcome this last attempt to eat fat-forming foods.

After a few days you will start feeling different, particularly in the morning. During the night your body experiences its longest period without food, so your morning appetite and cravings are mirrors of your state of health. This is why Starvation Response sufferers want to eat Bad Calorie breakfasts, bursting with fatty foods or high-sugar cereals. Once you recover, Good Calorie breakfasts taste better than do Bad Calorie ones.

Appendix A presents menus that illustrate the principles of this chapter.

THE GOLDEN DOZEN IN DETAIL
...

1. Eat primarily Good Calories. It should be no surprise that the first rule of the Good Calorie Diet is to eat a diet that is high in Good Calories. Please note that I did not say that you have to avoid all Bad Calories.

PRACTICAL SUGGESTIONS: Don't deemphasize Good Calories once you lose weight. Good Calories may not inhibit the formation of fat in people who are not experiencing the Starvation Response, but this does not mean that they are not still vitally important.

Good Calories are also a preventive medicine. Eating them will prevent you from eating so many Bad Calories that you bring on a new bout of the Starvation Response. Therefore, you should remind yourself that you will always need Good Calories, even after you lose weight. Our genetic inheritance makes them necessary. Good Calories are as essential as is anything else you do to keep yourself healthy.

2. Combine Good and Bad Calories using the four-to-one ratio. Not every food must be a Good Calorie. Your stomach can hide Bad Calories in a mass of lower glycemic-index food. It is as though you ate a single food with a glycemic index that is the average of all the foods you consumed. In most cases, that will be the equivalent of a food with a moderate glycemic index.

Consider this example. If you eat equal calories of carbohydrates with glycemic indexes of 33 (lentil soup) and 100 (bread), the resulting glycemic index of the mixture is only 66. The glycemic index of table sugar—the benchmark—is in the seventies; therefore, 66 is still within the bounds of Good Calories. When you combine these foods, it is as if you never ate the high glycemic-index food.

So go ahead and eat Bad Calories, but counter them with Good Calories.

You could counter a cookie with nonfat yogurt or an overly ripe banana with cherries. The possibilities are endless. All you have to do is remember two simple conditions.

First, you must eat both foods at the same time. Averaging glycemic indexes works only if the foods are consumed at the same time, in the same part of the meal. A Good Calorie main course cannot balance a Bad Calorie appetizer, since the appetizer will boost your blood sugar long before you get to the main course, creating the conditions for the formation of excess fat. Once your hormonal balance is thrown off, all future food, even Good Calorie foods, will make excess fat. Thus, whenever you combine Good and Bad Calories, you should make sure that your first few mouthfuls of food are Good Calories.

Second, you need enough Good Calories to counter the effect of the Bad Calories. The question is, how many Good Calories are needed?

Scientists can compute the average glycemic index of food combinations by applying a fairly difficult series of equations. I hate doing it. And if I, a trained scientist, find it too much of a hassle to compute these indexes, then I can't expect others to do so.

Instead, I discovered that if you eat four times more Good Calories than Bad Calories, you cannot go wrong. This rule of thumb comes from a simple mathematical truth. Take the worst-case situation, a meal of Good and Bad Calories with glycemic indexes of 76 (buckwheat) and 131 (French baguette bread), and eat four times more Good Calories than Bad Calories. The glycemic index of the resulting mixture is 87, barely into the Bad Calorie range. Almost all real-life situations involve foods with lower glycemic indexes than this hypothetical one; therefore, the four-to-one combination ratio almost always works.

The four-to-one ratio combination works only when Good and Bad Calories are combined in the same dish, such as in a casserole or curry, or when they constitute separate dishes, such as bread and mixed vegetables. Either method is a valid way to combine foods as long as you eat the foods at the same time.

Choose from the lists of Good and Bad Calories (Appendixes 1–30). There is no math to do or calories to add. You can ignore the numbers associated with the glycemic index. Everything is simple as long you eat four times more Good Calories than Bad Calories. There is no need to weigh the food or count calories; just estimate its weight and calories. I know that this method sounds unscientific, but I have found that such seat-of-the-pants estimates are amazingly accurate. You do not have to be exact. If you think you are eating a four-to-one ratio, you are probably safe.

PRACTICAL SUGGESTIONS: The four-to-one rule applies to combining two or more ingredients in a single dish. Thus, creative cooks can make almost anything into a Good Calorie dish just by adding enough Good Calorie ingredients.

Many ethnic cuisines, including Mexican, Indian, Chinese, Japanese, and Italian, feature a Good Calorie that is added to almost every main dish. Mexicans add beans; Indians add dal, a lentil soup; Chinese and Japanese serve food on rice; and Italians add pasta as a preliminary course before the main dish. These are examples of how people in different cultures develop tricks to keep themselves healthy. These Good Calories balance whatever Bad Calories are served in the same meal.

Becoming accustomed always to having a Good Calorie dish with your meal is a trick that you can emulate. It gives you more freedom. Certainly, it is better to eat a Good Calorie food, rather than the Bad Calorie bread that accompanies so many American meals.

3. Eat Good Calorie breakfasts. If you eat Good Calorie breakfasts, you will eat less food later in the day, make less blood sugar from the food you eat, and inhibit food cravings. Good Calorie breakfasts, such as oatmeal, orange juice, fruit, and decaffeinated coffee, are essential to the Good Calorie Diet.

A breakfast of Bad Calories almost doubles the blood sugar produced at lunch 3¾ hours later (see Figure 5-1).[1] Even if you have a Good Calorie lunch, it does not help. The poor breakfast makes the Good Calorie lunch produce the same blood sugar as it would if it were composed of Bad Calories.

This is called "the second-meal effect," and it is why breakfast can set the mood for the entire day.[2] If you have a Bad Calorie breakfast, you will probably suffer from the equivalent of a Bad Calorie lunch. The high blood sugar that follows lunch raises your blood sugar at dinner. In other words, a Bad Calorie breakfast can ruin an entire day.

Skipping breakfast is almost as bad. It also raises your blood sugar response to lunch. Therefore, you must eat a Good Calorie breakfast.

There is an additional, and extremely helpful, effect of eating only Good Calorie breakfasts: Good Calories decrease your sense of hunger and

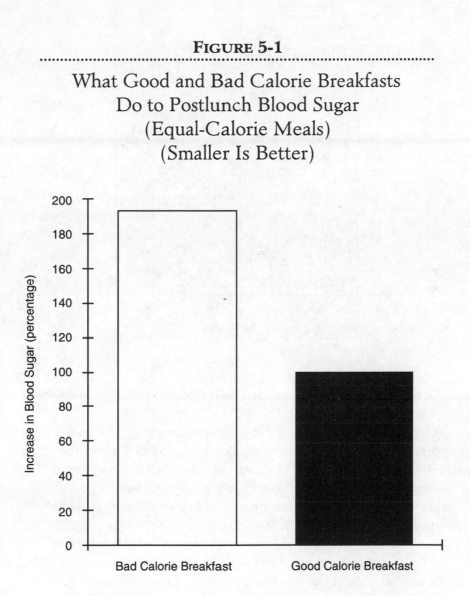

FIGURE 5-1

What Good and Bad Calorie Breakfasts
Do to Postlunch Blood Sugar
(Equal-Calorie Meals)
(Smaller Is Better)

minimize the carbohydrate addiction that causes you to choose fatty foods and Bad Calories throughout the day.[3]

One of my friends, John, is a perfect example of how Bad Calorie breakfasts sabotage your entire day. John has founded more than three companies. His car carries not one, but two, cellular telephones. The second phone is cross linked to his portable fax machine, so he can receive and send documents while talking to someone on the first phone. John is on the go from the moment he awakens. It is a rare morning when he stops to eat breakfast. Generally, his secretary brings donuts to his desk.

As one would expect, John has a weight problem. I tried to convince him that his basic problem was his breakfast habits. John refused to believe me. He said that the problem was that he craved greasy lunches of hamburgers and french fries.

John refused to try the Good Calorie Diet. However, I soon found a backdoor method to experiment on John. When we went on a working vacation in the Caribbean, I insisted on breakfast meetings. Every morning John and I sat down to a feast of fresh fruits and slow-cooked oatmeal.

All our lunches were at the hotel's buffet, which featured everything from greasy meats to pasta. At the beginning of our trip, John would choose the worst Bad Calories for lunch—roast beef, deep-fried shrimp, and pastries. I said nothing, curious to see if the Good Calorie breakfasts would take hold. After the first week, I noticed that John had switched to foods with a lower fat content—primarily grilled fish—and had stopped eating sweets.

I tried to convince John that the Good Calorie breakfasts accounted for the difference in his food preferences at lunch. I failed. John said that it was the sunshine. He almost convinced me. So I decided to do another experiment. I canceled our breakfast meetings. Without the moderating influence of those Good Calorie breakfasts, it was only a few days before John's plate was piled with fried foods and sweet rolls. There was no doubt in my mind: Good Calorie breakfasts work.

PRACTICAL SUGGESTIONS: Americans seem to be addicted to Bad Calorie breakfasts for a simple reason: They also eat Bad Calorie dinners, and eat them late at night. These dinners create an abnormal hormonal flow that alters one's sense of taste in the morning. Therefore, if you have trouble adjusting to Good Calorie breakfasts, the first place you should look is at your evening meals. Change them, and Good Calorie breakfasts will taste better than Bad Calorie ones.

Some people find that their quest for Good Calories takes them beyond their traditional concept of breakfast food. Some Oriental cultures eat rice for breakfast. Pacific Islanders eat fruit. I found that rice and slow-cooked oatmeal work best for me. It is a manifestation of modern society that we have come to think of breakfast as being composed of only Bad Calorie convenience foods.

4. Eat the most fat-forming foods for lunch, not for dinner. Despite the American tradition of eating a big evening meal, it is one of the worst habits for proper weight loss. At night, our bodies do not remove excess blood sugar but seek to conserve it as a means of ensuring a constant supply of blood sugar while we sleep and cannot eat. So when we eat late in the day, each calorie creates extra fat.

Jack used to work in the computer industry as a programmer. His workday started in the afternoon and lasted until the early hours of the next morning. When Jack went home, he would eat a huge meal and then go to sleep. He was obese. Although he was unwilling to go on a diet, I finally convinced him to eat his large meal at noon, shortly after awakening. It soon became apparent that this simple trick stopped Jack from continuing to gain two pounds every week as he had been doing for the previous six months.

Bad Calorie foods should not be eaten at dinner. Not only do they immediately create extra fat, but they increase the blood sugar that is created after the next morning's breakfast and probably the next lunch as well.[4] So if dinner is composed of animal protein or Bad Calories, you will have a greater appetite and create more fat throughout the next day.

Under ideal conditions, you should eat Good Calorie foods at both breakfast and dinner. That leaves lunch as the optimal time for protein and Bad Calories. Just following this simple rule will make a huge difference in your weight.

The rule against late-night Bad Calories applies to more than dinner. Late-night snacks and alcoholic drinks will also march straight to the nearest fat cell. Since we tend to indulge in these foods well after normal dinner hours, they can be even more devastating than can a Bad Calorie dinner. If you are up late at night and want a snack, make sure it is a Good Calorie snack, such as fruit. Avoid all foods that contain or will make excess fat.

What are the consequences of violating these rules? A University of Minnesota study, published in the proceedings of the Tenth International Congress on Nutrition, showed that people gained weight when fed a diet late in the day and lost weight when fed the same diet at breakfast. With a 2,000 calorie diet, the difference between the two groups was an amazing 2.3 pounds per week.

These studies were so startling that scientists repeated them. Instead of a set diet, participants could eat whatever they wanted in a single meal. There were no caloric limitations. One group ate breakfast within one hour of rising. Another group ate after 6 P.M. The result was that the breakfast group had a weight-loss advantage of 1.8 pounds per week.

PRACTICAL SUGGESTIONS: This rule is practically tailor-made for those who must eat out for lunch. Since lunch is when you should eat protein or other Bad Calories, choosing from a restaurant menu is fairly easy.

There's no doubt that it can be troublesome to eat Good Calorie dinners at restaurants. But there are always good choices, especially pasta and vegetables—skip the cream sauces. Since restaurants are in the business of selling food, they will try to sell the maximum amount of food at dinner, especially the more expensive main courses that feature animal protein. It is important to be strong and limit your intake of Bad Calories and animal protein. If you order a dinner that includes these items, eat sparingly while filling up on salad and vegetables. Take home a doggie bag of the excess food.

For many of us, dinner has become the prime forum for intimacy and the expression of love. Lovers or the family gather together for the evening meal. If your love relationship or family has been oriented around these principles, then you must gain a consensus as to your proposed change in eating habits. Dinner can still be a large meal. The only difference is that it will be composed of Good Calories.

If you must have your large meal in the evening, it does not mean that you cannot lose weight. It will just be more difficult to do so. However, you should try to have nothing but Good Calorie evening meals that do not feature animal products.

5. Eat Good Calorie snacks. Eating more frequently reduces insulin, blood sugar, and fat in the blood.[5] This is how our ancestors ate as they foraged for food; only when they started to hunt did they eat a single big meal. If you get hungry between meals, you should eat Good Calorie snacks.

You do not have to snack, but it will give you more latitude during meals. The lower the glycemic index of the snack, the more it aids the digestion of future meals.

PRACTICAL SUGGESTIONS: Fruit is a great snack. So is fat-free bean dip.

Obviously you should avoid Bad Calorie snacks, such as potato chips, corn chips, candy, hamburgers, and french fries.

6. Don't miss a meal. Never starve yourself. It is the one thing guaranteed to induce the Starvation Response. Just a few days of starvation can increase your fat-forming potential more than fourfold. Skipping a single meal can change your brain biochemistry and make you eat fattening foods in future meals.

PRACTICAL SUGGESTIONS: Although this would seem to be an easy rule, it goes against the long experience of most habitual dieters. Whereas conventional diets make you eat less, the Good Calorie Diet works by making you choose the proper foods while eating fully. You must remind yourself that your job is not to punish your body, but to make it feel comfortable.

If you cannot eat a full meal, you should make sure that you have several Good Calorie snacks, each a few hours apart. The ingestion of Good Calories will, via the second-meal effect, decrease your response to future meals.

7. Avoid combining excessive amounts of animal protein with starchy carbohydrates or fruit. This is a case in which red meats, poultry, fish, and dairy products all create the same problem. Combining anything that creates large amounts of blood sugar, such as starches or fruits, with animal protein inhibits the enzyme that places excess blood sugar into glycogen storage, thus elevating blood sugar and insulin levels and diverting large amounts of blood sugar into triglyceride fats.[6]

Figure 5-2 shows that combining protein with white potatoes or spaghetti almost doubles the peak insulin response.[7] It also shows that animal protein will increase the fat-forming potential of both Good and Bad Calorie carbohydrates. Spaghetti is a Good Calorie, and white potatoes are Bad Calories. Yet, the increase in insulin is roughly equal when either is combined with animal protein. This is one of the few cases in which Good Calories cannot prevent the formation of excess fat. Part of the problem is the saturated fat that accompanies animal protein.

The combination of starch and animal protein also causes us to overeat because it also inhibits the release of glucagon, the enzyme that signals when our stomachs are full.[8]

I have already mentioned that wheat bread is one of the worst Bad Calories. Now, you can see that the fat-forming potential of bread is further enhanced if it is included in meat sandwiches. Hamburgers, even low-fat hamburgers, can never be Good Calories. The same admonition applies to fish sandwiches, such as tuna.

Pizza appears to be an acceptable food, one that should cause no problems as long as it does not have meat toppings. Cheese topping, used in moderation, does not appear to evoke the problems outlined in this section. Of course, you should use low-fat cheese or normal cheese in sufficient moderation that less than 30 percent of the calories come from fat.

While I was writing this book, I decided to test what would happen if I combined excessive amounts of animal protein and starches. I had already cured the Starvation Response, and my weight was low. I ate animal protein with mashed potatoes. For four days nothing happened, and then the Starvation Response appeared. Within two weeks I had gained eight pounds.

FIGURE 5-2

Increases in Peak Insulin When Protein
Is Combined with Carbohydrates
(Smaller Is Better)

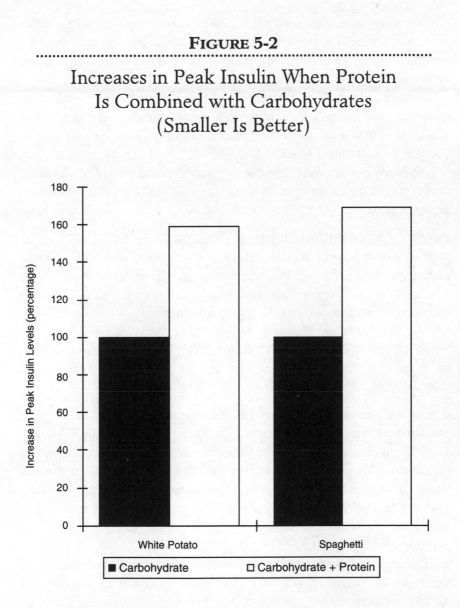

Not wanting to carry the experiment too far, I began to eat meals with no animal protein, but that change was not enough. Until I returned to a diet of Good Calories, thereby thwarting the Starvation Response, my weight did not return to normal.

Combining animal protein and starch gave me a clear message, and it will do the same for you. When you are suffering from the Starvation Response, vegetable proteins are better because they do not create excess fat when combined with starches or fruit.

When eating animal protein, combine it with either salads or vegetables that don't have as much potential to raise your blood sugar. You can also eat animal protein with meals in which starch or fruit predominate if you limit your intake of animal protein. It's simple.

Finally, do not interpret this rule to mean that you should totally avoid either protein or carbohydrates. Both are fine foods. Just have them in separate meals.

PRACTICAL SUGGESTIONS: If you eat grilled fish as the main course, so the meal is mainly protein, then do not have white potatoes or rice as a side dish. Don't panic; this rule is not as restrictive as it seems at first. You can have meat-based sauces with spaghetti and clams with linguine. The key is that the protein must be a minor part of the meal.

After the Starvation Response has subsided, you can eat sandwiches. However, you should realize that they are Bad Calories and treat them as such (see Rule 11). Sandwiches should be preceded and followed by Good Calorie meals.

8. Avoid excessive amounts of animal products while curing the Starvation Response. As long as you suffer from the Starvation Response, you should not eat meals in which animal products are the primary ingredients. Ingesting animal flesh turns off the normal mechanisms of energy storage, the deposition of energy in muscle and liver glycogen, and switches to mechanisms that create fat. Remember that only two days of eating high-protein foods or saturated fat can increase your blood sugar over fourfold.

This rule does not mean that you have to avoid animal products totally. But until the Starvation Response vanishes, you should eat only low-fat animal products and only as side dishes. For example, you can add small amounts to pasta sauce, a little tuna to a salad, or a few ounces of chicken to a meal that features Good Calorie vegetables and fruit.

During this period, avoid animal products that are high in saturated fat, such as red meat. Chicken and turkey are better than red meat, but still have more saturated fats than do some fish.

Don't be concerned about eating less protein. Our protein needs are much less than we may think. The World Health Organization estimates that people need a half gram of protein per kilogram of body weight, meaning that a 140-pound person needs 30 grams of protein per day (6 ounces of fish, 4 ounces of beefsteak, or 4 ounces of cheese). Others estimate that we need no more than 20 grams per day.[9]

Several lines of evidence suggest that we are healthier when we eat less protein. The average American consumes over 100 grams of protein per day, which contributes to obesity, diabetes, and osteoporosis.[10] Seventh Day Adventists, a vegetarian religious group, have lower rates of cancer and heart disease and live longer.

I don't expect all readers to eliminate animal products from their diets permanently. In fact, such a practice may be counterproductive. Serotonin, the neurotransmitter that controls appetite and cravings, measures the balance between sugar and protein in the bloodstream. When either substance is disproportionately low, serotonin makes you crave it. When you eat Bad Calorie carbohydrates, the resulting rise in blood sugar makes it seem as though you have eaten an enormous quantity of carbohydrates: Therefore, you'll crave protein. After you overcome the Starvation Response, your blood sugar will return to normal, and you will need less protein to maintain the balance.

If you find that you crave protein when you eat no animal products, eat a little animal protein. However, be careful not to pay attention to this craving until you have been following the first ten rules for several weeks. The avoidance of animal protein during this period allows your body to overcome the artificial needs imposed by the Starvation Response.

PRACTICAL SUGGESTIONS: Vegetable proteins should be a mixture of legumes (beans) and grains in a ratio of 1 to 2½, for example, 2½ parts rice to 1 part beans. This mixture will provide all the amino acids necessary for building muscle. The process of combining different vegetables is called protein complementation. Until recently, it was thought that both legumes and grains had to be eaten in the same meal, but some scientists now say that the two foods can be eaten in different meals. I have not had any problem eating a diet that does not always combine legumes and grains in the same meal.

71

AVOID THINGS THAT INCREASE FAT FORMATION

Avoid foods that are high in fat.

Avoid saturated fats; substitute unsaturated fats.

Avoid overcooked carbohydrates.

Avoid overly ripe fruit.

Avoid processed foods.

Avoid canned starches and legumes.

Avoid fructose.

Avoid alcohol before a meal.

Avoid smoking before a meal.

Avoid Bad Calories before and during exercise.

Some people may experience intestinal gas until they become accustomed to their new diet. If this happens to you, you may wish to take pills, such as Gas-X, that are designed to help with this problem. Don't worry. The discomfort is only temporary, and your digestive muscles will soon become accustomed to transporting Good Calorie foods.

9. Avoid the Starvation Response triggers. Chapter Three discussed the conditions that increase the fat-forming potential of all food, even Good Calories. They are repeated here. Keep them in mind.

10. Avoid vitamin and mineral deficiencies. Humans evolved to eat plants that are rich in vitamins and minerals. In times of starvation, one of the signals of the need to create excess fat was vitamin and mineral deficiencies. Today, such deficiencies are strongly associated with the Starvation Response, whose victims excrete significantly more, and absorb fewer, vitamins and minerals than do normal people.[11] Therefore, if you are experiencing the Starvation Response, a normal, well-balanced diet is not enough; you must take vitamin and mineral supplements.

Vitamin C. The Starvation Response induces Vitamin C deficiencies.[12] When you lack Vitamin C, blood sugar does not become glycogen and is thus made available for forming fat.[13] You also need Vitamin C for the proper release of insulin.[14]

Vitamin D. Levels of Vitamin D are much lower in people with the Starvation Response.[15] You should be concerned because Vitamin D deficiencies may cause the abnormal regulation of blood sugar.[16]

Vitamin E. Vitamin E supplementation decreases blood sugar.[17]

Magnesium. Magnesium deficiencies have been linked to insulin resistance, a primary symptom of the Starvation Response.[18]

Potassium. In normal people, insulin stimulates the entry of potassium into the liver and muscles, where blood sugar is converted into glycogen.[19] With the Starvation Response, insulin loses its ability to stimulate the uptake of potassium.[20]

Copper. The average American is likely to have a copper deficiency.[21] Copper supplements lower the triglyceride levels of copper-deficient people who are experiencing the Starvation Response by more than 70 percent, but do nothing for normal people with the same copper deficiency.[22]

Unfortunately, fructose aggravates a copper deficiency, and the combination of a copper deficiency and a high-fructose diet increases the risk of heart attacks in men.[23]

Chromium. Ninety percent of Americans are so deficient in chromium that the normal regulation of blood sugar is nearly impossible.[24] Food processing, Bad Calories, and caloric restriction all induce chromium deficiencies that elevate blood sugar, insulin, insulin resistance, cholesterol, and triglycerides.[25] Chromium supplements counteract these problems.[26]

Only a handful of modern foods contain significant quantities of chromium. They include brewer's yeast, beer, black pepper, liver, lobsters, oysters, mushrooms, shrimps, and whole grains.

Almost nobody can live on a diet of these foods, although I once watched a friend try. He was about to be fired from his job and wanted to charge his company for outlandish meals. I know it sounds bizarre, but every day he ate at least five lobsters and washed them down with the finest imported beers. At the end of the week he dreaded the moment he would step on the scales. To his complete amazement, he had not gained any weight. Rather, he had lost five pounds. Although seafood restaurants may love it, I am not about to write *The Lobster and Beer Miracle Diet*. It is not healthy. I suspect, however, that this certainly shows what can happen when you get enough chromium.

You should take chromium supplements, but chromium must be in a special form before it will do anything in the body. Chromium picolinate has received massive publicity, but numerous authorities have questioned whether it is effective or even safe.[27] Of the many chromium supplements that are available, chromium–nicotinic acid complexes appear to be the most active, producing a 15 percent decrease in blood sugar, a 20 percent to 30 percent decrease in cholesterol, and decreased triglycerides.[28]

RECOMMENDED SUPPLEMENTS: To counter any vitamin or mineral deficiencies while you're on the Good Calorie Diet, I recommend that you take the following supplements: 200 mg of chromium nicotinate, 300 mg of vitamin C, at least the RDA of vitamin B complex, the RDA of Vitamin D, and a good mineral tablet (with at least the minimum recommended daily allowance of calcium, zinc, potassium, and magnesium). You also need 3 mg of copper if you eat fructose, especially if you are a man.

BEFORE YOU ENJOY THE FREEDOM OF THE LAST TWO RULES, DETERMINE WHEN YOU HAVE OVERCOME THE STARVATION RESPONSE

•••

Until you overcome the Starvation Response, a process that should take fewer than two weeks, you do not have the freedom to relax the first ten rules of the Good Calorie Diet. To figure out when you can relax the rules, examine the list of symptoms of the Starvation Response. Compare the symptoms to the symptoms you experienced before you went on the Good Calorie Diet. If several have disappeared, then you have probably overcome the Starvation Response and are ready to move on. For most people, observing the first ten rules for two weeks is enough to do the trick.

Remember, the symptoms are as follows:

SYMPTOMS OF THE STARVATION RESPONSE

1. Regular overeating.
2. Eating rapidly.
3. Difficulty knowing when one's stomach is full.
4. Strong or persistent hunger.
5. Craving high-fat or high-sugar food.
6. Occasional binge eating.
7. Snacking at night.
8. Gaining weight on less food.
9. Regaining weight easily.
10. Gaining weight after a pregnancy or while taking either birth control or estrogen-replacement pills.

If you still exhibit a majority of the symptoms after two weeks, then you should reexamine your activities. Are you following the dietary instructions properly? Have you eaten protein-rich or high-fat meals? Are you snacking inappropriately? Do you still drink alcohol before a meal or on an empty stomach? Do you drink too much alcohol? If you look long enough, you will find what you are doing wrong and can easily correct it.

After your symptoms subside, you are free to move on to the last two rules. They help you to select the greatest variety of foods that your genetics will allow. They may allow you to eat Bad Calorie meals and other junk foods while still losing weight.

During the first several weeks after you have cured the Starvation Response, follow the suggestions in Appendix A on how often to have meals containing animal proteins. During this time, the stress of introducing animal proteins makes them count as Bad Calorie meals. Treat them as such and avoid other Bad Calorie meals.

11. Good Calorie meals should precede and follow Bad Calorie meals. After you have cured the Starvation Response, you can enjoy Bad Calorie meals. To avoid reevoking the Starvation Response, you should make sure that you precede and follow Bad Calorie meals with two days of Good Calorie meals. If you have been eating Good Calorie meals for the past few days, then your body will not overreact if you eat a Bad Calorie meal. Similarly, a few days of Good Calorie meals will normalize your system after a Bad Calorie meal.

Avoid eating any more food, either Good or Bad Calories, while digesting a Bad Calorie meal or snack. If you wait long enough for your next meal, then you will make less fat.

How long do you have to wait before the wrong enzymes subside? You have already seen that 3¾ hours is too short a time (see Rule 3); however, by 5¾ hours after a Bad Calorie breakfast the second-meal effect has dissipated.[29] So, simply wait six hours before eating the next meal. This rule does not mean that you have to wait six hours between *all* meals, just after a Bad Calorie meal. If you cannot wait six hours, then wait at least five hours.

Felicia is a magazine editor. She claims to have read more than a hundred diet books and certainly knows about conventional diets. When she read an early version of the Good Calorie Diet, she was filled with questions about why my advice was so different from conventional diets. After she read the manuscript, our first phone calls were filled with her skepticism. Then she went on vacation. Naturally, she went to a good restaurant and had a fat-filled lunch. Remembering my rule, she waited six hours before having dinner. The next day, she phoned me and was full of excitement. Ordinarily, the large lunch would have made her ravenously hungry at dinner. But after waiting six hours, she was *less* hungry than normal. Several times she tried this trick, and it always worked. Then, and only then, did she decide to try the rest of the Good Calorie Diet.

PRACTICAL SUGGESTIONS: While you are curing the Starvation Response, you meals will not include animal sources of protein. You avoid animal protein to reassure your body that it does not face starvation. After you have cured the Starvation Response, you should *gradually* reintroduce animal low-fat protein into your diet, if that is your nutritional preference. Remember, you do not have to eat animal protein, but neither do you have to avoid it.

While you are gradually reintroducing your body to animal protein, remember that meals with animal products count as Bad Calorie meals. Therefore, you must initially precede and follow them with several days of Good Calorie meals. Later you can introduce more meals containing animal products until you are eating them every other day. Remember that if you start to reexperience the symptoms of the Starvation Response, you should immediately discontinue whatever form of Bad Calories you are eating, including animal products. Fortunately, this is a rare response, and most people can tolerate some animal products.

After you have become reaccustomed to eating animal protein without evoking the Starvation Response, then these meals no longer count as Bad Calories. That is why low-fat animal proteins are listed as being Good Calories. After you have stabilized your intake of animal products at your desired level for two weeks, then you can try substituting meals that contain other forms of Bad Calories. Appendix A contains meal plans that illustrate these principles.

Remember, you can minimize the effects of discretionary Bad Calories by eating them at lunch, rather than at dinner. This suggestion is critical for eating animal protein. Lunch is the only time when you should subject your body to that stress.

You can prepare for a forthcoming party by eating nothing but Good

Calorie meals for several days, to normalize your system. Then you can enjoy Bad Calories at the party. Afterward, you should eat nothing but Good Calorie meals for several days.

While recovering from a Bad Calorie meal, you should also remember that Good Calorie meals can include Bad Calories via the four-to-one rule. There is no reason to be unnecessarily hard on yourself.

Finally, you should never atone for junk-food binges with caloric restriction. A Bad Calorie meal followed by starvation is the classic signal to initiate the Starvation Response. A Bad Calorie lunch is better than a Bad Calorie dinner. If you have a Bad Calorie lunch, you can compensate for it with a Good Calorie dinner. Eating a Bad Calorie dinner means that you must wait overnight before eating again, and that is too long a time to go without food.

12. Find your personal limits of freedom. The Starvation Response emerges differently in each person. Therefore, if you want to enjoy the maximum freedom, then you must experiment. I can give a list of rules that will work for everybody, but that list will include rules that you do not need. Different people are sensitive to different aspects of the Good Calorie Diet. For example, I am most sensitive to proper mineral supplementation. The wife of a good friend of mine is most sensitive to alcohol before meals. My daughter appears to be intolerant of excessive fat in her food.

After you start losing weight on a regular basis, you can slowly push the bounds of dietary freedom and occasionally enjoy a sinfully delicious meal that goes against the principles you learned in this book. Months later, you will be able to do so more often. A good rule is to explore alternative meals once a week after you have been on the diet for three months and twice a week during the following month.

If you go too far in your experiments, the Starvation Response reappears. You will stop losing weight or crave unusual foods and develop a larger appetite. When that happens, you should celebrate, for you now have one of the most valuable pieces of information—knowledge of what it takes for your body to become ill. You know exactly how much freedom you can enjoy without worrying.

PRACTICAL SUGGESTIONS: Remember, the operative word in the previous paragraphs is *slowly*. If you have just overcome the Starvation Response, you also have to be careful not to violate the other rules of the Good Calorie

Diet. Later, after you've established a healthy state, you can *gradually* expand the boundaries of your explorations.

Our bodies are in the same situation as is a small child awakening from a nightmare. As we comfort our bodies, we must train them to do nothing that reintroduces the fear and panic that lurks just below the surface. We must teach our bodies to recognize that occasional Bad Calories are not a sign of impending starvation.

Only with time will you determine your limits. Sometimes you may go too far. Your body may have a greater or lesser tolerance for cheating. The only way to know is to experiment—slowly and sanely.

To lose weight, all you have to do is limit yourself to the first ten rules of this section. At some point, you will find that the symptoms of the Starvation Response have disappeared, and you can then expand your freedom somewhat. As long as you stay within the limits that apply to you, you will lose weight.

DAILY AND RESTAURANT MENUS
...

So how do you incorporate the Golden Dozen Rules into your daily life? To make your job easier, I have compiled two appendixes.

Appendix A presents two sets of daily menus, one to use while combating the Starvation Response and one for afterward. Clearly, you can use the menus designed for combating the Starvation Response even after you have overcome that condition.

Appendix C helps you to eat in American, Chinese, fast-food, French, Italian, Japanese, Mexican, and seafood restaurants. Of course, the main problem with listing restaurant menus is that the recipes vary. So use these menus as a guide, not as absolute rules. They are also a good guide for home menus.

CHAPTER SIX

WHAT TO DO IF YOU DO NOT LOSE WEIGHT

ARE YOU FOLLOWING THE PROGRAM?
...

The Good Calorie program works, without modifications, for the vast majority of people who experience the Starvation Response. It will not make you look like an underfed youngster, but it will restore you to a healthy body without excessive concentrations of fat.

But what if it doesn't work for you? There may be medical reasons, but before you start looking for them, you should ask yourself one question: Did you follow the program?

Jackie Alexander is a thirty-five-year-old hospital administrator, who

exercises regularly and exudes good health. I first met her in the gym. She walked up to me and said that she heard I had developed an amazing weight-loss program. She was five feet five and weighed 130 pounds, and she wanted to lose fifteen pounds. When she went on the Good Calorie Diet, she did not lose weight. Three weeks later she approached me and informed me that my diet was a failure. I spent the next half hour going over everything she ate. At first I was mystified. Then I discovered that she consumed several high-protein, high-sugar shakes after each exercise session. When I told her that drinking these shakes violated the rule against consuming protein combined with excess blood sugar, she was astonished. In her mind "protein" meant a piece of meat or fish on a plate.

Jackie stopped drinking the protein shakes and devoted herself to overcoming the Starvation Response. After ten days she started to lose two pounds per week. Within a few months she reached her target weight. Jackie was thrilled. She had been promoted at work and thought that her image was the deciding factor. While I prefer to think that her competence earned her the promotion, I was pleased that her weight loss had given her a psychological edge that might have helped.

Some people, like Jackie, find it hard to follow the rules. They have some habit that is so deeply ingrained that they do not think about it. Many people are so accustomed to their predinner alcoholic drinks that they allow this habit to persist even though it raises their blood sugar. Other people work late and eat dinner very late in the evening; it will be difficult for them to lose weight. Some people still mix protein and starchy carbohydrates, especially when they eat in restaurants and potatoes or rice are served as a side dish.

And there are always the anxious people who engage in Bad Calorie meals before they have cured the Starvation Response. It is important to complete the first ten rules of the Golden Dozen presented in Chapter Five before relaxing the program. If you enjoy the freedom of potentially fat-forming foods prematurely, you must start again from the beginning.

Another common problem is that some people think that the Good

Calorie Diet's freedom means that they can engage in gluttony. Following a diet that does not restrict the quantity of food does not mean you can behave as if you are at a Roman orgy. If you are overeating, slow down and realize that it induces the Starvation Response.

Some people will need to combine exercise with weight loss. These are the people who suffer from a double problem—they make too much fat and they burn too little fat. However, *fewer* people than one would think require vigorous exercise for weight loss once they overcome the Starvation Response. *Do not* automatically assume that exercise is necessary for weight loss. However, don't ignore the benefits of exercise for general conditioning and cardiovascular health.

STRESS CAN AGGRAVATE THE STARVATION RESPONSE

...

When you suffer from the Starvation Response, you are at war with yourself. Insulin and high blood sugar send abnormal signals to your brain and alter more than your appetite. Like anyone whose body is at war with itself, you suffer from abnormal stress that pervades every thought. To be healthy, you must undo the damage that the Starvation Response has done to your mental health.

Mental stress has numerous measurable effects, many of which strengthen the Starvation Response. During mental stress, fat cells are activated, so that more blood circulates through them and more blood sugar flows within them, maximizing the formation of fat.[1] Furthermore, blood sugar is routed way from pathways that would burn it. Mental stress also alters the activity of the sympathetic nervous system, the same system that helps determine appetite and food preferences.[2] Finally, stress increases the secretion of glucocorticoid, which promotes a response that closely resembles that seen in starvation.[3]

Mental stress also severs the connection between your mind and your body, making it difficult to listen to the messages that ordinarily control your eating patterns. More than appetite controls, these messages contain the intelligence of your body, the same intelligence that will steer you to the proper combinations of Good and Bad Calories.

The bottom line is that mental stress creates a deadly positive feedback loop that locks you into the formation of excess fat. The Starvation

Response creates mental stress, and that stress strengthens the Starvation Response, which, in turn, creates more stress.

The way out of these problems is to reduce your levels of physical and mental stress. Some people find that exercise helps relieve stress, whereas others engage in meditation. Whatever technique you choose, you will find that lowering stress can frequently provide the last needed bit of momentum to overcome the Starvation Response.

PERSISTENT CASES OF THE STARVATION RESPONSE

...

Suppose you are eating reasonably, exercising, and following the rules, but you are still not losing weight. The first thing to do is see your physician to make sure that your weight problem is not a symptom of a serious disease. If you find out that you are in good health, you should realize that you suffer from a special form of the Starvation Response.

A small percentage of people, unfortunately, can never rid themselves of the Starvation Response. Their bodies are so strongly programmed that Bad Calories will always evoke the Starvation Response. For these people, there is a simple solution: Follow the first ten rules of the Golden Dozen in Chapter Five, but not the last two.

If you suspect that you are among this group, practice these first ten rules for five weeks. If you lose weight during that time, then continue on to the next two rules. If you stop losing weight at that point, return to and continue to follow only the first ten rules. Although the first ten rules are more stringent, you should find relief in the knowledge that you will lose weight while following them.

People who have to lose more than sixty pounds are another exception. They have a special set of problems. Not only will they have to remain within the bounds of the first ten rules, but they frequently have to decrease the amount of foods they eat because they suffer from other forms of excess fat formation and decreased fat burning, in addition to the Starvation Response. They are the *only* people who should follow the rules of the next section.

COMBINING GOOD CALORIES AND
CALORIC RESTRICTION
...

I do not normally recommend caloric restriction as a method of weight loss, but the experience of my friend George taught me the value of Good Calories in such a program.

George used to weigh well over 400 pounds. He had to modify his car so he could fit into the driver's seat. His clothes were like bags, hanging over a mass of flesh that he could barely move. George wanted to follow the Good Calorie Diet, but there was no time. His physician said that George's health was at risk and that he had to lose huge amounts of weight immediately. I knew that George could not lose several hundred pounds in six months on the Good Calorie Diet. Such a drastic loss of weight is medically inadvisable except under a physician's direct, and constant, supervision. Therefore, George and I decided to try an experiment. He would restrict himself to 1,000 calories a day of the Good Calories with the lowest glycemic indexes (see Appendix D) and would also follow the first ten rules of the Golden Dozen.

George liked the combination of caloric restriction and Good Calories because he could eat a greater volume of food; 1,000 calories a day felt more like 2,000 or 3,000. However, I did not expect much from the combination of caloric restriction and Good Calories. To my surprise, Good Calories prevented many of the food cravings and irritability that normally accompany caloric restriction. However, it was clear that George still suffered from the Starvation Response. He would experience hunger and excess blood sugar whenever he ate any Bad Calories.

George lost weight fairly rapidly—more rapidly than he had with liquid shakes and starvation. I remember the day he proudly showed me his new car. It was showroom perfect and completely unmodified. I do not know how much weight he lost, but it was well in excess of a hundred pounds.

When it was obvious that George's diet was coming to an end, I waited anxiously to see how much weight he would regain. Since he was suffering from a controlled case of the Starvation Response, I suggested that he devote himself to overcoming the Starvation Response by limiting himself to the first ten rules of the Good Calorie Diet. Perhaps immediately attacking the Starvation Response would prevent him from once again requiring a custom car.

85

Overcoming the Starvation Response was a pleasure for George. It was just like his old diet except that he could eat more food. Every time I saw George, he would smile and tell me how many second helpings of food he had enjoyed.

We extended the diet to six months and then *very gradually* introduced many of the freedoms of the last two rules. He regained a few pounds, but so few that his report was my only clue.

I was curious: Was this success a generalized phenomenon, or was it something unique to George? I tried a modified form of George's diet with Ann and Jill, both of whom were impatient to lose weight. Instead of 1,000 calories, they ate 1,500 calories a day. Other than that, they followed the same restrictions as did George. In two months, Ann lost twenty pounds, and Jill lost twenty-five. However, this is where their stories diverge.

Ann's goal had been to look good in a bathing suit because she was going on a Caribbean vacation. She did nothing to prevent the Starvation Response while on vacation. In two weeks she regained fifteen pounds.

Jill stayed in town and worked on overcoming the Starvation Response. She then spent another two months gradually easing into the freedom of the last two rules. After four months she had regained only two pounds. She looked great and felt great.

These case histories illustrate the possibilities and traps of restricting food while eating Good Calories. You will lose weight faster, but you will suffer from a greater case of the Starvation Response. Without the *strictest* recovery period, you will regain every pound. You must stick to only the first ten rules. Because Ann never took the time to prevent the Starvation Response, she regained every pound. Jill took the time, and she is still slim.

Though I am generally pretty easygoing about violating the rules, I am now going to sound like a drill sergeant addressing new recruits. If you go on a caloric-restriction diet, you should not break the first ten rules for at least *six months* after you stop restricting calories. The last two rules are no longer operative. You cannot eat unaccompanied Bad Calories. You cannot cheat if you want to lose weight and not regain it.

When you do follow caloric restrictions, be sure to consult Appendix D and eat only the foods with the lowest glycemic indexes. Although these foods will not provide as much of a taste treat, they will provide the maximum volume of foods.

Who should attempt to combine caloric restriction with the nutritional principles of the Good Calorie Diet? Obviously, people who have a lot of weight to lose. This combination will also work for people who must lose weight quickly.

I do *not* recommend caloric restriction for people who need to lose only thirty or forty pounds. The normal Good Calorie Diet is much more sensible, does not present the enormous threat of rebound weight gains, is easier to implement, and is more forgiving of deviations. It is also much faster in the sense that you spend less time thinking about strict food restrictions. I lost thirty pounds in just a few months on the normal program. Others have lost fifty to sixty pounds in less than a year.

I am not totally opposed to combining food restriction and Good Calories, especially since some scientists have suggested that malnutrition and other medical emergencies make the Starvation Response irreversible.[4] Those who experience an irreversible Starvation Response will not lose weight only by following the first ten rules of the Golden Dozen. They, and only they, should follow this program.

Using caloric restriction unnecessarily is like amputating your hands to cure hangnails. It will cure the problem, but it will create long-term consequences that are unnecessary. Most readers should enjoy the freedom of eating fully and losing weight without caloric restriction.

CHAPTER SEVEN

THE GOOD CALORIE SOLUTION

GOOD CALORIES THWART THE STARVATION RESPONSE

...

I have already presented many examples of how Bad Calories boost and Good Calories counter the Starvation Response. Chapters Two and Three reviewed scientific studies that have found that Good Calories reverse insulin resistance, lower blood sugar, and inhibit the synthesis of triglycerides, and many other studies have found the same results.[1]

Only one month of a Good Calorie diet decreases concentrations of triglycerides.[2] HDL triglycerides, the form of fat that moves into fat cells, are cut in half by Good Calories (see Figure 7-1).

FIGURE 7-1

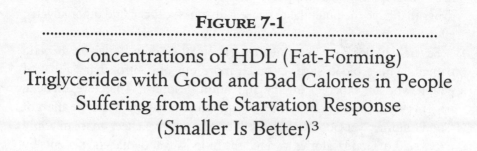

Concentrations of HDL (Fat-Forming)
Triglycerides with Good and Bad Calories in People
Suffering from the Starvation Response
(Smaller Is Better)[3]

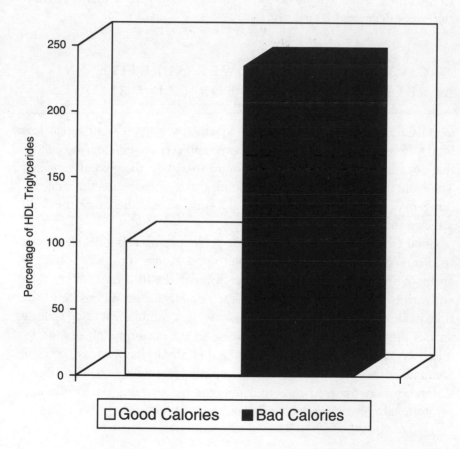

Good Calories lower triglycerides almost as effectively at cloibrate, a drug developed for that purpose.[4] Yet Good Calories are much safer than drugs that have the potential to cause gallstones, cancer, and other adverse effects.[5]

Several studies have examined the effects of Good Calories on diabetic patients whose blood sugar is much more out of control than is that of people who are experiencing the Starvation Response. Therefore, diabetic patients would seem to be in the worst possible situation to test the effect of Good Calories, yet Good Calories still have a positive effect on them. Only two weeks of Good Calories lowered the blood sugar of diabetic patients by 29 percent.[6] After five weeks on a low glycemic-index diet, their triglycerides decreased 20 percent.[7]

GOOD CALORIES LOWER APPETITE AND REVERSE CRAVINGS FOR BAD CALORIES

...

Good Calories change your brain biochemistry, so you want to eat less food.[8] In a pioneering study, Brand gave subjects six different breakfasts that contained foods that ranged from 43 to 116 on the glycemic index.[9] The higher the glycemic index of a food, the less it satisfied the subjects' hunger. Conversely, the lower the glycemic index, the more the food satisfied their hunger.

Good Calories not only reduce your present hunger, but decrease your food intake by allowing a longer time to pass before you become hungry again. When people eat shepherd's pie prepared with beans, rather than with white potatoes, for example, there is a significant difference in the time it takes for them to get hungry again.[10] Just eating a few Good Calorie snacks produces a spontaneous decrease in the consumption of food by 150 fewer calories per day.[11] If you eat Good Calories for breakfast, you will spontaneously eat less during lunch, but still feel totally satisfied.[12] Good Calorie carbohydrates reduce your appetite by reversing the insulin and serotonin abnormalities that cause you to crave food.[13]

GOOD CALORIES INCREASE FAT
BURNING

•••

The Starvation Response, malnutrition, and excess blood sugar all decrease
the rate at which fat burns, thereby allowing your body to hoard energy
stored as fat.[14] Because your body is sensitive to the ratio of fat to blood
sugar produced from food, extremely low-fat or high blood-sugar diets
comprised of Bad Calories can decrease your metabolic set-point. In contrast, lowering blood sugar increases the rate of fat burning.[15]

Therefore, you do not give up the metabolic advantages of conventional
diets when you pursue the Good Calorie Diet. I like to think that this diet
combines the best of both worlds.

MILLIONS HAVE USED GOOD CALORIES

•••

Scientists have studied representative samples of millions of people who
are fat when they eat Bad Calories and thin when they eat Good Calories.
Their stories gave me the idea for the Good Calorie Diet.

Studies have found that Native Americans, Australian Aborigines, Alas-
kan Eskimos, African Zulus, Asian Indians, Mexicans, and Yemenite Jews
are fat and diabetic on Bad Calories, but quickly lose both weight and
excess blood sugar when they eat Good Calories. The correlation between
blood sugar and weight is best seen in the Pima Indians of Arizona.

The Pima originally lived in the arid desert valleys of Arizona and
worked farms built around an elaborate system of irrigation canals.[16] Their
diet consisted of low glycemic-index carbohydrates: acorn stew, mesquite
cakes made from cacti, corn hominy made from low-sugar corn, tepary
beans, and lima beans. It is a diet that induces lower levels of blood sugar
than any other commonly used diet.[17]

The Pima abandoned their original diet a century ago when white
settlers appropriated their farmlands and water. Living on reservations,
they ate surplus wheat flour, sugar, coffee, processed cereals, and lard.
Although this diet sounds crude, it consists of about the same percentages
of fat, protein, and carbohydrate that are found in the typical American
diet. Unfortunately, it also induces high blood-sugar levels.

The Pima soon grew obese with their new diet. On some reservations three-quarters of the population is grossly fat, and over one half the residents suffer from diabetes, a disease that stems from dangerously high blood sugar.[18]

Realizing that they were poisoning themselves, some Pima returned to their traditional diet. When they ate native foods, both their obesity and high levels of blood sugar diminished. Other health problems, such as diabetes and heart disease, lessened as the pounds melted away. What is the magic of native foods?

At first, the physicians thought that a decrease in calories accounted for the weight loss. However, native foods proved to have more calories than they expected. Obviously, some other factor was at work. Now we know that it was the Good Calorie content of the diet.

GOOD CALORIES WORK ONLY ON THOSE WHO SUFFER FROM THE STARVATION RESPONSE
...

If Good Calories are such miracle workers, why have they remained unknown until now? To answer this question, you have to consider the nature of medicines. A headache tablet, for example, will do nothing for a person who does not have a headache. Similarly, Good Calories will do nothing for people who do not suffer from the Starvation Response. Replacing Bad Calories with Good Calories lowers blood sugar, insulin, and triglycerides in people who exhibit the Starvation Response, but does not have the same effect in normal people (see Figures 7-2, 7-3, and 7-4).

To study the Starvation Response properly, you must remove all the Starvation Response triggers and use the entire program on those who suffer from the Starvation Response.

ADDITIONAL BENEFITS OF THE GOOD CALORIE DIET
...

Weight loss is only one of the many benefits of the Good Calorie Diet. Here are just a few of the added health benefits:

Diabetes. The most common form of diabetes is adult-onset non-insulin-dependent diabetes melitus (NIDDM). When Australian physicians

FIGURE 7-2

Increase in Blood Sugar After Eating
Good and Bad Calorie Potatoes
(Smaller Is Better)[19]

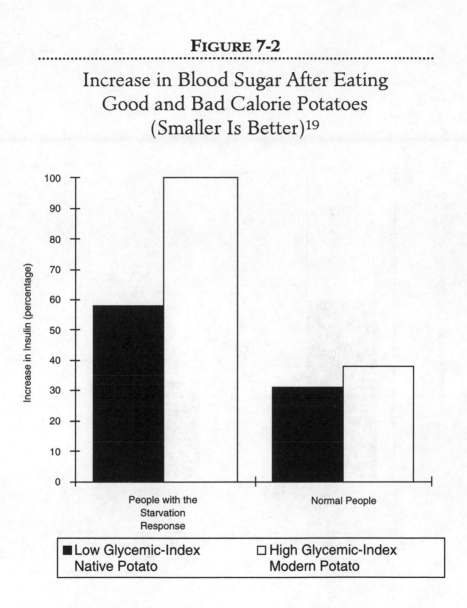

FIGURE 7-3

Increase in Insulin After Eating
Good and Bad Calorie Potatoes
(Smaller Is Better)[20]

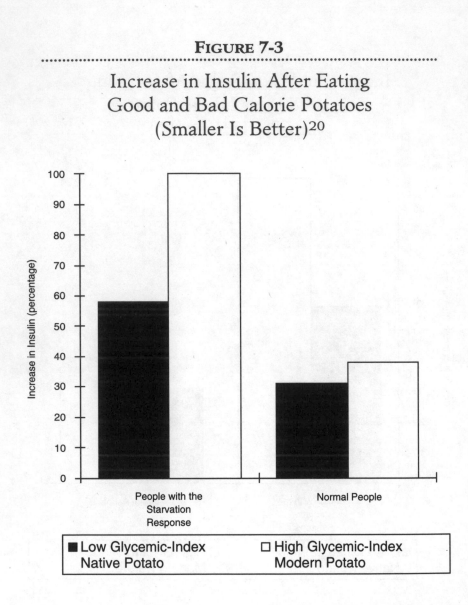

FIGURE 7-4

HDL Triglycerides
(The Most Fat-Forming Triglycerides)
After Eating Good and Bad Calories
(Smaller Is Better)[21]

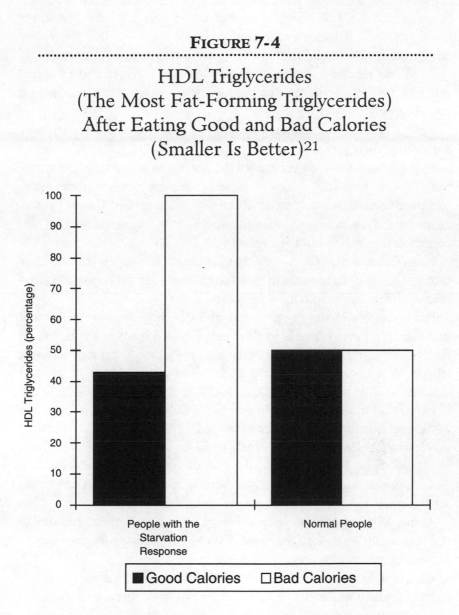

compared the effects of Good Calories versus the effects of the usual treatment for NIDDM, they found that Good Calories produced lower blood sugar and less urinary excretion of blood sugar.[22] Other physicians have confirmed the effectiveness of Good Calories in the treatment of NIDDM and insulin-dependent diabetes.[23] Good Calories also help prevent fat from binding to the protein in muscle—a primary cause of diabetic complications.[24]

Note: Persons with diabetes should not change their diets without consulting their physicians.

Hypoglycemia. Hypoglycemia is a disease of low blood sugar. Its symptoms include headache, fatigue, irritability, anxiety, confusion, sweating, and poor concentration. It usually occurs after eating Bad Calories and is characterized by initial increases in blood sugar followed by rapid decreases to lower-than-normal levels.

Good Calories are often an effective treatment for hypoglycemia. They promote the gradual increase in blood sugar that does not trigger the rapid release of insulin that produces low blood sugar.

Heart disease. A fifteen-year study of 7,038 French policemen found that the earliest marker of heart disease is elevated insulin, a symptom of the Starvation Response.[25] The Starvation Response also raises levels of triglycerides, cholesterol, and fatty acids, all of which contribute to heart disease.

Numerous studies have shown that Good Calories can lower, by nearly 30 percent, the low-density lipoproteins (LDLs) in people who experience the Starvation Response; high levels of LDLs are correlated with heart attacks.[26] Only three weeks of adding four ounces of beans—the best Good Calories—per day to a normal diet lowers cholesterol by more than 10 percent.[27]

Aging. As you age you develop insulin resistance and other symptoms of the Starvation Response. The Good Calorie Diet may be an easy way to counter or inhibit this process.

Cancer. One-third to one-half of all cancers may have a dietary origin.[28] Certainly, many researchers have noted a correlation between cancer and the ingestion of animal fats. Good Calories are known to help prevent prostate and colon cancer.[29]

Dental caries (cavities). Dental caries are caused when Bad Calories, which are easily digested, release sugar into the mouth. Therefore, Good Calorie foods may help prevent them.[30]

Endurance and fatigue. An additional advantage of Good Calories is that they foster endurance and lessen fatigue. Eating Good Calories (such as lentils) before exercise produces an 18 percent increase in endurance, whereas exercise drinks produce only a 9 percent increase.[31] Thus, a Good Calorie diet may be more than twice as effective as are many common exercise drinks in increasing endurance.

HISTORICAL PERSPECTIVE

...

*They are as sick that surfeit with too much as
they that starve with nothing.*

WILLIAM SHAKESPEARE (1564–1616),
The Merchant of Venice, I, ii

This is how *The Surgeon General's Report on Nutrition and Health* (1988) opens its discussion of obesity:

> Historians of obesity, finding few scientific records, have searched for clues in linguistics, history, and art and have concluded that obesity as it is now known did not occur in England, except in a few isolated instances, until it began to appear in the English upper classes in the 18th and 19th centuries.
>
> One hypothesis suggests the ability to store excess calories as fat in adipose tissue was useful during prehistoric times as a protection against food shortages. However, the ability later became a handicap in industrialized societies.

The report makes quite clear what many people have always known in their hearts—that modern eating habits are the source of excess fat. The problem has been that, until now, no one knew exactly what were the dangerous elements of the modern diet. Without this information, it is nearly impossible to correct the problem. Clearly, you cannot abandon everything just to eliminate a few harmful elements.

It is my hope that the Good Calorie Diet will give you the freedom to enjoy food, without the anxiety that you are eating the wrong thing. In this respect, it has been my intent to create a diet of freedom. If you enjoy yourself as you return to health, then you will have fulfilled my fondest wish.

Thank you for taking this journey with me.

97

Write to me about your experiences:
Box 322
20 Sunnyside
Mill Valley, CA 94965

I cannot promise to acknowledge all correspondence, but I will read as many letters as possible. I may use your story or suggestion in a future book. I am also interested in the experiences of alcoholics, drug users, migraine sufferers, and people with either mental or eating disorders.

These appendixes were designed to make it easy to implement the Good Calorie Diet. They may address some questions that were unanswered by the text. They should offer the examples and guidance needed to make implementing my program as painless as possible.

Appendix A offers a list of suggested menus for the two stages of the Good Calorie Diet: vegetarian menus for combating the Starvation Response and a program for introducing animal products during the weight loss and maintenance portions of the diet. Many menu items are preceded by an asterisk, indicating that the recipes for those items are presented in Appendix B. These menus are included only to help show you the great diversity of foods and meals available to you. Feel free to substitute comparable foods. The only guidelines that must be followed closely are those concerning the timing of meals containing animal products, given in a short section immediately preceding the sample menus.

Appendix C surveys many restaurant menus and indicates which items are your best bets. Unlike the other appendixes, this one is not strictly divided into Good and Bad Calories because of the immense variations in cooking styles among chefs. Instead, it highlights the items that are least likely to be harmful. You can also use Appendix C to get ideas for dishes that you may want to include in menus at home.

Appendix D is the most technical and, for most people, will be the least used. It lists the glycemic indexes of foods that have been actually measured. Most people do not need to know the glycemic indexes of the foods they eat. It is sufficient to know if they are Good or Bad Calories, something that is presented in Appendixes 1–30.

Sample Daily Menus

Please remember that the Good Calorie Diet offers a good deal of freedom. I have included these menus only as examples. I'm sure you will find that substituting many of your own low-fat recipes will work as well. Also, you should feel free to combine items from different parts of the menus. Just be sure to follow the Golden Dozen rules and avoid the Starvation Response triggers.

The suggested menus offer vegetarian options as well as ones that contain sources of animal protein. Remember that animal fat and protein can induce the Starvation Response. Therefore, you must be careful about eating them. When you reintroduce them into your diet after you have overcome the Starvation Response, they count as Bad Calories. Only later—about a month after you start eating animal protein—after your body is accustomed to digesting animal fat and protein do they count as Good Calories. At that time, you can start to experiment with Bad Calorie meals. However, most people find that they can tolerate animal fat and protein only every other day without reevoking the Starvation Response.

The following summarizes the maximum pace at which you can introduce animal fat and protein into your diet after conquering the Starvation Response. You should test yourself after ten and fourteen days to see if the symptoms of the Starvation Response have subsided. You may notice that the symptoms subside after three or four days, though such encouraging signs do not indicate that they have decreased as much as possible. Only when the symptoms have reached their maximum state of decrease should you consider moving to Day 1 of the menus for introducing animal fat and protein. Remember that it is better to stay on a diet that is free of animal fat and protein for a few extra days than to eat these products before you have fully overcome the Starvation Response.

Contents of menus for overcoming the Starvation Response

I recommend a diet of Good Calories that excludes animal fats and protein while you are overcoming the Starvation Response.

Contents of menus for reintroducing animal fat and protein

The *only* time you can eat animal fat and protein without cheating is at lunch. All other meals should be similar to those that are eaten while overcoming the Starvation Response.

Day 1	Lunch: animal protein, but no starch or high glycemic-index carbohydrates.
Days 2 and 3	No animal protein in any meal.
Day 4	Lunch: animal protein, but no starch or high glycemic-index carbohydrates.
Days 5 and 6	No animal protein in any meal.
Day 7	Lunch: animal protein, but no starch or high glycemic-index carbohydrates.
Days 8 and 9	No animal protein in any meal.
Day 10	Lunch: animal protein, but no starch or high glycemic-index carbohydrates.
Days 11 and 12	No animal protein in any meal.

Day 13   Lunch: animal protein, but no starch or
                          high glycemic-index carbohydrates.

Day 14   No animal protein in any meal.

Day 15   Lunch: animal protein, but no starch or
                          high glycemic-index carbohydrates.

Day 16 and onward   Alternate the plans for Day 14 and Day 15.

After two months without symptoms of the Starvation Response, animal protein meals eaten every other day are no longer considered to be Bad Calorie meals. At that point you can experiment with adding Bad Calorie meals according to the principles of Rules 11 and 12 of the Golden Dozen.

*Menus for use both while curing the Starvation Response
and on vegetarian days during weight loss**

This section contains only vegetarian meals. The next section features some lunches with animal products and contains vegetarian menus in all dinners and some of the lunches. Do not overlook this important source of new menus.

Vegetarian Menu 1

Breakfast: Extra Fiber All Bran Cereal (Kellogg's) with nonfat
                 milk
              orange juice
              nonfat unsweetened yogurt

Lunch: pasta with lemon and ginger
              fresh vegetable crudities with *dill-yogurt dip

Snack: nonfat bean dip, salsa, and vegetable crudities

Dinner: *vegetable medley soup
              pasta with garlic, olive oil, and broccoli

              fruit smoothie drink of frozen fruits blended with
                 nonfat plain yogurt

---

* An asterisk before a recipe means that it is included in Appendix B.

Vegetarian Menu 2

Breakfast: old-fashioned slow-cooked oatmeal
              grapefruit

Lunch: *lentil stew with garlic and ginger
              rice
              fruit salad

Snack: cooked rice topped with berries and flavored nonfat
                  unsweetened yogurt

Dinner: *spinach and garlic soup
              baked, vegetarian lasagna (seasoned and layered
                  eggplant pasta, zucchini, nonfat cheese and
                  tomato sauce)
              grapes

Vegetarian Menu 3

Breakfast: sliced bananas and low-fat plain yogurt
              Fiberwise cereal (General Mills) with nonfat milk
              orange slices

Lunch: tossed green salad with nonfat salad dressing
              pasta sautéed in olive oil with sun-dried tomatoes
              melon with strawberries

Snack: pumpernickel sandwich with nonfat cheese, nonfat
                  mayonnaise, sliced tomato, and lettuce

Dinner: *gazpacho
              *three-bean salad
              nonfat cottage cheese
              melon
              slice of whole-kernel rye bread

Vegetarian Menu 4

Breakfast: fresh fruit salad with nonfat plain yogurt
              melon
              old-fashioned slow-cooked oatmeal

Lunch: Vegetarian chili
garden salad with nonfat herb dressing
*pinto-bean dip with vegetable sticks

Snack: low-fat cottage cheese with assorted vegetable sticks

Dinner: *Cuban black bean soup
rice with salsa
sponge cake

Vegetarian Menu 5

Breakfast: broiled grapefruit
nonfat cottage-cheese crepes with nonfat yogurt and
    fresh fruit topping

Lunch: *Indian dal (lentil) soup
*baked tomatoes
*saffron rice
100 percent rye bread

Snack: slice of vegetable pizza with a moderate amount of
    cheese

Dinner: *miso soup with scallions and seaweed
*cucumber salad with vinegar-herb dressing
pumpernickel toast with corn oil margarine
*sugar-free strawberry jam

Vegetarian Menu 6

Breakfast: Fiber One cereal (General Mills) with nonfat milk
fruit

Lunch: *Russian borscht with nonfat yogurt
pasta with pesto
green salad with lowfat dressing

Snack: cheese sandwich on toasted rye bread

Dinner: *miso soup with scallions and seaweed
*three-bean salad
*roasted vegetables

Vegetarian Menu 7

Breakfast: fresh citrus slices
slice of dark pumpernickel bread
unsaturated-fat margarine and unsweetened jam
non-fat cottage cheese

Lunch: *tomato-herb soup
*roasted vegetables

Snack: rice mixed with cheese-free pesto

Dinner: mashed fresh tropical-fruit soup (chilled)
*Good Calorie vegetable medley
steamed rice
sponge cake

Vegetarian Menu 8

Breakfast: stewed fresh fruit medley with nonfat yogurt

Lunch: cold lentil salad on spinach with vegetable bacon
bits
pasta with low-fat marinara sauce
apple slices

Snack: fat-free cheese sandwich on toasted 100 percent rye
bread

Dinner: tomato juice
*white beans and garlic puree
broccoli with toasted sesame seeds and unsaturated
margarine
pumpernickel bread with unsweetened jam
sponge cake with banana (not overly ripe) and
strawberries

Vegetarian Menu 9

Breakfast: old-fashioned slow-cooked oatmeal with heated
fresh fruit
melon

Lunch: gazpacho
                *linguine with shiitake mushroom sauce
                fresh seasonal fruit

Snack: rye toast with *sugar-free jam

Dinner: cold asparagus with nonfat yogurt and curry sauce
                lentil soup
                herb-flavored rice
                mixture of star fruit, papaya, strawberries, and
                    raspberries

Vegetarian Menu 10

Breakfast: rice topped with *sugar-free strawberry jam
                orange juice

Lunch: grilled halibut with low-fat tomato sauce
                steamed vegetables with chutney
                *fruit ice or "granita"

Snack: melon

Dinner: *Middle Eastern chickpea-cabbage soup
                *stewed tomatoes and okra
                baked yams
                *cranberry-ginger-orange relish

Vegetarian Menu 11

Breakfast: Fiber One cereal (General Mills) with nonfat milk
                grapefruit

Lunch: *Indian dal (lentil) soup
                rice
                grilled vegetable kabobs (green peppers, tomato,
                    yam, orange, celery, and cabbage), marinated in
                    nonfat Italian dressing
                fresh strawberries

Snack: nonfat mild black-bean dip on rye bread

Dinner: nonfat coleslaw
                  *horseradish and beet puree
                  *puree of butternut squash

Vegetarian Menu 12

Breakfast: old-fashioned slow-cooked oatmeal
                  orange slices

Lunch: *lentil-stuffed zucchini
                  rice with herbs
                  melon

Snack: Dole Frozen Fruit bars

Dinner: *cucumber salad with vinegar-herb dressing
                  vegetarian chili
                  pumpernickel toast
                  fruit

Vegetarian Menu 13

Breakfast: Heartwise cereal (Kellogg's) with nonfat milk
                  fruit

Lunch: linguine with *yellow bell-pepper sauce
                  tropical fruit salad

Snack: fresh apple slices and nonfat cheese

Dinner: brown rice, lima beans, and steamed vegetables with
                      balsamic vinegar
                  green salad
                  macrobiotic wheat-free and sugar-free cookies

Vegetarian Menu 14

Breakfast: Extra Fiber All Bran cereal (Kellogg's) with nonfat milk
                  orange juice
                  pumpernickel toast
                  *sugar-free strawberry jam

Lunch: spinach salad with mushrooms and nonfat dressing
low-fat pizza

Snack: fresh vegetable crudities (cucumber, celery, and so
on) with *dill-yogurt dip

Dinner: *three-bean salad
steamed cauliflower and spinach with Old Bay
seasoning
herbed rice

Vegetarian Menu 15

Breakfast: cooked, cooled rice topped with *sugar-free
strawberry jam
orange juice

Lunch: mixed greens, arugula, and radicchio with balsamic
vinaigrette
*pasta primavera

Snack: *cottage cheese toasts

Dinner: *jasmine rice and split peas
fruit salad

Vegetarian Menu 16

Breakfast: old-fashioned slow-cooked oatmeal with nonfat milk
orange juice
pumpernickel toast
*sugar-free jam

Lunch: *gazpacho
*lentil stew with garlic and ginger
rice
fruit salad

Snack: cooked, cooled rice topped with berries and flavored
nonfat yogurt

Dinner: *savory baked yams
baked vegetarian lasagna with nonfat cheese
grapes

Vegetarian Menu 17

Breakfast: old-fashioned slow-cooked oatmeal
              melon
              juice

Lunch: *spring asparagus soup
              *black-eyed pea salad
              steamed or *roasted vegetables

Snack: broiled open-face pumpernickel sandwich with
                  nonfat cottage cheese, green onion, sweet basil,
                  and a thin slice of nonfat cheese

Dinner: *cucumber salad with vinegar-herb dressing
              *fresh broccoli with lemon vinaigrette
              *bean and pumpkin stew

Vegetarian Menu 18

Breakfast: flavored nonfat yogurt
              old-fashioned slow-cooked oatmeal with fresh fruit
                  cooked in the cereal

Lunch: tomato and onion salad with nonfat dressing
              pasta with steamed vegetables and pesto
              *fruit ice

Snack: *Russian borscht with a small amount of nonfat sour
                  cream and/or cucumber

Dinner: green salad with nonfat dressing
              *white beans and garlic puree
              rye toast
              sponge cake with partially thawed frozen berry
                  topping

Vegetarian Menu 19

Breakfast: sliced bananas (not overly ripe) and low-fat plain
                  yogurt
              Fiberwise cereal (Kellogg's) with nonfat milk
              toasted whole-kernel bread with low-fat unsaturated
                  oil margarine

Lunch: *Russian borscht
*chickpea flour "quiche"
*wild rice salad
papaya

Snack: cold tomato and basil soup garnished with nonfat
      yogurt

Dinner: *red and green salad with oriental dressing
pasta with olive oil and garlic

Menus containing animal products, to be introduced slowly after curing the Starvation Response*

Menu A

Breakfast: old-fashioned slow-cooked oatmeal
melon
juice

Lunch: shrimp cocktail with *horseradish dip
*Turkish cucumber-yogurt soup
*salmon and black bean sauce

Snack: fruit shakes made from fruit, nonfat yogurt, and
      ice, blended

Dinner: white bean soup
*eggplant-tomato stew
rice

Menu B

Breakfast: old-fashioned slow-cooked oatmeal
orange slices
whole-kernel bread, toasted

---

* An asterisk before a recipe means that it is included in Appendix B.

Lunch: vegetable soup with kidney beans
rye bread
*Mexican chicken fajitas
honeydew melon

Snack: Healthy Choice fat-free deli meat rolled around
                    nonfat cheese

Dinner: *creamy winter squash soup
pasta with low-fat marinara sauce

Menu C

Breakfast: fruit compote
Extra Fiber All Bran cereal (Kellogg's) with nonfat
                    milk

Lunch: *red and green salad with oriental dressing
*grilled sea bass with dill sauce
fresh apple and grapes

Snack: *gazpacho

Dinner: *cantaloupe soup
*pasta fagioli
cooked spinach with sesame seeds

Menu D

Breakfast: nonfat cottage cheese crepes with nonfat yogurt and
                    fresh fruit topping
low-fat turkey ham
grapefruit juice

Lunch: *Cuban black bean soup
*New Orleans fettucine with mussels
*fruit ice or "granita"

Snack: citrus fruit salad

Dinner: *eggplant-tomato stew
*pinto bean dip on pumpernickel toast
*savory baked yams

Menu E

Breakfast: papaya
baked yams with unsaturated fat margarine

Lunch: broiled trout with *yellow bell-pepper sauce
steamed green beans
curried unsweetened applesauce
fresh fruit

Snack: cold cooked rice with cinnamon and diced fruit
covered with nonfat milk to moisten

Dinner: *Middle Eastern chickpea-cabbage soup
*stewed tomatoes and okra
Dole Frozen Fruit bars

Menu F

Breakfast: Extra Fiber All Bran Cereal (Kellogg's) with nonfat
milk
orange juice
nonfat plain yogurt

Lunch: split-pea soup
*Good Calorie chicken salad
baked butternut squash
cantaloupe with berries and banana

Snack: low-fat or nonfat cheese sandwich on toasted 100
percent rye bread

Dinner: *Indian dal (lentil) soup
rice
grilled yams
fresh strawberries

Menu G

Breakfast: fresh citrus slices
slice of dark pumpernickel bread
unsaturated-fat margarine and unsweetened jam
low-fat cottage cheese

Lunch: Japanese-style clear miso broth with spinach and
                  cabbage
              *chicken and beet salad
              sliced orange and apple

Snack: nonfat bean dip, salsa, and low-fat tortilla chips

Dinner: *spinach and garlic soup
              grilled vegetable kabobs (green peppers, tomato,
                  yam, orange, celery, and cabbage), marinated in
                  nonfat Italian dressing
              grapefruit ice

Menu H

Breakfast: old-fashioned slow-cooked oatmeal
              nonfat plain yogurt over fresh fruit slices

Lunch: *Turkish cucumber-yogurt soup
              mixed baby greens with balsamic vinegar and olive
                  oil
              *marinated chicken breasts

Snack: mild black-bean dip spread on rye bread

Dinner: sautéed mushrooms and broccoli on rice
              *puree of butternut squash

Menu I:

Breakfast: sliced bananas (not overly ripe) and low-fat plain
                  yogurt
              Fiberwise cereal (Kellogg's) with nonfat milk
              toasted whole-kernel bread with low-fat unsaturated
                  oil or margarine

Lunch: *grilled halibut with green sauce
              *savory baked yams

Snack: low-fat cheese on whole-kernel bread

Dinner: mashed fresh tropical-fruit soup (chilled)
              stir-fried vegetables and rice
              sponge cake

Menu J

Breakfast: cooked white rice with *sugar-free jam
              fruit
              melted low-fat cheese on 100 percent rye toast

Lunch: *cantaloupe soup
              *spicy chicken salad
              steamed broccoli with cauliflower

Snack: fruit

Dinner: *marinated green tomato salad
              *pasta fagioli

Menu K

Breakfast: stewed fresh fruit
              Extra Fiber All Bran cereal (Kellogg's) with nonfat
                  milk

Lunch: *shrimps with lemon and ginger
              steamed rice
              brussels sprouts with light olive oil and lemon

Snack: fruit

Dinner: *cucumber salad with vinegar-herb dressing
              *winter vegetable puree
              *fruit ice or "granita"

Menu L

Breakfast: sliced bananas and low-fat plain yogurt
              Fiberwise cereal (Kellogg's) with nonfat milk
              toasted whole-kernel bread with low-fat unsaturated
                  oil or margarine

Lunch: *spinach and garlic soup
              *flounder with lemon-mustard sauce
              *baked tomatoes

Snack: vegetable crudities with *Tzatziki-Greek cucumber-
                  yogurt dip

Dinner: *vegetable medley soup
                pasta and non-fat tamato marinara with steamed
                  vegetables

Menu M

Breakfast: fresh citrus slices
                slice of dark pumpernickel bread
                unsaturated-fat margarine and unsweetened jam
                non-fat cottage cheese

Lunch: *creamy winter squash soup
                *shrimps with tomatoes

Snack: fresh vegetable crudities (cucumber, celery, and so
                  on) with *horseradish dip

Dinner: *oriental sweet potato stew
                rice

Menu N

Breakfast: fresh fruit salad with nonfat plain yogurt
                melon

Lunch: *orange-glazed turkey breast
                *horseradish and beet puree
                *Good Calorie vegetable medley

Snack: fresh apple slices and nonfat cheese

Dinner: *rice pilaf
                *mung bean–tomato stew

Menu O

Breakfast: grapefruit
                old-fashioned slow-cooked oatmeal with stewed
                  fresh fruit
                nonfat cottage cheese

Lunch: spinach salad with nonfat dressing
*turkey chili Diablo
*roasted vegetables
diet sorbet

Snack: fruit shake made from fruit, nonfat yogurt, and ice,
blended

Dinner: herbed spaghetti tossed with Molly McButter

Menu P

Breakfast: melon
old-fashioned slow-cooked oatmeal with berries

Lunch: *tomato-herb soup
*shrimps with lemon and ginger
*saffron rice

Snack: Dole Frozen Fruit bars

Dinner: *red bean pistou
cucumber and onion salad with seasoned nonfat
yogurt dressing

Menu Q

Breakfast: rice with *sugar-free jam
grapefruit

Lunch: *marinated chicken breasts
steamed vegetables
*fruit ice or "granita"

Snack: apple slices with low-fat cheese

Dinner: green salad with nonfat dressing
*wild rice salad
sponge cake with strawberries

Good Calorie Recipes

The main purpose of these recipes is to demonstrate the wonderful diversity of vegetarian meals, though these recipes certainly do not cover all the foods you can eat. Just look at Appendixes 1–30 for other choices.

I purposely did not choose recipes that are extremely low in fat. Such extraordinary measures are not necessary in the Good Calorie Diet. However, that does not mean that you should not eat such foods. They can be extremely useful in balancing a Bad Calorie food that is slightly high in fat served in the same meal.

When you use recipes from other books, you should make sure that they feature Good Calories in at least a four-to-one ratio with Bad Calories.

You should also make sure that your alternate recipes do not derive greater than 30 percent of their calories from fat. To calculate the percentage of calories that are derived from fat, multiply the grams of fat in one portion by 9 and divide that figure by the total number of calories in the portion. If you do not know the total calories in a food, multiply the grams of carbohydrate or protein by 4 and then add the calories derived from fat. I recommend Martha Rose Shulman's books because they give

the fat content and total calories of each recipe, making it easy to calculate fat content.

Among the several excellent books that feature useful recipes that are compatable with the Good Calorie Diet are these:

- *Friendly Foods: Gourmet Vegetarian Cuisine*
  by Brother Ron Pickarski, O.F.M.
  Ten Speed Press, 1991

- *The Silver Palate Cookbook*
  by Julee Rosso and Sheila Lukins
  Workman Publishing Co., 1982

- *The Greens Cookbook: Extraordinary Cuisine from the Celebrated Restaurant*
  by Deborah Madison
  Bantam Books, 1987

- *The Savory Way*
  by Deborah Madison
  Bantam Books, 1990

- *City Cuisine*
  by Susan Feniger and Mary Sue Milliken
  William Morrow, 1989

- *The California-American Cookbook*
  by Jeannette Ferrary and Louise Fiszer
  Simon & Schuster, 1985

- *Mediterranean Light: Delicious Recipes from the World's Healthiest Cuisine*
  by Martha Rose Shulman
  Bantam Books, 1989

- *Entertaining Light: Healthy Company Menus with Great Style*
  by Martha Rose Shulman
  Bantam Books, 1991

- *The Vegetarian Feast*
  by Martha Rose Shulman
  HarperPerennial, 1986

- *Moosewood Cookbook*
  by Mollie Katzen
  Ten Speed Press, 1977

- *Still Life with Menu Cookbook*
  by Mollie Katzen
  Ten Speed Press, 1988

SALADS

MARINATED GREEN TOMATO SALAD

5 medium green tomatoes,
  sliced
1½ teaspoons olive oil
salt and pepper
2 tablespoons red wine vinegar
  or apple cider vinegar

1 large clove garlic, minced
1 small red onion, sliced thin
2 tablespoons fresh tarragon,
  minced

Preheat the broiler.

Brush the tomato slices with olive oil. Sprinkle with salt and pepper and broil about 2 minutes on each side until lightly browned.

Place the tomatoes in a shallow dish and sprinkle with vinegar, garlic, onion, and tarragon. Marinate at least 4 hours or overnight.

Serve cold.

serves 6–8

THREE-BEAN SALAD

1 cup cooked fresh green beans
1 cup cooked or canned kidney
  beans, rinsed
1 cup cooked or canned white
  or pinto beans, rinsed
2 tablespoons olive oil

2 tablespoons balsamic vinegar
2 shallots, minced
2 tablespoons coarse-grained
  mustard
salt and pepper to taste
¼ cup fresh chopped dill

Combine the three types of beans in a large mixing bowl and set aside. Place the olive oil, vinegar, shallots, mustard, salt, and pepper in a small saucepan and heat, whisking constantly, until very hot, but not boiling. Pour the hot mixture over the beans and toss to coat thoroughly. Stir in the dill.

Can be served at room temperature or chilled.

serves 8–10

CUCUMBER SALAD WITH VINEGAR-HERB DRESSING

Salad:
2 small cucumbers, sliced thin
1 celery stalk, chopped

Dressing:
4 tablespoons rice vinegar
1 clove garlic, mashed
1 tablespoon chopped fresh dill
  or 1 teaspoon dried dill

In a blender or food processor, blend all the ingredients for the dressing and pour over the salad. Chill.

serves 4

RED AND GREEN SALAD WITH ORIENTAL DRESSING

Salad:
1 green pepper, cut in strips
1 red pepper, cut in strips
12 ounces spinach leaves
small head of radicchio

Dressing:
7 tablespoons nonfat Italian
  dressing
1 tablespoon fresh minced
  ginger
1 teaspoon orange zest
1 tablespoon fresh cilantro,
  chopped

Arrange the fresh vegetables attractively on a platter.
Blend all the ingredients for the dressing in a blender or food processor and pour over the vegetables.

serves 4

WILD RICE SALAD

4 cups cooked wild rice
1 pound fresh peas, parboiled
2 tablespoons white wine
  vinegar
3 scallions, minced

1 tart green apple, peeled,
  cored, and chopped
2 tablespoons olive oil
salt and pepper to taste

Combine all the ingredients in a medium-size bowl and mix. Serve with meat or fish.

serves 4–5

BLACK-EYED PEA SALAD

1 pound dried black-eyed peas,
  washed and sorted
4 cups cold water
2 medium onions, chopped
3 garlic cloves, minced
2 tablespoons olive oil

1 teaspoon dried marjoram
2 teaspoons salt
pepper to taste
3 tablespoons cider vinegar
⅓ cup chopped fresh parsley

Soak the beans for 2 hours in a large saucepan. Drain and cover with fresh water. Over medium heat, bring the beans to a boil. Cover and cook 1 hour. Drain the beans and transfer to a large bowl.

Add the onions, garlic, olive oil, marjoram, salt, pepper, and vinegar. Mix well. Add parsley and stir.

Chill several hours or overnight.

serves 10

SOUPS

BASIC VEGETABLE STOCK FOR SOUPS AND STEWS, No. 1

5 cups water
5 ounces dried wild or Japanese mushrooms or 3 tablespoons miso
3 carrots, shredded
3 tablespoons fresh chopped parsley

1 tablespoon dried marjoram
1 tablespoon soy sauce (wheat free)
salt and pepper to taste

Combine all the ingredients except the soy sauce, salt, and pepper in a large saucepan or stockpot and bring to a boil.

Reduce the heat to low and simmer 30 minutes. Add the soy sauce, salt, and pepper. Simmer an additional 5 minutes.

Experiment with the spices and herbs. Fresh herbs always give a wonderful taste; however, if you are short on time, bottled herbs and spices are fine. Adjust the seasonings to taste.

Check the seasonings. Cool and reserve.

BASIC VEGETABLE STOCK FOR SOUPS AND STEWS, No. 2

2 quarts water
1 medium onion, peeled and diced
3 carrots, shredded
2 celery stalks, halved
1 cup leeks, washed and coarsely chopped
1 tablespoon soy sauce (wheat free)

3 tablespoons fresh chopped parsley
1 tablespoon dried marjoram
½ teaspoon cayenne pepper
2 sprigs fresh thyme
1 bay leaf
salt and pepper to taste

Combine all the ingredients except the soy sauce, salt, and pepper in a large saucepan or stockpot and bring to a boil.

Reduce the heat to low and simmer 30 minutes. Add the soy sauce, salt, and pepper. Simmer an additional 5 minutes.

Experiment with the spices and herbs. Fresh herbs always give a wonderful taste; however, if you are short on time, bottled herbs and spices are fine. Adjust seasonings to taste.

Check seasonings. Cool and reserve.

CUBAN BLACK BEAN SOUP

4 slices turkey bacon
1 medium onion, chopped
4 cloves garlic, chopped
4 celery stalks, chopped
2 jalapeño peppers, seeded and diced
3 tablespoons ground cumin

3 tablespoons oregano
1 pound black beans, soaked overnight
4 quarts water
½ cup fresh lime juice
salt and pepper to taste
nonfat yogurt for garnish

Cook the turkey bacon in a large saucepan or stockpot until almost crisp. Remove and set aside. Chop.

Add the onion, garlic, and celery to the pot and sauté, stirring about 10 minutes. Stir in the jalapeño peppers and continue to cook approximately 5 more minutes. Stir in the cumin and oregano.

Rinse and drain the black beans and add to the pot with the water. Simmer until the beans are very soft, about 2 to 2½ hours. Thin with more water if the soup becomes too thick.

Stir in the lime juice and the reserved turkey bacon. Add salt and pepper. Garnish with nonfat yogurt. Serve.

serves 12

TOMATO-HERB SOUP

2 tablespoons olive oil
4 medium leeks (tender green and white parts only), washed thoroughly and sliced
2 carrots, shredded
1 medium onion, chopped
2 cloves garlic, minced
1 teaspoon lemon zest
1 teaspoon dried tarragon
1 teaspoon saffron

10 large ripe tomatoes, seeded and diced
28 ounces Italian plum tomatoes, canned
1 cup fresh orange juice
2 quarts vegetable stock, #1 or #2
1 cup chopped fresh basil
low-fat Parmesan cheese, grated (optional)

In a nonstick frying pan, heat the olive oil and add the leeks, carrots, onion, and garlic. Sauté until soft, about 15 minutes.

Add the sauté to a large saucepan or stockpot. Add the lemon zest, tarragon, and saffron and cook, stirring, for 3 minutes.

Add the fresh and canned tomatoes, orange juice, and vegetable stock and stir to combine.

Simmer over low heat for 30 minutes.

Remove from the heat and cool.

Puree the soup in batches in a blender or food processor and return to the stockpot. Before serving, warm the soup and stir in the basil.

Sprinkle with Parmesan cheese, if desired.

serves 12

INDIAN DAL (LENTIL) SOUP

1 cup chana dal (lentils, available in Indian or oriental groceries), or other varieties of lentil
5 cups water
3 cloves garlic, chopped
1 inch fresh ginger, peeled and minced

1 teaspoon turmeric
1 tablespoon cumin
salt to taste
cayenne pepper to taste (about ⅛ teaspoon)
½ teaspoon garam masala (available in Indian or oriental groceries)

Wash the dal thoroughly in several changes of water, drain, and pick over for any grit or particles.

126

Put the dal and water in a large saucepan or stockpot and bring to a boil. Skim off any scum from the surface.

Add the garlic, ginger, turmeric, and cumin; turn the heat to low; and cook, partially covered, for about 1½ hours, until the dal is soft. Stir frequently to prevent sticking.

After the dal is tender, add the salt, cayenne pepper, and garam masala. Stir and cook an additional 15 minutes.

Serve with rice.

serves 12

CREAMY WINTER SQUASH SOUP

2 tablespoons olive oil
1 bunch medium leeks (white and tender green parts only), washed thoroughly and sliced
3 cloves garlic, minced
2 pounds butternut or acorn squash (about 3 large), peeled and cubed
3 quarts vegetable stock, #1 or #2

1 tablespoon curry powder
1 teaspoon ground coriander
salt and pepper to taste
2 tablespoons peeled fresh ginger, minced
8 ounces nonfat yogurt
3 tablespoons fresh lime juice

In a skillet, heat the olive oil and sauté the leeks and garlic until soft. Reserve.

In a large saucepan or stockpot, add the squash and the vegetable stock.

Bring to a boil; turn the heat to low; and add the curry powder, coriander, salt, and pepper. Simmer while adding the sautéed leeks, garlic, and ginger and continue to simmer until the squash is very soft, about 45 minutes.

Let cool slightly.

Puree the soup in batches in a blender or food processor and return to the pot.

Adjust the seasonings. Stir in the yogurt. Add lime juice to taste. Serve hot or cold.

serves 12

MIDDLE EASTERN CHICKPEA-CABBAGE SOUP

1 cup dried chickpeas, rinsed
  and cleaned
1 medium onion, chopped
6 cups water
1 large yam, peeled and cubed
1 small can tomatoes

1 small head of cabbage,
  shredded
¾ cup minced fresh dill
2 teaspoons tomato paste
salt and pepper to taste

Cover the chickpeas with water and soak 12 hours or overnight. Drain and rinse.

Add the onion and chickpeas to a large saucepan or stockpot and cover with 5 cups of the water. Bring to a boil. Turn the heat to low, cover partially, and simmer for 1 hour.

Add the yam, tomato, cabbage, dill, tomato paste, salt, pepper, and the remaining cup of water. Cover, simmer for 1 more hour, adjust seasonings, and serve.

serves 8

RUSSIAN BORSCHT

1 pound beets, sliced and
  cooked
1 medium onion, chopped
2 carrots, shredded
1 leek (white and tender green
  parts only), washed thoroughly
  and sliced
2 celery stalks, chopped
1 bay leaf

salt and pepper to taste
1 tablespoon sherry or apple
  cider vinegar
8 cups vegetable stock, #1 or
  #2, or water
lemon juice to taste (2–4
  tablespoons)
1 cup plain nonfat yogurt

In a large stockpot, combine the beets, onion, carrots, leek, celery, bay leaf, salt and pepper, sherry or vinegar, and vegetable stock or water. Bring to a boil, reduce the heat to low, and simmer for 1 hour, or until the vegetables are very soft.

Strain all the vegetables and stock through a sieve and discard the vegetables.

Stir in the lemon juice and serve either hot or cold, topped with the nonfat yogurt.

serves 6–8

CANTALOUPE SOUP

2 large ripe cantaloupes
½ cup fresh orange juice
2 tablespoons sweet sauterne
1 teaspoon chopped fresh mint

1 teaspoon fresh grated ginger
½ cup nonfat yogurt
fresh strawberries (optional)

Cut the melons in half and remove the seeds. Remove the skin from the melons and dice the fruit.

Puree the cantaloupe, orange juice, sauterne, mint, and ginger in a blender or food processor.

Add the yogurt and blend.

Refrigerate and serve cold with fresh strawberries to garnish, if desired.

serves 6–8

SPRING ASPARAGUS SOUP

Prepare the stock (can be done
1 day ahead and refrigerated):

1 pound tender young
asparagus
1 small bunch leeks (about 4
small leeks, approximately 1½
cups chopped, tender green
and white parts only), washed
thoroughly and sliced

1 bay leaf
2 stalks celery, chopped
7 cups water
salt and pepper to taste

Chop the asparagus into small pieces. Combine all the ingredients in a large stockpot and bring to a boil. Reduce the heat to low and simmer for 30 minutes. Strain, discard the solids, and reserve the broth. Prepare the soup:

3 leeks (white and tender green
parts only), washed thoroughly
and sliced
2 cloves garlic, minced
1 pound trimmed asparagus
2 tablespoons chopped fresh
parsley

6 cups reserved stock
salt and pepper to taste
lemon juice (optional)
½ cup nonfat plain yogurt

Steam the leeks and garlic in a vegetable basket until tender.

Add the leeks and garlic, asparagus, parsley, stock, salt, and pepper to a large stockpot.

Bring to a boil, reduce the heat to low, and simmer until the asparagus is tender, about 8–10 minutes. Cool slightly.

Puree the soup in a blender or food processor and then strain.

Return the strained mixture to the pot; season with lemon juice, if desired; and stir in the yogurt. Serve.

serves 6–8

MISO SOUP WITH SCALLIONS
AND SEAWEED
....

4 cups water
1 strip chopped *kombu* seaweed
  approximately 10″ × 13″
  (available in oriental groceries)
4 tablespoons dark yellow miso

⅛ teaspoon 7-spice seasoning
  (available in oriental groceries)
chopped scallions
1 tablespoon Japanese chopped
  seaweed

Bring the water to a boil in a large saucepan or stockpot. Wipe the *kombu* with a damp cloth and immerse in the boiling water. Turn off the heat and steep the *kombu* about 3 minutes. Remove the *kombu*. Add the miso and seasoning and boil for an additional 5 minutes. Strain the broth through a fine sieve.

Serve with a garnish of chopped scallions and seaweed.

serves 4

GAZPACHO
....

2 cloves garlic, chopped
2 tablespoons lemon juice
5 large ripe tomatoes, coarsely
  chopped
1 bunch scallions, chopped fine
1 cucumber, peeled and very
  thinly sliced

1 green pepper, seeded and
  chopped fine
1 yellow pepper, seeded and
  chopped fine
1 small can V-8 juice
1 tablespoon balsamic vinegar
salt and pepper to taste

In a blender or food processor, puree the garlic and lemon juice to a smooth paste. In a large bowl, add all the vegetables to the garlic paste; toss to combine; and stir in the V-8 juice, balsamic vinegar, salt, and pepper.

Puree half the soup in a blender or food processor and recombine with the soup remaining in the bowl. Refrigerate until cold.

serves 4

RED BEAN PISTOU

Soup:
3 tablespoons olive oil
1 large onion, chopped
3 garlic cloves, minced
2 tablespoons oregano
1 tablespoon thyme
1 large can (28 ounces) Italian
  tomatoes
4 cups vegetable stock, #1 or
  #2
1 tablespoon Old Bay seasoning
salt and pepper to taste
2 small zucchini, diced
¼ cup rice
3 cups red kidney beans,
  cooked

Basil gremolata:
¼ cup fresh parsley leaves
2 cups fresh basil leaves
1 large garlic clove, minced
1 tablespoon olive oil
2 tablespoons low-fat Parmesan
  cheese

Prepare the soup:

In a large saucepan or stockpot, heat the olive oil over low heat. Add the onion, garlic, oregano, and thyme. Cook until the onion is soft, about 10 minutes.

Add the tomatoes, stock, and Old Bay seasoning. Salt and pepper to taste.

Bring to a boil, reduce the heat to low, and simmer for 25 minutes.

Add the zucchini, rice, and cooked beans. Simmer for an additional 20 minutes.

Prepare the gremolata:

Combine the parsley, basil, and garlic in a blender or food processor and process until finely minced. Add the olive oil and process to a paste. Add the Parmesan cheese and blend. Reserve.

Serve the soup hot with a dollop of gremolata.

serves 6–8

TURKISH CUCUMBER-YOGURT SOUP

2 cups plain nonfat yogurt
½ cup skim milk
1 medium cucumber, peeled,
  seeded, and diced
salt and pepper to taste

2 cloves garlic, mashed or
  pureed
1 tablespoon olive oil
1 tablespoon fresh dill, chopped

In a bowl, whisk together the yogurt and milk until smooth. Add the cucumber, salt, pepper, garlic, and oil and mix well. Serve chilled, garnished with dill.

serves 4

SPINACH AND GARLIC SOUP

2 quarts vegetable stock, #1 or
  #2, or water
2 teaspoons olive oil
6 large garlic cloves, sliced
1 medium onion, chopped

½ cup grated carrots
2 stalks celery, chopped
1½ cups stale rye bread crumbs
3 cups finely chopped spinach
salt and pepper to taste

Place the vegetable stock or water in a large stockpot and bring to a simmer. Add the olive oil, garlic, onion, carrots, and celery. Simmer approximately 25 minutes, until the vegetables are soft. Add the bread crumbs.

Remove from the heat and cool slightly. Puree the soup in a blender or food processor and return to the pot. Bring to a simmer and add the spinach, salt and pepper. Heat thoroughly to blend the flavors.

serves 6–8

VEGETABLE MEDLEY SOUP

2 tablespoons olive oil
1 large onion, chopped
4 garlic cloves, minced
4 quarts vegetable stock, #1 or #2
4 carrots, chopped
4 stalks celery, chopped
2 tablespoons dried rosemary
2 tablespoons Old Bay seasoning
2 tablespoons dried basil
salt and pepper to taste
2 yams, peeled and cubed
1 13.5-ounce package frozen lima beans, thawed
1 13.5-ounce package frozen escarole, thawed
1 28-ounce can Italian tomatoes

In a frying pan, heat the olive oil and sauté the onion and garlic until soft. Add the sautéed vegetables, vegetable stock, carrots, celery, and seasonings to a large stockpot and bring to a boil. Reduce the heat to a simmer, add the yams, and continue to cook until the yams are soft, about 45 minutes. Add the lima beans, escarole, and tomatoes and cook an additional 20 minutes. Correct the seasonings and serve.

serves 8

VEGETARIAN MAIN DISHES

MUNG BEAN-TOMATO STEW

1 cup whole mung beans (available in oriental or Indian groceries)
5 cups water
3 tablespoons olive oil
8 cloves garlic, minced
1 large onion, chopped
1 28-ounce can tomatoes
½ pound spinach, cleaned and chopped
salt and pepper
2 tablespoons fresh lime juice
lime wedges (optional)

Clean and pick over the mung beans. Wash thoroughly in several changes of water. Drain. Put the beans and water in a large saucepan or stockpot and bring to a boil. Turn the heat to low.

Cover and simmer 3 minutes.

Turn off the heat and allow to rest, covered, for 1 hour.

Bring to a boil, reduce the heat to low, and simmer an additional 1½ hours until the beans are slightly mushy. Stir to avoid sticking. Drain the beans and reserve. Reserve water to add to sauce if thinning is needed.

Heat the olive oil in a large saucepan and add the garlic. Stir-fry the garlic until it is slightly browned. Add the onion and sauté until translucent.

Add the tomatoes and stir-fry 4–5 minutes. Add the beans and bring to a simmer. Cook for 5 minutes.

Add the spinach, salt and pepper, and lime juice and simmer an additional 5 minutes until the spinach is cooked.

Serve with rice and lime wedges, if desired.

serves 8

ORIENTAL SWEET POTATO STEW

2 tablespoons olive oil
3 cloves garlic, minced
2 tablespoons fresh ginger, peeled and minced
1 pound sweet potatoes, peeled and cubed
½ pound fresh green beans, trimmed and cut in half-inch pieces

2 carrots, peeled and cut in half-inch slices
6 ounces mushrooms
2 cups water
¼ cup soy sauce
1 tablespoon sherry (optional, alcohol will cook away)

Heat the olive oil in a heavy frying pan over medium heat. Add the garlic and ginger and stir-fry for 1 minute. Using a slotted spoon, transfer the vegetables, not the oil, to a large, heavy saucepan.

Add the sweet potatoes, green beans, and carrots and stir-fry 1 minute.

Add the mushrooms and stir-fry another minute.

Add the water, soy sauce, and sherry.

Cover and simmer over low heat until the sweet potatoes are tender, about 25–30 minutes. Remove the cover, raise the heat to high, and boil until the sauce is reduced and slightly thickened. Stir gently.

Serve with rice, if desired, or as a side dish.

serves 6

EGGPLANT-TOMATO STEW

1 large purple eggplant, peeled and cubed
4 tablespoons olive oil
3 cloves garlic, minced
1 inch fresh ginger, peeled and minced
3 large tomatoes, chopped
½ cup fresh parsley

1 cup cooked baby lima beans
2 tablespoons soy sauce (wheat free)
salt and pepper to taste
1 bunch scallions, chopped

Preheat the oven to 350°. Bake the eggplant cubes until almost tender, about 25 minutes.

Meanwhile, heat the olive oil in a small saucepan and sauté the garlic and ginger, stirring, until soft, about 7–8 minutes. Do not brown. Remove the vegetables and transfer them to a large saucepan.

Add the tomatoes, parsley, lima beans, soy sauce, salt, and pepper to the saucepan and simmer on low heat for 20 minutes, stirring and mashing the tomatoes with the back of a wooden spoon.

Add the reserved eggplant to the saucepan and continue to cook until soft.

Correct the seasonings and garnish with scallions.

serves 6

LENTIL STEW WITH GARLIC AND GINGER

8 ounces dry lentils, rinsed
4 quarts water
1 tablespoon curry powder
2 tablespoons turmeric
1 tablespoon Old Bay seasoning
1 teaspoon coriander
1 teaspoon ground cumin
1 teaspoon dried basil

salt and pepper to taste
2 celery stalks, chopped
2 large yams, peeled and cubed
½ inch piece of fresh ginger, peeled and minced
5 large garlic cloves, minced
3 tablespoons tomato paste

In a large saucepan, cover the lentils with the water and bring to a boil. Stir in all the dry seasonings, turn the heat to low, and simmer 30 minutes. Add the vegetables, ginger, garlic, and tomato paste and cook until the yams are tender. Adjust the seasonings and serve.

serves 8–10

BEAN AND PUMPKIN STEW

1 cup white or pinto beans
1 medium onion, chopped
3 cloves garlic, minced
2 tablespoons olive oil
1-pound can tomatoes
1 teaspoon ground cinnamon
1 tablespoon ground cumin
1 teaspoon Old Bay seasoning

2 whole cloves (do not eat!)
1 tablespoon Hungarian-style hot paprika
2–3 cups vegetable broth
1 small sugar pumpkin, peeled, seeded, and diced
salt and pepper to taste

Soak the beans for 6 hours or overnight. Drain and rinse. Reserve.

In large, heavy saucepan, sauté the onions and garlic in the olive oil until soft, about 5–6 minutes. Do not brown.

Add the tomatoes, cinnamon, cumin, Old Bay seasoning, cloves, paprika, and 1 cup of the vegetable broth. Simmer for 10 minutes, then add the remaining broth, beans, pumpkin, salt, and pepper.

Cook on low heat for about 1–1½ hours, until the pumpkin is very tender.

Adjust the seasonings; add additional salt, if necessary.

serves 6–8

LINGUINI WITH SHIITAKE MUSHROOM SAUCE

1-ounce package dried shiitake
  mushrooms
1 cup boiling water
3 tablespoons olive oil
4 shallots, minced
5 ounces fresh crimini
  mushrooms, sliced

½ teaspoon dried rosemary
1 cup vegetable stock
1 cup nonfat yogurt
1 pound dried linguini

Soak the dried mushrooms in boiling water until soft, about 30 minutes.

Drain and squeeze out the excess water. Discard the stems and reserve the mushrooms and liquid separately.

Heat the olive oil in a saucepan and sauté the shallots until tender. Add the dried reserved mushrooms, fresh mushrooms, and rosemary.

Add the vegetable stock and the reserved mushroom liquid.

Boil until reduced to a thick glaze, about 10 minutes.

Add the yogurt and blend.

Cook the linguini. Serve with the sauce.

serves 4

WINTER VEGETABLE PUREE

2 yams
3 pounds celery root
10 medium turnips
3 cloves garlic
4 medium leeks
1 cup nonfat yogurt
salt and pepper to taste

Bouquet garni:
3 thyme sprigs
1 bay leaf
2 cloves garlic
6 parsley sprigs
10 black peppercorns

Peel the yams, celery root, turnips, and garlic. Trim the leeks and wash well. Chop the vegetables coarsely and make a bouquet garni by encasing the herbs in cheesecloth or a cloth tea bag.

Place all the vegetables in a large saucepan with barely enough water to cover them and the bouquet garni. Bring to a simmer and cook, covered, about 20 minutes, or until the vegetables are tender.

Remove the bouquet garni, drain the vegetables, and puree them in a blender or food processor, adding the yogurt, until smooth.

Add salt and pepper to taste.

Keep warm in a double boiler and serve.

serves 8–10

CHICKPEA FLOUR "QUICHE"

2½ cups sifted chickpea flour
4½ cups water
4 cloves garlic, minced
½ teaspoon grated ginger
1 teaspoon ground cumin
½ teaspoon turmeric
⅛ to ¼ teaspoon cayenne
  pepper (to taste)

1 tablespoon fresh parsley,
  minced
3 tablespoons olive oil
1 medium onion, sliced
1 tablespoon lemon juice
2 teaspoons salt
red and yellow pepper slices, for
  garnish

In a large mixing bowl, slowly add the water to the chickpea flour, smoothing out any lumps. Set aside.

Add the garlic, ginger, parsley, cumin, turmeric, cayenne, and parsley to ¼ cup of additional water; mix; and set aside.

Heat the olive oil in a large saucepan, add the onion, and stir-fry 3–4 minutes.

Add the spices and stir-fry 1 more minute.

Add the chickpea mixture and bring to a boil, stirring constantly.

Turn the heat to medium low and continue stirring about 15 minutes until the mixture begins to leave the sides of the saucepan.

Add the lemon juice and salt. Taste.

Empty the mixture into a 9-inch cake pan and allow to cool to room temperature.

Add slices of red and yellow peppers to garnish.

serves 6–8

LENTIL-STUFFED ZUCCHINI

4 medium zucchini (about 2 pounds), scrubbed with ends trimmed
2 tablespoons olive oil
1 medium onion, chopped
3 cloves garlic, minced

1 teaspoon cumin
salt and pepper to taste
1 cup cooked lentils
1 cup cooked rice
nonfat Parmesan cheese

Scoop out the center of the zucchini. Steam, covered, for 8 minutes.

Heat the olive oil in a frying pan and add the onion and garlic. Sauté until soft.

Add the cumin, salt, and pepper. Stir-fry 1 minute.

Combine the lentils and rice. Mix the onion mixture into the combined lentils and rice and stuff the zucchini with the mixture. Sprinkle with Parmesan cheese and place under the broiler until lightly browned. Serve hot.

serves 8

ROASTED VEGETABLES

This method is a wonderful way to serve fresh asparagus and can be used with eggplant, peppers, broccoli, and cauliflower as well. The roasting time for the vegetables varies, broccoli and cauliflower taking the longest. Check the tenderness of the vegetables during cooking.

1 pound fresh asparagus, stalks trimmed
2 tablespoons coarse kosher salt

1 tablespoon dried rosemary
olive oil

Preheat the oven to 375°. Arrange the asparagus in a single layer in a large baking pan or cookie sheet with sides. Sprinkle the salt and rosemary over the asparagus and drizzle sparingly with olive oil. Roast for about 6–7 minutes, or until crisp-tender.

serves 6

PASTA PRIMAVERA

2 tablespoons olive oil
2 garlic cloves, minced
1 medium red onion, sliced
2 carrots, coarsely shredded

1 small bunch broccoli, cut into
  florets
salt and pepper to taste
1 pound cooked linguine
nonfat Parmesan cheese

Begin cooking the pasta. Meanwhile, in a large skillet heat the olive oil, add the garlic, and sauté until soft. Add the onion, separating the slices, and sauté an additional 3 minutes. Add the carrots and broccoli.

Cover and steam, stirring occasionally, until the vegetables are crisp-tender. Add salt and pepper to taste.

Toss the vegetable mixture with the cooked pasta and sprinkle with Parmesan cheese. Serve immediately.

serves 4

PASTA FAGIOLI

2 cups dried white beans,
  soaked overnight in water
2 tablespoons olive oil
1 medium onion, chopped
3 cloves garlic, chopped
1 32-ounce can crushed Italian
  plum tomatoes
¾ cup pastina

1 tablespoon Old Bay seasoning
1 tablespoon paprika
1 tablespoon oregano
salt and pepper to taste
nonfat Parmesan cheese

Drain and rinse the beans. Place them in a large saucepan, cover with fresh water, and bring to a boil. Reduce the heat to a simmer and cook until very soft, about 1½ hours. Meanwhile, heat the olive oil in a skillet, sauté the onion and garlic for 8–10 minutes, and reserve.

Drain the beans, reserving the cooking liquid. Puree the beans in a food mill, blender, or food processor, adding small amounts of liquid, if needed. Return to the pot. Add the tomatoes, 4 cups cooking liquid, pastina, seasonings, salt, and pepper.

Over low heat, cook until the pasta is tender, about 30 minutes. Sprinkle with Parmesan cheese, if desired.

serves 8–10

NONVEGETARIAN MAIN DISHES

CHICKEN AND BEET SALAD

1 tablespoon Dijon mustard
2 scallions, chopped
3 tablespoons minced fresh dill
1 teaspoon olive oil
salt and pepper to taste

1 large chicken breast (skin removed), cooked and cubed
4 medium beets, cooked and diced (may use canned, drained beets)

Combine all the ingredients for the dressing—mustard, scallions, dill, olive oil, salt, and pepper—and whisk until well blended.

Mix the chicken cubes and the beets in a large bowl.

Pour the dressing over the chicken and beets, toss, and chill several hours.

Serve.

serves 2

GRILLED SEA BASS WITH DILL SAUCE

Sauce:
¾ cup nonfat yogurt
2 tablespoons fresh chopped dill
¼ cup chopped cornichons (optional, available in gourmet food shops)
2 teaspoons Dijon mustard
1 tablespoon fresh chopped tarragon

Fish:
4 8-oz. fillets of sea bass
Fresh lemon juice
salt and pepper to taste

Sauce:

Combine all the ingredients in a small bowl. Whisk until thoroughly combined. Reserve.

Fish:

Preheat the broiler or grill. Sprinkle the fish with lemon juice and season with salt and pepper.

Broil until cooked through, about 3 minutes per side.

Serve with the sauce.

serves 4

GRILLED HALIBUT WITH GREEN SAUCE

Green sauce:

1 bunch fresh parsley

1 bunch fresh cilantro

4 cloves garlic, minced

3 anchovy fillets

¼ cup fresh lemon juice

3 tablespoons olive oil

4 6- to 8-oz. halibut fillets

Add all the ingredients for the sauce to a food processor and process until smooth. Reserve.

Grill the fish over hot coals or under the broiler about 4 minutes per side.

Serve with the green sauce.

serves 4

NEW ORLEANS FETTUCINE WITH MUSSELS

2 tablespoons olive oil

1 medium onion, chopped

2 cloves garlic, minced

1 tablespoon Cajun seasoning
  (Chef Louis)

2 cups sliced fresh mushrooms

1 can (16 ounces) tomatoes

1 cup frozen peas (thawed)

24 fresh mussels, scrubbed

salt and pepper

1 pound cooked fettucine

Heat the olive oil in a saucepan. Add the onion, garlic, and Cajun seasoning. Sauté about 5 minutes. Add the mushrooms and cook an additional 5 minutes. Add the tomatoes and simmer 10 minutes on low heat, stirring constantly.

Stir in the peas and the mussels. Cover and cook, still on low heat, until the mussels have opened. Season with salt and pepper.

In a large bowl, pour the sauce over the cooked pasta and serve immediately.

serves 4

GOOD CALORIE CHICKEN SALAD

3 cups cooked skinless white-meat chicken, cubed
2 stalks celery, chopped
1 tablespoon shallots, minced
½ cup fresh grapes
2 tablespoons chopped fresh dill

1 tablespoon fresh chopped parsley
salt and pepper to taste
½ cup nonfat plain yogurt
greens for garnish
sliced orange for garnish

Combine all the salad ingredients in a large bowl and chill. Serve on a bed of fresh greens with sliced orange.

serves 6

MARINATED CHICKEN BREASTS

Marinade:
¼ cup coarsely ground Dijon mustard
7 garlic cloves, minced
¼ cup fresh ginger, peeled and minced
½ cup soy sauce (wheat free)

¼ cup sherry or apple cider vinegar
3 tablespoons olive oil
2 pounds skinless chicken breasts

Whisk all the ingredients together in a small bowl.

Pour over the chicken breasts and marinate at least 3 hours or overnight until chilled.

Discard the marinade and grill the chicken over open coals or under a broiler until browned on both sides.

serves 4

TURKEY CHILI DIABLO

3 tablespoons olive oil
1 cup chopped onions
5 garlic cloves, minced
2 tablespoons ground cumin
2 pounds ground turkey
2 15½-ounce cans chickpeas or white beans
1 jalapeño pepper, seeded and minced
5 cups vegetable stock, #1 or #2, or water

1 tablespoon oregano
1 teaspoon basil
1 teaspoon marjoram
½ cup water with 1½ tablespoons arrowroot, dissolved
salt and pepper to taste
chopped scallions

In a large saucepan, heat the olive oil and sauté the onions and garlic until soft. Add the cumin and cook, stirring to release the spice's fragrance, about 5 minutes.

Add the ground turkey, stirring to break it up, until the meat loses its pink color. Add the chickpeas or beans, jalapeño pepper, vegetable stock or water, oregano, basil, and marjoram. Simmer, covered, for about 1 hour. Stir occasionally.

Add the arrowroot-water mixture and simmer an additional 10 minutes. Season with salt and pepper and garnish with scallions.

serves 6–8

SPICY CHICKEN SALAD

Chili Salsa:
4 large fresh tomatoes, chopped
1 tablespoon jalapeño pepper,
  finely chopped
1 red onion, chopped
1 garlic clove, minced
1 teaspoon lime juice
1 teaspoon salt

Chicken Base:
2 whole chicken breasts,
  skinless and boneless
3 cups vegetable stock, #1 or
  #2
1 pound good-quality spaghetti
salt and pepper to taste
chopped scallions

Chili Salsa:

Combine all the ingredients in a bowl and mix well. Correct the seasonings. Cover and refrigerate.

Chicken Salad:

In a large saucepan, place the chicken and vegetable stock and bring to a boil. Add water, if necessary, to cover the chicken.

Simmer the chicken until tender, about 10 minutes. Cool the chicken, dice it, and reserve.

Cook the spaghetti in salted water, drain, and set aside.

Combine the chicken, pasta, and 2 cups of salsa in a large bowl. Correct the seasonings and add salt and pepper.

Serve at room temperature or chilled, with chopped scallions for garnish.

serves 4

SHRIMPS WITH TOMATOES

2 garlic cloves, minced
1 16-ounce can Italian tomatoes
4 tablespoons olive oil

12 jumbo shrimps (about 1
  pound), peeled and deveined
¼ cup dry white wine (optional)
salt and pepper to taste

In a nonstick saucepan, cook the garlic and tomatoes in 1 table-spoon olive oil, stirring to prevent sticking, for about 15 minutes.

Heat the remaining oil in a large skillet and sauté the shrimps for 1–2 minutes until pink. Add the wine and heat. Deglaze the skillet, scraping the browned bits.

Add the tomato mixture and heat until the shrimps are cooked through. Season with salt and pepper to taste.

Serve with cooked rice or pasta.

serves 4

MEXICAN CHICKEN FAJITAS

3 tablespoons olive oil
1 green pepper, seeded and cut in narrow strips
1 red pepper, seeded and cut in narrow strips
1 large onion, thinly sliced
1 pound skinless, boneless chicken breasts, cut in strips
1 teaspoon ground cumin
salt and pepper to taste

Toppings:
chopped scallions, cubed tomatoes, nonfat yogurt
Soft corn flour tortillas

In a large, heavy skillet, heat the olive oil, add the peppers and onion, and sauté until crisp-tender. Set aside. Add the chicken to the hot skillet and sprinkle with cumin, salt, and pepper. Sear the chicken, stirring until cooked through and sizzling. Return the vegetables to the skillet just to heat. Serve the chicken and vegetables on tortillas topped with scallions, tomatoes, and yogurt.

serves 4

ORANGE-GLAZED TURKEY BREAST

1 cup orange juice
½ cup fresh cranberries
2 tablespoons fresh rosemary, chopped

1 teaspoon sugar
1 teaspoon olive oil
4 turkey breast fillets
salt and pepper to taste

Preheat the oven to 350°. Heat the orange juice in a saucepan and add the cranberries, rosemary, and sugar. Cook about 15 minutes until the cranberries pop. Let cool thoroughly. Puree the orange-berry mixture in a blender or food processor. Season the turkey breasts with salt and pepper. In a lightly oiled baking pan, roast the turkey breasts until almost done, brushing with the olive oil to prevent drying. During the last 10 minutes of cooking, brush the turkey breasts with the orange-berry glaze, reserving some to serve as an accompaniment. The breasts may also be cooked on an open grill.

serves 4

FLOUNDER WITH LEMON-MUSTARD SAUCE

4 teaspoons olive oil
2 shallots, minced
1 tablespoon dried tarragon
¼ cup cognac (optional, the alcohol will cook away)
½ cup tarragon vinegar

pinch of cayenne pepper
1 tablespoon coarse-grained mustard
1 tablespoon fresh lemon juice
1 pound flounder fillets

In a small nonstick saucepan, heat 2 teaspoons of the olive oil and add the minced shallots. Sauté the shallots until very soft, about 6–7 minutes. Add the tarragon, cognac, tarragon vinegar, and cayenne pepper and cook until almost all the liquid has evaporated. Stir in the mustard and lemon juice and set aside.

Brush the fish fillets with the remaining oil and panfry them quickly until they turn white and are cooked throughout. Serve the fish with a small portion of the lemon-mustard sauce.

serves 4

SHRIMPS WITH LEMON AND GINGER

2 tablespoons olive oil
1 tablespoon fresh ginger, minced
½ teaspoon Old Bay seasoning

1 pound fresh shrimps, peeled and deveined (about 18 shrimps)
salt and pepper to taste
juice of 1 large lemon

In a large skillet, sauté the ginger in the olive oil until soft, about 5–6 minutes. Add the Old Bay seasoning and stir an additional minute. Add the shrimps and stir-fry until pink throughout. Season with salt and pepper. Transfer to a plate and drizzle lemon juice over the shrimps.

serves 4

SALMON AND BLACK BEAN SAUCE

3 tablespoons canned black
  beans, drained of fluid
1 tablespoon ginger, peeled and
  minced
2 tablespoons chopped onions
2 cloves garlic, minced

1 teaspoon sugar
2 tablespoons cooking sherry
4 teaspoons sesame oil
1 pound salmon fillets
2 tablespoons chives

Blend all the ingredients except the salmon and chives. Coat both sides of the salmon fillets with the mixture and refrigerate in a covered container until thoroughly cooled.

Broil on a preheated grill or under a broiler for 2 minutes. Turn and broil until the fish turns milky (2–3 minutes). Garnish with a light sprinkling of chives.

serves 4

SIDE DISHES

BAKED TOMATOES

8 red tomatoes
½ cup tomato juice or V-8 juice
1 cup fresh 100 percent rye-
  bread crumbs
½ cup nonfat yogurt
2 tablespoons coarse-grained
  mustard

2 tablespoons chopped fresh
  parsley
1 shallot, minced
salt and pepper to taste
nonfat Parmesan cheese
  (optional)

149

Preheat the oven to 350°. Cut the tops off the tomatoes and remove the seeds.

In a mixing bowl, combine the tomato juice or V-8 juice, bread crumbs, yogurt, mustard, parsley, shallot, salt, and pepper. Stir to blend. Correct the seasonings.

Spoon the mixture into the tomatoes and place in a lightly oiled baking dish.

Sprinkle with Parmesan cheese, if desired.

Bake for 25 minutes, or until hot and bubbly.

Serve.

serves 8

JASMINE RICE AND SPLIT PEAS

⅓ cup yellow split peas
2 cups jasmine rice
3 tablespoons olive oil
½ teaspoon garam masala
1 teaspoon salt

4 tablespoons fresh chopped dill
3 cups vegetable stock, #1 or #2

Soak the split peas in hot water for 2 hours.

Soak the rice in water (6 cups) for 1 hour.

Drain the split peas and rice.

Heat the olive oil in a heavy saucepan and add the split peas and rice. Stir-fry a few minutes to coat with oil.

Add the garam masala, salt, and dill.

Stir-fry an additional 2 minutes.

Add the vegetable stock and bring to a boil. Reduce the heat to low, cover, and cook gently for about 25 minutes.

Turn off the heat and allow to sit 15 minutes, covered.

Serve.

serves 6–8

WHITE BEANS AND GARLIC PUREE

2 cups cooked or canned white
  or cannellini beans (liquid
  reserved)
4 large garlic cloves, peeled and
  mashed in a garlic press

2 tablespoons olive oil
salt and pepper to taste
1 tablespoon fresh lemon juice

In a food processor combine the beans, ½ cup bean liquid, garlic, olive oil, salt, pepper, and lemon juice and process until smooth.
  Correct the seasonings and add liquid, if necessary.
  Heat over simmering water or a double boiler.
  Serve.

serves 6–8

GOOD CALORIE VEGETABLE MEDLEY

1 cup dried yellow split peas (or
  lentils)
½ teaspoon turmeric
5½ cups cold water
1 large tomato
1 teaspoon lemon juice
1½ tablespoons olive oil
1 teaspoon black mustard seeds

¼ teaspoon fenugreek seeds
2 teaspoons garlic, chopped
1 tablespoon garam masala
1 pound brussels sprouts
½ pound green beans
2 teaspoons salt
2 tablespoons chopped
  coriander leaves

Clean and wash the split peas. Combine the split peas, turmeric, and 4 cups of the cold water in a large saucepan. Bring to a boil; reduce the heat to medium low; and cook until the split peas are tender, about 30 minutes. Add 1 more cup of water and continue cooking until the split peas are mushy. Remove from the heat.
  Clean and wash the vegetables. Puree the tomato in a blender with the lemon juice and set aside.

In large saucepan heat the olive oil until very hot and add the mustard seeds. Add the fenugreek seeds and stir for approximately 1 minute until they start to darken. Add the garlic and garam masala. Add the vegetables and cook for 5 minutes. Add the reserved tomato puree, salt, and an additional ½ cup water. Cover the saucepan and cook over low heat for 25 minutes. Add the split peas and stir. Continue cooking for 15 minutes until all the vegetables are tender. Stir in the coriander leaves. Correct the seasonings and serve.

serves 6–8

FRESH BROCCOLI WITH LEMON VINAIGRETTE

1 large bunch fresh broccoli, trimmed
lemon slices (for garnish)

Dressing:
2 tablespoons fresh lemon juice
1 tablespoon white wine vinegar
1 teaspoon Dijon mustard
1 tablespoon olive oil
1 tablespoon fresh tarragon, chopped
salt and pepper to taste

Steam the broccoli until crisp-tender, drain, and chill.
Whisk all the dressing ingredients in a small bowl.
At serving time, toss the broccoli with the dressing and garnish with lemon wedges, if desired.

serves 4–6

COTTAGE CHEESE TOASTS

2 slices whole-kernel or 100 percent rye peasant bread
Molly McButter flavor sprinkles

2 ounces nonfat cottage cheese
cinnamon

Preheat the broiler.

Spread the sliced bread with a thin coating of butter spread, top with cottage cheese, and sprinkle with cinnamon.

Broil about 10 inches from the heat, until warm and melted.

Serve immediately.

serves 1

YELLOW BELL-PEPPER SAUCE

2 yellow bell peppers, seeded
  and roasted
2 cups vegetable stock, #1 or
  #2

½ cup nonfat yogurt
salt and pepper to taste

To roast the peppers: Broil peppers on the rack of a broiler pan about 2 inches from the heat, turning frequently, until the skins are blistered and charred. Transfer to a brown paper bag and let them steam until cool enough to handle. Peel off the skins and discard the ribs and seeds.

Sauce: Combine the vegetable stock and peppers and simmer for 15 minutes. Stir in the yogurt. Cool.

Puree the mixture in a blender or food processor and process until smooth.

Season with salt and pepper.

Serve with grilled meats or fish.

serves 2

CRANBERRY-GINGER-ORANGE RELISH

2 teaspoons fresh ginger, peeled
  and minced
1 large navel orange, peeled,
  seeded, and chopped

1 12-ounce bag cranberries
¼ teaspoon cinnamon

153

In a food processor, finely chop the ginger and orange. Add the cranberries and cinnamon and process until the berries are finely chopped. Chill and use as a condiment for meats and poultry.

makes 2 cups

DILL-YOGURT DIP

8 ounces plain nonfat yogurt   salt and pepper to taste
2 tablespoons minced fresh dill

Whisk the ingredients in a mixing bowl. Use as a dip for fresh vegetable crudities or as a garnish for Russian borscht.

makes 1 cup

TZATZIKI: GREEK CUCUMBER-YOGURT DIP

1 32-ounce container nonfat   2 tablespoons olive oil
  plain yogurt   1 tablespoon fresh dill, minced
2 medium cucumbers, peeled   1 tablespoon red wine vinegar
  and coarsely grated   or apple cider vinegar
3 garlic cloves, minced   pepper to taste

Place the yogurt in a very fine sieve over a bowl in the refrigerator overnight to drain the excess moisture.

Squeeze the cucumbers to remove the excess liquid.

In a bowl, combine all the ingredients and add pepper to taste. Serve with whole-kernel bread or vegetable crudities.

makes 4 cups

STEWED TOMATOES AND OKRA

cooking spray
1 medium onion, chopped
¼ cup green peppers, finely
  chopped
4 to 5 small okra, ¼-inch slices
3 large tomatoes, coarsely
  chopped, unpeeled, seeds
  removed

¼ teaspoon hot pepper sauce
1 teaspoon dried ground
  oregano
1 tablespoon lemon juice
salt to taste

Coat a frying pan with cooking spray and place over medium heat until hot. Add the onion and pepper and cook 2 minutes, stirring constantly. Add the okra, tomatoes, and remaining ingredients. Cover and cook over medium-low heat for 15 minutes or until the okra is tender. Stir occasionally.

serves 4–6

PINTO BEAN DIP

1 15½-ounce can plain pinto
  beans
1 green pepper, chopped
¼ cup apple cider vinegar

1 jalapeño pepper, seeded and
  chopped
2 garlic cloves, minced
½ teaspoon ground cumin
water, as needed

Place all the ingredients in a food processor bowl and process until smooth. Add water as needed. The mixture should be the consistency of a paste.

Use as a dip for vegetables, crackers, or chips.

makes approximately 3 cups

SAVORY BAKED YAMS

3 large yams, peeled and cubed
3 medium leeks (white and
tender green parts only), thinly
sliced

1 clove garlic, minced
salt and pepper to taste
1 tablespoon olive oil
¼ teaspoon ground sage

Coat a large piece of aluminum foil with olive oil to prevent sticking.

Place the vegetables and seasoning on the foil and wrap tightly. Bake in a 400° oven for 30 minutes or on an outside grill.

serves 4–6

HORSERADISH DIP

1 cup plain nonfat yogurt
2 tablespoons horseradish
(white)

2 tablespoons ketchup
salt and pepper to taste
1 tablespoon lemon juice

Mix all the ingredients well in a small bowl. Refrigerate. Serve with shrimp cocktail or cold fish.

makes approximately 1 cup

HORSERADISH AND BEET PUREE

2½ pounds beets, scrubbed and
trimmed
2 teaspoons freshly grated
horseradish, or strong white
bottled horseradish

2 teaspoons red wine vinegar
salt and pepper to taste

In a large saucepan, cover the beets with water and bring to a boil. Simmer covered for 40 minutes, or until tender. Drain and skin the beets. In a food processor, puree the beets with the horseradish and vinegar. Add salt and pepper to taste.

Reheat in the saucepan over low heat before serving.

makes approximately 1 cup

PUREE OF BUTTERNUT SQUASH

1 large butternut squash   ¼ cup apple cider
1 tablespoon ground cinnamon   salt and pepper to taste
¼ teaspoon nutmeg

Preheat the oven to 350°.

Halve the squash lengthwise.

Peel and seed the squash and place the two halves, cut side down, in a large baking pan. Add about 1½ inches of water.

Cover and bake until the squash is very tender, about 1 hour. Remove from the oven and cool slightly. Drain.

Puree the squash in a blender or food processor and then place the puree in a large bowl. Stir in the cinnamon, nutmeg, apple cider, salt, and pepper.

Serve hot.

serves 6–8

RICE PILAF

3 tablespoons olive oil   2 teaspoons garam masala
1 teaspoon black mustard seeds   (available in Indian groceries)
1 medium onion, chopped   1½ teaspoons ground coriander
1 teaspoon fresh ginger, minced   salt and pepper to taste
4 garlic cloves, minced   4 cups boiling water
2 cups basmati rice   3 tablespoons fresh parsley,
¼ pound sliced mushrooms   chopped

Preheat the oven to 325°. Heat the olive oil in a large, heavy skillet on high heat until hot. Add the mustard seeds and heat until they begin to pop, a few seconds. Add the onion and fry about 5 minutes, or until lightly browned. Add the ginger and garlic and fry about 1 minute.

Reduce the heat to medium low and add the rice, mushrooms, garam masala, coriander, salt, and pepper. Sauté, stirring, about 10 minutes, until the rice turns translucent and the vegetables are well coated with oil.

Add the boiling water and parsley. Turn the heat to high and cook, stirring, for about 5 minutes, or until most of the water is absorbed. Cover tightly with aluminum foil, dull side down, and then cover with the pot lid. Bake for 1 hour. Serve hot.

serves 6–8

SAFFRON RICE

2 cups vegetable stock, #1 or
  #2, or water
½ teaspoon salt
1 tablespoon olive oil

¼ teaspoon Spanish saffron
  threads
1 cup rice, washed

Bring the vegetable stock or water to a boil in a heavy saucepan. Add the salt, olive oil, and saffron. Reduce the heat to low and add the rice, stirring with a fork. Cover tightly and cook for about 15 minutes until the water is absorbed.

serves 4–6

SUGAR-FREE STRAWBERRY JAM

1 pound fresh strawberries,
  sliced (or other fresh berries)
2 vanilla beans, split lengthwise
1 tablespoon lemon zest

¾ cup frozen unsweetened
  white grape juice concentrate
½ cup water

In a heavy saucepan, cook the strawberries, vanilla beans, lemon zest, and grape juice concentrate until very thick. Stir frequently. Add water, if necessary, cooking about 45 minutes. Remove the vanilla beans.

Remove from the heat, cool, and chill.

Store in the refrigerator approximately 3 weeks.

Serve on cooked cereal, toast, or yogurt.

makes approximately 2 cups

FRUIT ICE OR "GRANITA"

3 cups unsweetened fresh fruit
(berries, pineapple, mango, or
papaya)

½ cup water
1 tablespoon fresh lemon juice
fresh mint leaves

Puree the fruit, water, and lemon juice in a blender or food processor. Freeze the mixture in a gelato machine or ice cream maker according to the manufacturer's directions. Garnish with fresh mint leaves before serving.

serves 2

Eating in Restaurants

In this appendix, following a general discussion of each cuisine, you will find a list of menu items in which Good Calories and the least harmful Bad Calories are in boldface. Bad Calories are in regular type. Remember that these lists are based on approximations. Preparations and recipes vary, so you must use your judgment based on the guidelines in Chapters 3 and 4. Don't be afraid to ask your waiter for low-fat alternatives.

This list is *not* designed for people who eat every meal at a restaurant. Some of the choices are slightly too high in fat for continuous consumption. Millions of dieters know that it's not possible to eat out continually and lose weight. In the other appendixes the foods would be listed as Bad Calories. **You should use this list for the occasional treat.**

If you dine at a restaurant and innocently order a dish that is high in fat, do not panic. You can compensate by eating low-fat meals for the next day or two. Do not compensate by starving yourself.

Some foods are followed by suggestions regarding alternative preparations that you can request. Avoid the foods described in the discussion as being Bad Calories. Remember to seek low-fat foods.

If you are still treating the Starvation Response, you should be extremely careful about what you eat. Do not use this list.

AMERICAN FOOD

...

This section does not include fast food. Instead, it refers to the typical food you will find at almost any restaurant that does not have an ethnic theme.

In many ways, it is easy to choose the proper foods in an American restaurant because the dishes do not generally contain unknown ingredients. If you follow the Golden Dozen rules, you cannot go wrong.

Remember, the biggest problems are combining starch and protein, eating bread before the meal, deep-fried foods, desserts, excessive protein, and high-fat foods.

APPETIZERS

barbecued ribs
buffalo wings
calamari, deep fried
cheese, deep fried
chicken nuggets
clams Casino
clams, fried
crab cocktail

crab Louis
deep-fried vegetables
escargot
mussels, steamed
oysters on the half shell
oysters Rockefeller
potato skins
shrimp cocktail

SOUPS

borscht (no sour cream)
chicken noodle
chicken rice
cioppino
corn chowder
cream of asparagus
cream of chicken
cream of mushroom
lentil

lobster bisque
Manhattan clam chowder
matzo ball
New England clam chowder
onion soup with cheese
onion soup without cheese
split pea
vegetable

SALADS

avocado salad
avocado, stuffed
Caesar salad
chicken tostada salad
Cobb salad
fruit salad
**green salad with low-fat
  dressing**

spinach salad with low-fat
   dressing and no bacon
tomato and onion
tortilla salad
**turkey salad with low-fat
  dressing**

ENTRÉES

barbecued chicken, the sauce is on the skin, which should be avoided

barbecued ribs

beef stew

blackened fish

blackened steak

chicken à la king

chicken-fried steak

chicken tetrazzini

chicken, no skin

chicken, Southern fried

chili, beef

chili, chicken or bean

corned beef hash

Cornish hen, no skin

crab cakes

crabs, soft shelled

filet mignon

fish and chips

fish, broiled, from an acceptable fish listed in the seafood section

fish, deep fried

fish, grilled, from an acceptable fish listed in the seafood section

flank steak, not marinated

ham

hot dogs

jambalaya

lamb

lasagna

liver

Lobster Newburg

lobster

London broil

New England boiled dinner

pasta, no cream sauce

pot pie

prime rib

quail

rib roast

spaghetti

spareribs

steaks, beef, except those listed

veal chop

CHINESE FOOD

•••

Chinese food is really a variety of cuisines: Cantonese, Szechwan, Beijing, Hunan, Shantung, Honan, Shanghai, and others. There are three major styles of preparation: deep frying, stir-frying, and steaming. Deep-fried foods are Bad Calories because of the fat. Steamed foods are almost always Good Calories. Stir-fried foods, which predominate, can be either Good Calories or Bad Calories, depending on their fat content.

Although Chinese fast food is almost universally high in fat and salt, you can still get a great healthy meal at a Chinese restaurant. I live outside San

Francisco, and one of my favorite evenings out is to eat in Chinatown. I concentrate on steamed foods and eat smaller portions, along with lots of steamed rice.

Styles of rice preparation also vary. Watch out for the glutenous rice that is featured in some restaurants and has a high glycemic index. You should also avoid rice that is cooked so that the kernels stick together, making it easy to eat with chopsticks. Since this kind of rice is prevalent in Chinese restaurants, you should be very careful about eating rice.

Egg rolls, fried shrimp, fried wontons, fried dim sum, pork strips, tofu (bean curd), sweet fried foods and sour sauces, sweet sauces, bird's nest, plum sauce, cashews, peanuts, duck, and beef should all be avoided. This means that almost all the appetizers are off-limits. You might make sure that vegetable oils are used for cooking. Fortunately, peanut and sesame oils are prevalent.

On the positive side, Chinese cuisine features rice, vegetable dishes, and Chinese noodles (not fried noodles), all of which are Good Calories.

Appetizers

chicken wings
combination platters
crab puff
dim sum, fried
dim sum, steamed, no tofu
egg rolls
fried shrimp
fried wontons

pork strips
shrimp balls
shrimp toast
spareribs
spring rolls
steamed vegetarian and seafood dim sum

Soups

chicken and asparagus, creamed
combination (pork, chicken, and beef)
crab meat and asparagus
egg drop
fun see, ham and egg
hot and sour soup

sam shin (noodles, chicken, seafood, and vegetables)
shark fin
shredded pork
sizzling rice
watercress
wonton soup

164

ENTRÉES

....

abalone with mushrooms
barbecued spareribs
bean curd
beef and broccoli
braised pork
cashew shrimp
chicken and cashews
chicken with brocolli
chicken with chestnuts
chop suey
chow mein
crab meat and eggs
crispy beef or pork
crispy whole fish
deep-fried chicken, seafood, or
   beef
**drunken chicken, marinated
   in wine**
duck
egg dishes
eggplant (without meat sauce)
fried food
fried rice with chicken, seafood,
   pork, or beef
General Tso's chicken
goose
hot and sour shrimp
Hunan chicken
lamb
**lo mein (noodles), chicken,
   vegetable, or seafood**

lobster
lychee chicken
**Moo Goo Gai Pan (sautéed
   chicken)**
Moo Shi shrimp (stir fry)
Moo shu pork
mushrooms and broccoli
panfried noodles
poached fish
pork sausage
pork, barbecued
pork, roast
sautéed prawns
shrimp with broccoli
shrimp with tomato sauce
sizzling beef
spareribs
spicy green beans
steamed chicken
sweet and sour chicken, pork,
   and shrimp
Szechuan beef
Szechuan fish
tofu (bean curd)
twice-cooked pork
vegetarian stir-fry
velvet chicken
**Yu Hsaing chicken (chicken
   with bamboo shoots)**

FAST FOOD

•••

The greatest problem in compiling a list of fast-food Good Calories is that restaurants are constantly adding new low-fat menu items. It is simply impossible to keep up with the tens of thousands of possible items, most of which are Bad Calories. In any case, you should be careful, since not all low-fat items are Good Calories. Many are high in blood sugar-inducing carbohydrates and should be rejected.

This section lists only generic fast-food items. Foods with a fat content of less than 31 percent are in bold face; foods with a fat content of 31 percent to 40 percent are also in bold face, but they are followed by an asterisk. The only restaurant-specific listings are for pizza, perhaps the best fast food when it is low in fat.

Fast-food items, such as sandwiches and pizza, combine protein and starches. This combination raises their fat-forming capacity. There are two ways to combat this problem. First, make sure that you do not eat other carbohydrates, such as french fries or milk shakes, with sandwiches or pizza. Second, you should realize that sandwiches tend to be Bad Calories because they combine starches and protein; therefore, you should eat them only as part of meals in a controlled program. These meals should be followed and preceded by several days of Good Calorie meals.

GENERIC FAST-FOOD ITEMS

biscuit
biscuit and egg
biscuit and meat
brownie
burrito, bean
burrito, bean and meat*
burrito, beef
cheeseburger
chicken fillet, fried
chicken, grilled*
chicken, breaded
chicken nuggets
chili

chimichanga, beef
chimichanga, beef and cheese
chimichanga, beef and peppers
clams, fried
coleslaw
cookies
crab, baked*
croissant
egg and cheese
enchilada, cheese
enchilada, cheese and beef
enchilada, cheese, beans, and
    beef

enchirito, cheese, beans, and beef

fish fillet

french fries

French toast

frijoles, cheese*

ham and cheese

ham, egg, and cheese

hamburger, large patty

hamburger, small patty* (moderate fat, but combines protein and starch)

hot chocolate, milk based

hot chocolate, water based and sugar free

hot dog

hush puppies

ice cream

juice, grapefruit

juice, orange, no sweetener

juice, orange, sweetener

juice, tomato

lemonade

milk

nachos, cheese

nachos, cheese, beans, and beef

onion rings

oysters, fried

pancakes

pie, fruit

pizza, cheese*

pizza, meat

potato chips

potato salad

potato, baked

potatoes, hash browns

roast beef* (moderate fat, but combines protein and starch)

roast beef and cheese

salad, cheese and egg, no dressing

salad, chef, no dressing

salad, green, with nofat dressing

salad, seafood pasta, no dressing

salad, vegetable, with nofat dressing

salad, with shrimp and nofat dressing

sausage

scallops, fried

shakes

shrimp, fried

shrimp, grilled

sodas

sodas, artificial sweetener

steak sandwich* (moderate fat, but combines protein and starch)

submarine sandwich, cold cuts

taco

taco salad

turkey, club sandwich

Domino's Pizza

pizza, deluxe*
pizza, cheese
pizza, ham
pizza, pepperoni*

pizza, sausage and
    mushroom*
pizza, vegetarian*

Godfather's Pizza

pizza, original, cheese
pizza, original, combo*

pizza, stuffed, cheese*
pizza, thin, cheese*

Little Caesar's Pizza

cheese pizza*
cheese pizza meal*
pepperoni pizza*

pizza meal*
tossed salad

McDonald's

pan pizza, cheese*
pan pizza, pepperoni*
personal pan pizza,
    pepperoni*

personal pan pizza, supreme*
pizza, thin 'n crispy, cheese*

Pizza Hut

hand-tossed pizza, cheese*
pan pizza, cheese*
pan pizza, pepperoni*

personal pan pizza,
    pepperoni*
personal pan pizza, supreme*
thin 'n crispy pizza, cheese*

SHAKEY'S

....

pizza, pan crust, cheese*   **pizza, thin crust, cheese***
pizza, pan crust, vegetables*   **pizza, thin crust, vegetables***
pizza, thick crust, cheese*   **spaghetti, meat sauce***
pizza, thick crust, vegetables*

FRENCH AND CONTINENTAL-STYLE FOOD

...

Classic French food is high in saturated fats, primarily because butter is used so liberally. However, the "nouvelle" French cuisine, which originated in health spas, has steered away from the excessive use of fat. Almost all French restaurants now feature elements of the nouvelle cuisine. Therefore, choosing the proper foods is as simple as discarding much of the classic cuisine and determining what foods are nouveau and therefore probably low in fat. Any good waiter will be glad to help you make this distinction.

Remember that certain classes of French food are high in fat. Avoid heavy sauces (béchamel, bearnaise, cheese, cream, hollandaise, and mornay), cheeses, goose, duck, sausage, lamb, and beef.

APPETIZERS

....

artichoke with butter or   fondue
  vinaigrette sauce   **grilled asparagus**
carpaccio of tuna or beef   **grilled shrimp**
caviar   mussels au gratin
cheese   pâté
confit of duck   terrine
escargots

SOUPS

....

bisques   **consommé**
bouillabaisse   cream soups
broth (bouillon) **onion soup without cheese**

SALADS

fresh seafood salad (not in a mayonnaise dressing)

green salad (generally acceptable if without cheese and in a light dressing)

house salad (generally acceptable if without cheese and in a light dressing)

marinated tomatoes

niçoise (do not eat the egg yolk)

seafood salad with mayonnaise

spinach salad (generally acceptable if without cheese or bacon and in a light dressing)

ENTRÉES

beef Wellington

blackened fish

bouillabaisse

braised fish (with no or low-fat topping)

brochette of chicken

chicken Kiev

coq au vin

Dover sole

duck

filet mignon au jus (with no or low-fat topping)

grilled chicken (with no or low-fat topping)

grilled fish

poached fish

rabbit (lapin) (with no or low-fat topping)

rack of lamb

sautéed chicken (with no or low-fat topping)

steaks, rib eye, New York, and sirloin

sweetbreads

veal Oscar

ITALIAN FOOD

...

Italian cuisine is really two different styles. The southern style, heavy on pasta and tomato sauces, predominates in the United States. The northern style resembles a lighter version of French cooking and is considered to be one of the world's great cuisines. This discussion focuses on the southern style simply because it is more common.

An increasing number of Italian restaurants serve olive oil with bread.

This combination lowers the glycemic index of the bread. However, you should avoid eating too much or you will consume too much fat.

Remember, pizza can be a Good Calorie food. Avoid deep-dish pizzas, which tend to be higher in fat. You should also avoid an excess of cheese; double cheese is forbidden. Play it safe and request lighter-than-normal cheese. You should also avoid fatty toppings, such as sausage and pepperoni. Vegetable toppings, except olives, are a good bet. If the pizza is made with unsaturated oils, then it can be a great choice.

Pasta is an excellent choice, but avoid eating too much protein with it. Stuffed pasta is frequently filled with high-fat ingredients or cheese; avoid it. I don't recommend pesto or creamy Alfredo either. Order a light sauce, in a minimal quantity.

Avoid all breaded and deep-fried foods. Also avoid foods with cheese toppings, such as veal and eggplant parmigiana. Most risotto dishes are high in fat and cheese; substitute a rice-vegetable combination.

APPETIZERS

antipasti di molluschi (assorted shellfish)

antipasto

bruschetta (grilled bread)

calamari, deep fried

calamari, in tomato sauce

calamari, marinated

carciofi al forno (artichokes baked with oil)

carpaccio (paper-thin sliced beef)

clams, steamed

cozze della riviera (mussels in red sauce)

eggplant, baked with cheese

funghi marinati (marinated mushrooms)

garlic bread

peperonata (pimentos, onions, and tomato sautéed in oil)

peperoncini arrostiti (roasted peppers)

pizza, no excess of cheese or meat

pompelmo (grapefruit)

prosciutto

sarde all'olio (sardines in oil)

SOUPS

brodetto pasquale (meat, vegetables, and egg yolks)

brodo (broth)

busecchina (chestnuts and milk)

cassola (fish stew)

crema (cream soup)

lentil

lentil and sausage

minestrone

panata (bread with cheese)

pasta e fagioli (bean and pasta)

ribbollita (vegetables with bread)

stracciatella fiorentina (Italian chicken soup with dumplings)

wedding soup

zuppa alla marinara (fish stew)

zuppa di cozze (mussel soup)

zuppa di fagioli ed orzo (bean and barley)

zuppa di pesce (fish)

zuppa di spinaci (spinach)

zuppa di vongole (clams steamed in wine)

zuppa pavese (topped with cheese and egg)

SALADS

arugula and Belgian endive

Caesar salad

insalata composta (mixed salad)

insalata cotta (cooked vegetable salad)

insalata di casa (house salad)

insalata di fagiolini (green bean salad)

insalata di gamberi (shrimp)

insalata di limone, cetriolo, e peperone (lemon, cucumber, and pepper)

insalata di patate con la pancetta affumicata (potato salad with bacon)

seafood, marinated on greens

seafood, on greens

tortellini salad with pesto

ENTRÉES

agnolotti

aragosta fra'diavolo (lobster braised in wine)

arrosto alla bolognese (roast chicken with ham)

bigne di peci misti (deep-fried seafood)

bistecca (beef steak)

branzino alla griglia (grilled snapper)

brodetto (fish stew)

calamari barcaiola (squid in wine sauce)

calzone (folded pizza; limit cheese and meat fillings)

cannelloni (stuffed pasta)

capelli d'angeli (angel-hair pasta)

cassola (fish stew)

chicken cacciatori (chicken in mushrooms, tomatoes, and herbs; be careful because the sauce can be full of fat)

chicken in wine sauce (with no pasta accompaniment)

chicken parmigiana

costoletta di pollo (chicken breast; ask about preparation)

cozze a vapore (steamed mussels)

egg dishes

eggplant parmigiana

fagioli (white beans)

fettuccine alle vongole (clam pasta; limit the fat content, no cream sauce)

fettucine Alfredo

filetti di tacchino (turkey-breast slices)

gamberetti (small prawns)

gnocchi (pasta filled with starches)

lasagna

manicotti (pasta stuffed with cheese)

medaglioni di bue (filet mignon)

molecche (soft-shell crabs)

pasta ai quattro formaggi (pasta with four cheeses)

pasta al marscarpone (creamy pasta)

pasta Alfredo (pasta with cream sauce)

pasta all'uovo (egg pasta)

pasta e ceci (pasta and chickpeas)

pasta e fagioli (pasta and white beans)

pasta primavera (if not heavy with cream or cheese; ask)

pasta with Bolognese sauce

pasta with cheese or cream sauces

pasta with tomato sauce and/ or minimal cheese

pesce passera (flounder)

pesce spada alla griglia (grilled swordfish)

pizza al pomodoro (pizza with tomato sauce and no cheese)

pizza al rosmario (pizza with rosemary)

pizza vegetale (pizza with vegetables)

pizza, with meat or excess cheese

pizza, with vegetables and limited cheese

polenta

pollo al vino bianco (chicken in white wine; ask if it is low fat and make sure olive oil is substituted for butter)

pollo alla cacciatore (chicken in mushrooms, tomatoes, and herbs; be careful because the sauce can be full of fat)

pollo alla griglia (grilled chicken)

pollo alla zingara (chicken baked in a clay pot)

pollo arrostito (roasted chicken)

pollo al forno (baked chicken; avoid the skin)

pollo piccata (chicken sautéed in olive oil)

ravioli (stuffed pasta)

risotto (rice with butter and cheese)

riso (rice, with low-fat toppings)

sarde (sardines)

scallops Marsala

scampi

scampi al vino bianco (shrimps sautéed in wine; request that the dish is cooked in olive oil, not butter)

scampi fra'diavolo (shrimps in tomato sauce)

seafood, grilled, poached, or baked

shrimp marinara

shrimp primavera (if not heavy with cream or cheese)

shrimp scampi

spaghetti (with low-fat sauce)

spaghetti alla carbonara (pasta with bacon, butter, and egg)

tacchino arrostito (roast turkey, white meat only)

tetrazzini (chicken or turkey casserole)

veal

JAPANESE FOOD

...

The Japanese have a longer life expectancy than do people in other industrialized countries—perhaps the longest in the world. Japanese women live to be 81 years old, on average. One reason for this longevity may be that the Japanese diet is one of the best low-fat Good Calorie diets.

There are those who claim that the United States and Japan are in some sort of competition. If the two countries are, then there is a real question of who is winning. Japanese goods have flooded the United States, and American food is flooding Japan. The result is already predictable. Americans will have less money, and Japanese will die sooner.

Almost all Japanese dishes are Good Calories. There are only a few significant problems. Avoid eating too much rice with animal protein. Sushi (cold rice wrapped around fish or vegetables) should not be mixed with sashimi, in which fish is the main ingredient. Avoid tempura and agemano dishes because they are deep fried and generally high in fat.

Some sushi and sashimi dishes feature fish that are excessively high in fat. Therefore, I will comment on a list of the Japanese names for the various fish ingredients.

Although salt is not directly linked to weight loss unless you suffer from water retention, you should be aware that soy sauce, shoga (the pickled ginger that is served with every meal) and teriyaki are high in salt.

Tofu is high in fat and should be avoided. Miso soup is tofu based and should also be avoided.

Finally, the February 1987 bulletin of the Food and Drug Administration recommended against eating raw fish, such as that found in sushi and sashimi because a disease called anisakiasis can result from parasites that are sometimes found in raw fish.

APPETIZERS

agedashi tofu

ebi-su (shrimp)

gyoza (fried dumplings)

kani-agemano (fried crab)

kushiyaki (chicken on a stick)

ohitashi (spinach with soy sauce)

oshinko (pickled vegetables)

shumai (steamed shrimp dumplings)

tempura

yakitori (teriyaki chicken on skewers)

yutofu (tofu)

Soups

miso
susmashijiru (clear broth)
susmono (clear broth)

tempura-udon (tempura with
noodles)
**yaki udon (noodles with
vegetables)**

Salads

**cucumber and seafood with
vinegar dressing**
**seafood sunomono (seafood
with vegetables in vinegar
dressing)**

tofu salad with miso dressing
tossed salad with miso dressing
**wakame-su (seaweed and
cucumber)**

Maki, Sushi, and Sashimi

aji (mackerel)
amaebi (sweet shrimp)
anago (eel)
awabi (abalone)
California maki (crab and
avocado)
ebi (shrimp)
hirame (halibut)
ika (squid)
ikura (salmon egg)
kainahira (scallop)
kaki (oyster)
kani (crab)
kappamaki (cucumber)

magura (dark tuna)
masago (smelt egg)
saba (mackerel)
saba (mackerel)
sake (salmon)
shinkomaki (pickled radish)
tako (octopus)
tamago (poultry egg)
tobiko (flying-fish egg)
toro (fatty tuna meat)
**umekyumaki (plum and
cucumber)**
unagi (freshwater eel)

ENTRÉES

··

agemano (breaded and deep-
fried crab)

**donburi (low-fat course over
rice; avoid tempura and
teriyaki)**

**shabu-shabu (sliced beef
cooked at the table)**

**soba (buckwheat noodles with
anything that is low in fat;
no tempura)**

sukiyaki (ask for no tofu)

tempura

teriyaki

tofu dishes (dengaku,
hiyayakko, iridofu,
mabodofu, yudofu)

**udon (noodles with anything
that is low in fat; no
tempura)**

udon sauté

**yosenabe (noodles,
vegetables, and seafood)**

MEXICAN FOOD

···

Mexicans are genetically susceptible to the Starvation Response, so it makes sense that they would develop a Good Calorie cuisine. Beans appear in most dishes and will lower the glycemic index of the entire meal. Mexican food is also good in that it does not stress high-protein dishes.

Unfortunately, the restaurant version of Mexican food is frequently high in fat. Animal lard is dripped onto beans and meat, making it hard to eat healthily in some restaurants. Many foods are deep fried. Avoid foods, such as taco shells, and substitute tortillas that are not fried, such as soft tacos and enchiladas. Ask your servers about the preparation.

The use of saturated animal fats is particularly troubling. Some Mexican restaurants may offer special low-cholesterol meals. These dishes will probably be lower in fat and feature unsaturated vegetable oils. Ask your server to hold the sour cream, guacamole, deep-fried chips, fried tortilla shells, hard taco shells, cheese, bacon, chorizo (Spanish sausage), and refried beans, since these foods are high in fat.

APPETIZERS

....

baked chips with salsa
chips with guacamole or melted
　cheese
ceviche (marinated fish)
nachos
pescado espada y melon en
　brocheta (kabob of fish and
　melon)

tostada chips, deep fried
tostada chips, oven baked
deep-fried chips with salsa
**almejas al vapor (steamed
　clams)**

SOUPS

....

**black bean (without sour
　cream)**

**gazpacho (without sour
　cream)**

SALADS

....

**dinner salad (without cheese;
　use salsa for dressing)**
Mexican salad (without cheese
　and do not eat the tortilla

shell, or ask for a soft corn
　tortilla for the shell and salsa
　for the dressing)
taco salad

ENTRÉES

....

arroz con pollo (boneless
　chicken on rice; excessive
　starch with protein)
burritos, meat
**burritos (without high-fat
　refried beans or cheese)**
**camerones de hacha (shrimp
　in tomato sauce)**
carne asada
**chicken chimichangas
　(without high-fat refried
　beans or cheese)**

**chicken enchiladas (without
　high-fat refried beans or
　cheese)**
**chicken fajitas (avoid
　guacamole, cheese, and
　sour cream)**
flautas con crema
mole pollo
tacos
tortillas (corn)
tostadas

SIDE DISHES

....

black beans
guacamole
refried beans

rice (if not in a protein-rich
   meal)
salsa
tortilla chips (baked only)

SEAFOOD

...

Seafood is the fastest-growing segment of the restaurant market. It is usually a low-fat alternative to red meat. Blackened, grilled, raw broiled, sautéed in wine sauce, steamed, and kabobed seafoods are generally good choices.

However, you should be careful, since many of the most popular seafood dishes are as high in fat as is red meat. Butterfish, catfish, caviar, mussels, roughy, sable, and salmon are all Bad Calories, even when grilled.

Many methods of seafood preparation create Bad Calories. Many seafoods, such as shrimp, lobster, and tuna salads, are full of fatty mayonnaise. Deep-fried fish, clams, shrimps, and crabs are Bad Calories. Drawn butter is another no-no. Creamy sauces, stuffed fish, casseroles, Newburg, and Thermador preparations are generally high in fat. Remember to avoid combing seafood with starches, such as rice or potatoes.

Fast-food seafood shops are full of the worst Bad Calories. All their breaded and deep-fried foods should be avoided. If they have a grilled or baked alternative, take it.

Salmon is increasingly available as farm-bred salmon flood restaurants and stores. Many of these salmon have a high fat content. It is generally better to eat wild salmon, which get more exercise.

APPETIZERS

calamari, fried
calamari, marinated
calamari, steamed
clams casino
clam fritters
oysters Rockefeller
raw clams

raw oysters
raw sashimi (if the fish is a Good Calorie)
shrimp cocktail
steamed clams
tempura

SOUPS

bisque, shrimp or lobster
bouillabaisse
chowder, Manhattan

chowder, New England
cioppino
gumbo

ENTRÉES

abalone
alewife (herring)
anchovy
anchovies (canned)
barbecued shrimp
bass, black
bass, freshwater
bass, striped
bluefish
butterfish
carp
carp, fried
carp, roe
carp, smoked
casserole
catfish
caviar
chub
clams, breaded and fried

clams, canned
clams, steamed
cocktail sauce
cod
cod, frozen, raw
crab salad
crab, deviled
crab, Dungeness
crab, imitation
crab, king
crab, soft shell, fried
crayfish
cuttlefish
dock
dogfish
eel
fish and chips
flounder
flounder, baked with butter

flounder, baked, no butter
flounder, raw, frozen
gefilte fish
grouper
haddock
haddock, breaded and fried
halibut, batter fried
halibut, broiled with butter
halibut, broiled, no butter
halibut, raw
halibut, smoked
herring
herring, kippered
jambalaya (avoid the sausage)
kabobs (see listings for
   individual seafood)
king crab
lobster
lobster, boiled or broiled
   (without drawn butter)
lobster, Newburg
mackerel
mackerel, canned
monkfish
mussels
octopus
oyster stew
oysters, breaded and fried
oyster, canned
oyster, fresh
paella (avoid the sausage)
perch, bread and fried
perch, freshwater
perch, ocean
pies, lobster or other seafood

pike
pompano
rockfish
roughy
sable fish
salmon cake
salmon, Atlantic
salmon, blueblack, canned
salmon, chinook
salmon, chum
salmon, chum, canned
salmon, coho
salmon, pink, canned
salmon, smoked, lox
salmon, sockeye, fresh
salmon, sockeye, canned
sardines
scallops
scallops, breaded and fried
scrod
sea bass
sea trout
seafood creole
shad
shark
sheepshead
shrimps
shrimps, canned
smelts
snapper
sole
stuffed fish
swordfish (trimmed of fat)
tuna, canned in oil
tuna, canned in water

THAI FOOD

...

Thai cuisine, when properly prepared, is low in fat and meat and features vegetables, seafood, rice, and rice pasta that are Good Calories. It is easy to maintain the Good Calorie Diet while enjoying frequent Thai meals.

Coconut milk is the most fattening ingredient of Thai cooking. It is not the clear juice found in coconuts, but white pulp mashed into a paste. Not only is it extremely high in fat (97 percent), but it is composed of saturated fats that resemble animal fats. Thus, it easily induces the Starvation Response. Coconut milk is found in many soups, such as Tom Ka Gai, and curries. Avoid dishes that contain coconut milk. Don't eat these dishes even during a Bad Calorie splurge.

Animal lard and coconut oil are used for stir-frying in the rural areas of Thailand. Although most restaurants in the United States use vegetable oils, I have found a few that cling to traditional ways. Ask your server.

The other major problems are with deep-fried items and nuts. Consult the discussion of Chinese food and apply those principles to Thai cuisine.

APPETIZERS

satay (meat or chicken marinated in coconut milk)
seafood kabob (if you are not having a rice-laden entrée)
steamed mussels

Tao Hoo Tod (fried tofu)
Thai rolls
Tod mon (fish cake)
Tod mun (deep-fried seafood)

SOUPS

Poh Taag (hot-and-sour seafood)
Tom Ka Gai (chicken with coconut)
Tom Ka Pak (vegetable with coconut)

Tom Yum Gai (hot-and-sour chicken)
Tom Yum Koong (lemon grass and shrimp)

SALADS

Laab (meat salad)
Pla Goong (charbroiled prawn salad)
Pla Koong (shrimp salad)
spiced beef salad
Talay Thong (chili seafood)
Thai salad

yam yai (combination salad)
Yum Pla Muk (calamari salad with lemon juice)
Yum Saw Menu (eggplant salad)
Yum Yai (Thai green salad without the egg)

ENTRÉES

beef, basil
chicken, basil
chicken, tomato sauce
chili beef
curry, green, red, yellow, or Mussaman (curry sauce is in many dishes; ask)
deep-fried fish
duck dishes
Gai Him Ma Pan (cashew chicken)
Gai Pad Khing (ginger chicken)
Gai Pad Praw (basil chicken)
Gai Yang (barbecued chicken, discard the skin and eat only the white meat)
Gang Pug (vegetable curry)
garlic shrimp
Goong Choop Pang (fried prawns)
Goong Gra Tiem (garlic prawns)
Goong Ob Maw Din (clay-pot prawns)

Goong Pea Seau (fried prawns with crab stuffing)
Gra Praw Neau (basil beef)
Moo Pad Ma Keau (eggplant pork)
Moo Yang (barbecued pork)
Nea Yang (barbecued beef)
Neau Pad Nam Mon Hoy (oyster beef)
Pad Jay (rice noodles and vegetables)
Pad Kao Pod (corn beef)
Pad Kao Pod (corn chicken)
Pad Kao Pod (corn pork)
Pad Ma Keau (sautéed eggplant)
Pad Sai Roong (rice noodles with tofu)
Pad Thai Jai (noodles with prawn, tofu, and egg)
Pad Thai Jai (noodles with tofu and egg)
Pad Thai, (rice noodles and shrimp; without the peanuts)

peanut sauces

Pla Laad Prik (fried whole spicy fish)

Pla Muk Choop Pang (fried calamari)

Pla Muk Gra Praw (basil sautéed calamari)

Pla Song Kreug (deep-fried whole fish)

Praram Long Song (beef with curry)

Pug Raum Mit (sautéed mixed vegetables)

scallops

seafood platter (without curry sauce)

spinach with peanut sauce

Thai chicken

tofu

Glycemic Indexes of Common Foods

This appendix lists the glycemic indexes of foods that are known to have been measured. Most of you will never use these figures, but will rely on Appendixes 1–30 to tell you what foods are Good or Bad Calories, which is generally all you need to know.

However, there are two situations, both of which involve a variation of the basic simple program, in which these figures may be of use to you. If you are cheating on your diet and want to counter Bad Calories with the best possible Good Calories, then you may wish to consult this list to find the foods with the lowest glycemic indexes. If you are combining caloric restriction with Good Calories, then you will also want to know which are the best possible Good Calories.

One note of caution in interpreting these numbers: Just because a food has lower glycemic index than table sugar (78) does not necessarily mean that it is a Good Calorie. Foods with unacceptably high fat contents can also have low glycemic indexes. Clearly, they are not Good Calories. Use your judgment.

Remember that glycemic indexes do not measure the total blood sugar that will be produced by a given food but rather how efficient one calorie is in producing an increase in blood sugar. Thus, it is not necessary to specify the quantity of food to use these numbers.

MEASURED INDEXES OF FOODS SORTED BY FOOD GROUPS

FOOD	GLYCEMIC INDEX
Breads	
barley, coarse	57
barley, coarse, scalded kernels	48
barley, whole meal	93
crackers, plain	100
oat, coarse	93
rye, crisp bread	95
rye, pumpernickel	68
rye, whole grain	42
rye, whole meal	89
wheat, whole meal	100
wheat, coarse	73
wheat, French baguette	131
wheat, puffed crisp bread	112
wheat, white bread	100
Pasta	
macaroni, white, boiled 5 minutes	64
spaghetti, white, boiled 15 minutes	67
spaghetti, brown, boiled 15 minutes	61
spaghetti, white, boiled 5 minutes	45
spaghetti, protein enriched	38
star pasta, white, boiled 5 minutes	54

Food	Glycemic Index
Cereal Grains	
barley, pearled	36
buckwheat	78
bulgur	65
couscous	66
millet	103
rye kernels	47
sweet corn	80
wheat kernels	63
wheat kernels, quick cooking	75
wheat kernels, steamed	41
Rice and Rice Products	
bran	31
brown	81
Chinese glutenous rice	98
waxy rice, boiled 14 minutes	120
white, instant, boiled 1 minute	65
white, instant, boiled 6 minutes	121
white, parboiled, boiled 15 minutes	68
white, parboiled, boiled 5 minutes	54
white, polished, boiled 5 minutes	58
white, polished, boiled 10–25 minutes	81
Breakfast Cereals	
40% Bran Flakes	104
All Bran	74
Corn Flakes (Kellogg's)	121
Muesli	96
oat bran	85
oats, rolled	85
oatmeal, long cooking	49
porridge oats	89
puffed rice	132
puffed wheat	122
Rice Krispies (Kellogg's)	112
Shredded Wheat (Nabisco)	97
Weetabix	109

FOOD	GLYCEMIC INDEX
Desserts	
custard	55
digestive biscuits	82
oatmeal cookies	78
tea cookies, "rich"	80
shortbread	88
sponge cake	46
ice cream	80
tofu ice cream substitute	155
ice cream, high fat	36
Root Vegetables	
beets	64
carrot	92
parsnip	97
potato, instant	120
potato peeled, sliced, and microwaved	117
potato, mashed	98
potato, white (new), boiled	80
potato, russet, baked	116
sweet potato	59
yam	62
Legumes	
baked beans, canned	70
black-eyed peas	33
butter beans	46
chickpeas, dried	47
chickpeas, canned	60
dal, Bengal gram lentils	12
garbanzo beans	61
green peas, dried	50
green peas, frozen	65
kidney beans, dried	43
kidney beans, canned	74
lentils, green, dried	33
lentils, green, canned	74

FOOD	GLYCEMIC INDEX
lima beans	36
navy beans	40
pinto beans, dried	60
pinto beans, canned	64
peas, dried	49
peas, frozen	51
peanuts	15
soybeans, dried	20
soybeans, canned	22
white beans, Haricot, dried	54

Ethnic Foods and Meals

Greek: lentils and bread	54
Italian: spaghetti Bolognese	70
East Indian: lentils and rice	81
Chinese: glutenous rice	98
Lebanese: bread and chickpeas	116
East Indian: gram, black	58
East Indian: gram, green	51
East Indian: gram, horse	64
East Indian: raggi	92

Fruit

apple	49
apple juice	45
applesauce	41
apricots	94
banana, green	56
banana, ripe	90
cherries	23
grapes	45
grapefruit	26
mango, ripe	81
orange	54
orange juice	65
papaya, ripe	81
peaches	29
pears	34

FOOD	GLYCEMIC INDEX
plums	25
raisins	93
Sugars	
fructose	25
glucose	138
honey	126
lactose	57
maltose	152
sucrose	78
Dairy Products	
custard	59
skim milk	39
whole milk	41
yogurt	44
yogurt, nonfat	39
yogurt, nonfat peach	32
Snack Foods	
corn chips	99
fish sticks	38
potato chips	77
tomato soup	38

Good and Bad
Calories by Category

Good Calories are in boldface. Bad Calories followed by an asterisk (*) have 31 percent to 40 percent fat and are suitable for occasional use, as the best Bad Calories to use after you have overcome the Starvation Response.

1. Bakery items
2. Beverages
3. Cereals
4. Chili
5. Condiments
6. Dairy products
7. Dinners, frozen
8. Entrées, canned
9. Entrées, frozen and refrigerated
10. Fish
11. Fruit, fresh
12. Fruit, canned
13. Fruit, frozen
14. Legumes
15. Meat
16. Meat, luncheon
17. Meat substitutes
18. Nuts
19. Pasta and Pasta Sauces
20. Pasta, frozen
21. Pizza, frozen
22. Poultry
23. Rice dishes
24. Rice dishes, frozen
25. Snacks
26. Soups, canned
27. Sugars
28. Vegetables, fresh
29. Vegetables, canned
30. Vegetables, frozen

APPENDIX 1:
BAKERY ITEMS
...

Wheat flour is one of the greatest sources of Bad Calories, since it causes up to twice as much blood sugar as table sugar does. There are almost no bakery products that are acceptable in the Good Calorie Diet.

Rye flour has a lower blood sugar-producing potential. Rye breads, such as pumpernickel, are generally acceptable. However, you must make sure that rye flour is the dominant ingredient.

bagels
BREAD
   corn
   rye, crisp bread
   rye, pumpernickel
rye, whole grain
rye, whole meal
wheat, diet
wheat, Ezekiel 4:9 Sprouted Grain Bread

Bread (cont.)
    wheat, French baguette
    wheat, puffed crisp bread
    wheat, Shiloh Farms 100
        Percent Whole Grain
    wheat, Shiloh Farms
        Sprouted Wheat Bread
    wheat, Vermont Bread
        Company's 100%
        Stoneground
        WholeWheat
    wheat, Vermont Bread
        Company's 100% Whole
        Grain
    wheat, Wild's Whole Grain
        Bread
    wheat, whole meal
    wheat, white bread
  breadsticks
  breakfast bars, Carnation

brownie
cake
cake, sponge
cookies, sugar
crackers, plain
crisp bread rye
crisp breads
croissant
croutons
croutons, cheese
Danish pastry
donut
matzo
matzo meal
muffins
pies, fruit and nut
rolls
rye kernels
rye, whole grain

APPENDIX 2: BEVERAGES
···

As a general rule, juicing fruits or vegetables will only increase the blood sugar-producing potential of the ingredient. The physical forces involved in juicing destroy the fibers that are essential for lowering the amount of blood sugar it produces. Therefore, if the fruit or vegetable is a Bad Calorie, it will be an even worse juice.

Many beverages have added sugar, and such drinks usually have too high a blood sugar-producing potential.

During the Good Calorie Diet, you should minimize your intake of caffeine. When possible, drink caffeine-free beverages.

If you are going to drink beer, drink low-calorie beers that have a high chromium content (see Chapter 5). Beers that are high in chromium include Carling's Black Label, National Bohemia, Moosehead, Schaefer, Miller, Miller Lite, and Pabst.

APPLE-BASED DRINKS
  apple berry drink
  apple cranberry drink
  apple cider
  apple drink
  apple juice
  apple juice cocktail
  apple cranberry juice
apricot nectar
BEERS
  lite
  normal
berry drinks
carrot juice
cherry drink
cherry juice, unsweetened
cocoa, Baker's
cocoa, Hershey's
cocoa, Nestle's*
cranberry apple drink
fruit drinks
fruit punch
grape juice cocktail, sweetened
grape juice, red
grape juice, unsweetened
grapefruit juice, unsweetened

grapefruit juice, sweetened
lemonade
orange drink
orange juice, sweetened
orange juice, unsweetened
papaya nectar
passion fruit
peach nectar
pineapple juice, sweetened
pineapple juice, unsweetened
raspberry-cranberry cocktail
soft drinks
soft drinks, diet
SOY DRINKS
  Edensoy, carob
  Edensoy, original*
  Edensoy, vanilla
  Health Valley, Soy Moo
  Isomil, infant formula with
    iron
  Isoyalac, infant formula
  Vitasoy, creamy original
  Vitasoy, vanilla delite
  Westsoy, nondairy
tomato juice

APPENDIX 3: BREAKFAST CEREALS

...

Most breakfast cereals are Bad Calories. There are three reasons for their high fat-forming potential. First, many cereals are made with wheat flour, a Bad Calorie. Second, many cereals have a high sugar content. Finally, many cereals have been processed so much (into flakes or puff balls) that their fiber content is destroyed.

Oat cereals are one of the few types of Good Calorie cereals. However, it is important that they not be overly processed. For example, instant oatmeal is unacceptable whereas regular oatmeal is a Good Calorie.

40% Bran Flakes (Kellogg's)

All Bran (Kellogg's)

corn flakes

Corn Flakes (Kellogg's)

corn grits

Extra Fiber All Bran (Kellogg's)

Fiber One (General Mills)

Fiberwise (Kellogg's)

granola

Heartwise (Kellogg's)

hominy

Muesli (Ralston)

oat bran cereal

oat bran flakes

oat bran, dry, 100 percent

oat bran, flaked

oatmeal, long cooking

oatmeal, instant

oats, rolled

porridge oats

puffed rice

puffed wheat

Rice Krispies (Kellogg's)

Shredded Wheat (Nabisco)

APPENDIX 4: CHILI

...

This all-American favorite is too high in fat unless it is made with chicken or vegetarian substitutes or is fat free. Even most products made with beans alone are too high in fat.

Armour Star, no beans

Armour Star, with beans

Cimarron, canned chicken

Cimarron, with beans*

Dennison's, with beans

**Dennison's, Lite Chicken with
  beans**

Estee, with beans

HAIN

  canned chicken

  **tempeh, vegetarian, reduced
    sodium**

  vegetarian

HEALTH VALLEY

chili, fat free

lentil

vegetarian, mild

vegetarian, spicy

Heinz, with beans

Hormel, no beans

Hormel, with beans

Libby's, no beans

Libby's, with beans

STAGG

  Steak House, no beans

  chili, canned chicken*

  chili with beans

Van Camp's, no beans

Van Camp's, with beans   Wolf, with beans
Wolf, no beans

APPENDIX 5: CONDIMENTS
···

The only key to these products is their fat content. Very few have high blood sugar-producing potential.

One tricky choice is mayonnaise. Choose nonfat mayonnaise; diet mayonnaise is still too high in fat content, and the nondairy mayonnaises made with tofu or soybean oils are Bad Calories.

bacon bits, Betty Crocker   **carob powder**
bacon bits, vegetarian,   **catsup**
  Bac'N Pieces   mayonnaise
bacon bits, vegetarian,   **mayonnaise, fat free**
  Bac'Os*   mayonnaise, light
barbecue sauce   **mustard**
bearnaise sauce   **salsa**
carob chips

APPENDIX 6: DAIRY PRODUCTS
···

In this category, fat content is the problem. If you look carefully, you will see that most of the acceptable choices are followed by an asterisk, indicating that they have a fat content of 31 percent to 39 percent. These products should be avoided until you cure the Starvation Response and used sparingly thereafter.

On the other hand, just because a dairy product may have a high fat content does not mean that you cannot use it for cooking. As an ingredient, it forms such a small part that the resulting dish is low fat.

butter   **American, Heart Beat***
butterfat   **American, Lite-Line, 8%**
cheese substitute, Formagg, all   **milk***
  except ricotta   **American, Weight**
cheese substitute, Formagg, ricotta*   **Watchers***
CHEESE   **American, Weight**
  all are Bad Calories, except low-fat   **Watchers, singles cheese**
    ones and those listed below   **food***

Cheese (cont.)
    Kraft Light Singles Swiss*
    Land O'Lakes, pot*
    Lite-Line, mozzarella, 8%
        milk*
    Sargento, ricotta, Lite*
    Weight Watchers Swiss*
    Weight Watchers, port
        wine*
    Weight Watchers, sharp
        cheddar*
  COTTAGE CHEESE
    all regular
    Borden's 4% milk fat*
    Carnation Slender 1½%
        milk fat
    Knuden 4% milk fat
    Land O'Lakes 2% milk fat
    Lite Line low fat
    Lite N' Lively
    Weight Watchers
  cream cheese, all
  cream, all
  EGGNOG

  all regular
  Borden, canned
  Carnation Lite
  Land O'Lakes
  eggs, chicken
  eggs, duck
  eggs, quail
  ICE CREAM
    all normal and high fat
    Baskin Robbins light, praline,
        low fat
    Baskin Robbins, light, low-
        fat strawberry
    Baskin Robbins low-fat sugar
        free*
    Dreyers Light, low fat*
    Dreyer's Grand Light, low fat*
    Kemp's low fat*
    Lucerne Light, low fat*
    Weight Watchers low fat
  Tofutti
  margarine
  sherbet
  sorbet

APPENDIX 7: DINNERS, FROZEN

•••

Many of these entrées are low on the glycemic index only because they combine fatty meats with starchy carbohydrates. This combination presents two problems: First, if you do not eat the entire dinner, there is an excellent chance that you will eat only the high-fat portion of the meal. Second, combining starches and proteins is not recommended because it can raise the fat-forming potential of both kinds of foods. They are not recommended for more than occasional use.

Though it would be tempting to term most frozen dinners Bad Calories, they are not listed as such in this appendix, on the basis that you can eat less of the protein section of dinners that combine both starch and protein. Clearly, eating less starch would only raise the fat content of the meal.

ARMOUR, DINING LIGHT
  cheese cannelloni
  cheese lasagna
  chicken à la king
  chicken chow mein
  chicken with noodles
  fettuccine
  lasagna with meat sauce
  Salisbury steak*
  sauce and Swedish meatballs*
ARMOUR CLASSICS
  barbecue chicken
  beef stroganoff*
  boneless beef short ribs
  chicken and noodles*
  chicken fricassee
  chicken Hawaiian
  chicken Milan
  chicken Parmesan
  chicken with wine and
    mushroom sauce
  ham steak*
  light, sweet and sour
    chicken
  light, baby bay shrimp
  light, beef pepper steak
  light, beef stroganoff
  light, chicken à la king
  light, chicken and noodles*
  light, chicken breast with
    mushroom and tomato
    sauce
  light, chicken burgundy
  light, chicken cacciatore
  light, chicken fettuccine*
  light, chicken mesquite*
  light, chicken oriental
  light, chicken parmigiana

light, chicken with wine and
  mushroom sauce*
light, glazed chicken
light, meat loaf*
light, Salisbury steak with
  mushroom gravy, peas,
  carrots, and potatoes
light, seafood with natural
  herbs
light, shrimp Creole
light, steak Diane
light, Swedish meatballs
light, tortellini with meat*
light, turkey with dressing
  and gravy
light, veal parmigiana
Salisbury steak
seafood Newburg*
sirloin roast
Swedish meatballs
turkey and dressing*
veal parmigiana
Yankee pot roast*
BANQUET
  barbeque sauce with sliced
    beef
  Beans & Frankfurters Dinner
  beef with gravy
  breaded veal parmigiana
  chicken nuggets
  chicken à la king
  chicken and vegetables
    primavera
  Chopped Beef Dinner
  creamed chipped beef*
  Fried Chicken Dinner
  gravy and Salisbury steak
  gravy and sliced beef

Banquet (cont.)
- gravy and sliced turkey
- macaroni and cheese, frozen
- Meat Loaf Dinner
- meat loaf
- spaghetti*
- **mostaccioli**
- mushroom gravy and charbroiled beef patty
- Noodles & Beef with Gravy*
- **spaghetti with meat sauce**
- **Stroganoff Sauce with Beef & Noodles**
- supreme microwave, turkey pot pie
- **sweet and sour chicken**
- Turkey Dinner
- turkey Dijon, frozen*
- Western Dinner

BANQUET, EXTRA HELPING DINNER
- All-White Fried Chicken
- Beef Dinner
- Fried Chicken
- Lasagna*
- Salisbury Steak
- Turkey

BANQUET, FAMILY ENTRÉE
- Beef Stew*
- Chicken & Dumplings
- **Chicken & Vegetables Primavera**
- Gravy & Salisbury Steak
- **Gravy & Sliced Beef**
- Gravy & Turkey
- Lasagna & Meat Sauce*
- Macaroni & Cheese*

- **Mostaccioli & Meat Sauce**
- Mushroom Gravy & Char broiled Beef Patties
- **Noodles & Julienne Beef with Sauce**
- Onion Gravy & Beef Patties
- Veal Parmigiana Patties

BANQUET, FAMILY FAVORITES
- Chicken & Dumplings
- Macaroni & Cheese
- Noodles & Chicken*
- **Spaghetti & Meatballs**

BANQUET, PLATTERS
- All-White Fried Chicken
- All-White Hot 'n Spicy Chicken
- Beef Platter
- Boneless Chicken Drumsnacker*
- Boneless Chicken Nuggets
- Boneless Chicken Pattie Platter
- Fish Platter
- Ham Platter*
- Salisbury Steak Dinner
- Salisbury steak

BANQUET, SUPREME ENTRÉES
- **Beef Stew**
- Chicken & Dumplings*
- Chicken à la King*
- **Lasagna with Meat Sauce**
- **Macaroni & Beef**
- **Macaroni & Cheese**
- Macaroni & Cheese with Frankfurters

Banquet, Supreme Entrées (cont.)
Mini Ravioli
Spaghetti & Meat Sauce
BUDGET GOURMET, LIGHT &
    HEALTHY
Beef Pot Roast*
Chicken Breast Parmigiana
Herbed Chicken Breast with
    Fettuccine
Italian-Style Meatloaf*
Sirloin Salisbury Steak*
Sliced Sirloin in Wine
Special Recipe Sirloin Beef*
Stuffed Turkey Breast
Teriyaki Chicken Breast
BUDGET GOURMET, LIGHT
    ENTRÉES
Beef Stroganoff*
Cheese Ravioli*
Chicken Au Gratin*
Chicken Enchilada Suiza*
French Recipe Chicken &
    Vegetables*
Glazed Turkey
Lasagna with Meat Sauce*
Mandarin Chicken
Oriental Beef
Sirloin Beef in Herb Sauce*
Sirloin Salisbury Steak
BUDGET GOURMET,
    REGULAR ENTRÉES
Cheese Manicotti with Meat
    Sauce
Chicken & Egg Noodles with
    Broccoli
Chicken Marsala
Chicken with Fettuccine

Italian Sausage Lasagna
Italian Style Meatballs with
    Noodles & Peppers*
Linguini with Shrimp
Pasta Shells & Beef*
Pepper Steak with Rice
Roast Sirloin
Seafood Newberg*
Shrimp Fettuccine
Sirloin Tips with Country-
    Style Vegetables
Spaghetti with Italian Sausage
Swedish Meatballs with
    Noodles
Sweet & Sour Chicken with
    Rice
Three-Cheese Lasagna*
Turkey à la King with Rice
BUDGET GOURMET, SIDE
    DISHES
Cauliflower in Cheddar
    Cheese Sauce
Cheddared Potatoes
Cheddared Potatoes &
    Broccoli
Cheese Tortellini
Country-Style Corn*
BUDGET GOURMET, SLIM
    SELECTS
Beef Stroganoff*
Cheese Ravioli*
Chicken Au Gratin
Chicken Enchilada Suiza*
Enchilada Ranchero
Fettuccine with Meat Sauce*
French Recipe Chicken*
Glazed Turkey

Budget Gourmet, Slim Selects (cont.)
  Ham & Asparagus Au
    Gratin*
  Lasagna with Meat Sauce*
  Linguini with Scallops &
    Clams*
  Mandarin Chicken
  Oriental Beef
  Salisbury Steak
  Sirloin of Beef in Herb Sauce*
BUDGET GOURMET, THREE-
  DISH DINNERS
  Beef Mexicana
  Chicken Cacciatore*
  Chicken Mexican
  Roast Chicken
  Scallops & Shrimp Mariner
  Sirloin Salisbury Steak
  Sirloin Tips in Burgundy
    Sauce*
  Sliced Turkey Breast
  Swiss Steak
  Teriyaki Chicken
  Turkey Breast Dijon*
  Veal Parmigiana
  Yankee Pot Roast
CAMPBELL'S, SOUPER-COMBO
  Chicken & Stars & Breaded
    Chicken Nuggets
  Chicken Noodle Os Soup &
    Hot Dog on a Bun
  Chicken Noodle Soup &
    Grilled Ham & Cheese*
  Chicken Rice Soup &
    Vegetable Egg Rolls*
  Chili with Beans & Hot Dog
    on a Bun

Cream of Broccoli & Ham &
  Cheese Croissant
Cream of Mushroom &
  Breaded Chicken
Minestrone Soup & Breaded
  Mozzarella
New England Clam Chowder
  & Breaded Fish Sandwich*
Tomato Soup & Grilled
  Cheese Sandwich
Vegetable Soup & Cheeseburger
CELENTANO
  Baked Pasta & Cheese*
  Broccoli Stuffed Shells*
  Cannelloni Florentine*
  Cavatelli
  Chicken Cutlets Parmigiana
  Chicken Primavera
  Eggplant Parmigiana
  Eggplant Rolletes
  Lasagna
  Lasagna Primavera
  Manicotti with Sauce
  Manicotti without Sauce
  Mini Ravioli
  Ravioli
  Stuffed Shells with Sauce
GOLDEN
  Apple Blintz
  Apple Raisin Blintz
  Blueberry Blintz
  Blueberry-Cheese Blintz
  Cheese Blintz
  Cherry Blintz
  Potato Blintz
  Potato Cheese Pierogie*
  Potato Onion Pierogie

Potato Pancakes
Strawberry-Rhubarb Blintz
HEALTHY CHOICE
Dinners, Beef-Pepper Steak
Dinners, Breast of Turkey
Dinners, Chicken & Pasta
Divan
Dinners, Chicken Oriental
Dinners, Chicken
Parmigiana
Dinners, Herb-Roasted
Chicken
Dinners, Mesquite Chicken
Dinners, Oriental Pepper
Steak
Dinners, Salisbury Steak
Dinners, Shrimp Creole
Dinners, Shrimp Marina
Dinners, Sirloin Tips
Dinners, Sole Au Gratin
Dinners, Yankee Pot Roast
Entrées, Baked Cheese
Ravioli
Entrées, Beef Pepper Steak
Entrées, Cheese Manicotti
Entrées, Chicken à
l'Orange
Entrées, Chicken Chow
Mein
Entrées, Fettuccine Alfredo
Entrées, Glazed Chicken
Entrées, Lasagna with Meat
Sauce
Entrées, Linguini with
Shrimp
Entrées, Roasted Turkey &
Mushroom Gravy
Entrées, Seafood Newburg

Entrées, Sole with Lemon
Butter Sauce
Entrées, Spaghetti with
Meat Sauce
Entrées, Zucchini Lasagna
HORMEL, MICROCUP
Chickens & Noodles
Chili Mac
Chili No Beans
Chili with Beans
Dinty Moore Beef Stew
Hot Chili with Beans
Lasagna
Macaroni & Cheese
Pork & Beans
Ravioli in Tomato Sauce
Scalloped Potatoes &
Ham
Spaghetti & Meatballs*
HORMEL, TOP SHELF
Beef Oriental*
Beef Stroganoff*
Boneless Beef Ribs
Breast of Chicken Acapulco*
Cheese Tortellini in
Marinara Sauce
Cheese Tortellini with
Shrimp & Seafood
Chicken à la King*
Chicken Cacciatore
Chili Con Carne Suprema*
Glazed Breast Chicken
Italian-Style Lasagna
Linguini
Salisbury Steak
Spaghettini
Sukiyaki
Sweet & Sour Chicken

Tender Roast Beef
Vegetable Lasagna
KIBUN GOLD
  Chicken Oriental
  Ellen's Homestyle Chicken
  Honey Garlic Chicken
  Lemon Ginger Beef
  Pasta & Chicken with
    Dressing*
  Pasta & Chicken without
    Dressing
  Pasta & Turkey Ham with
    Dressing
  Pasta & Turkey Ham
    without Dressing
  Sweet & Sour Chicken
KID'S CUISINE
  Eating Right Entrées, Cheese
    Beef Patty Sandwich
  Cheese Nuggets
  Cheese Pizza
  Chunky Chicken Supreme
  Fish Nuggets
  Fried Chicken
  Macaroni & Cheese with
    Mini Franks*
  Mini Cheese Ravioli
  Spaghetti with Meat Sauce*
KRAFT, EATING RIGHT
  Beef Pepper Steak*
  Beef Sirloin Tips &
    Noodles
  Chicken Breast &
    Vegetables
  Fettucine Alfredo
  Glazed Chicken Breast
  Lasagna with Meat Sauce
  Shrimp Vegetable Stir Fry

Sirloin Salisbury Steak*
Sliced Turkey Breast
Swedish Meatballs &
  Noodles
KRAFT
  Barbeque Beef with Corn*
  Beef Stew
  Cheese Enchilada
  Chicken à la Chicken*
  Chicken & Egg Noodles
  Chili with Beef and Beans
  Creamed Chipped Beef
  Fettucine Alfredo
  Lasagna with Meat Sauce*
  Macaroni & Beef*
  Macaroni & Cheese
  Ravioli*
  Salisbury Steak & Fries
  Spaghetti & Meatballs
  Tuna Noodle Casserole
  Turkey & Dressing
  Microwave, Beef Stew
  Microwave, Beef Stroganoff*
  Microwave, Cheese
    Tortellini
  Microwave, Chicken
    Cacciatore
  Microwave, Chicken
    Fettuccine
  Microwave, Lasagna*
  Microwave, Salisbury Steak*
  Microwave, Spaghetti &
    Meatballs
  Microwave, Sweet & Sour
    Chicken
LE MENU, DINNERS
  Beef Sirloin Tips
  Beef Stroganoff

Le Menu, Dinners (cont.)
    Chicken à la King*
    Chicken Cordon Bleu
    Chicken Florentine
    Chicken Parmigiana
    Chopped Sirloin Beef
    Ham Steak
    Pepper Steak*
    Salisbury Steak
    Sliced Breast of Turkey
        with Mushroom Gravy
    Sweet & Sour Chicken
    Veal Parmigiana
    Yankee Pot Roast*
LE MENU, ENTRÉES
    Beef Burgundy
    Chicken Kiev
    Manicotti with Cheese Filling
    Oriental Chicken
LE MENU, HEALTHY
    Chicken Cacciatore
    Chicken Cannelloni
    Chicken Chow Mein
    Glazed Chicken Breast
    Herb-Roasted Chicken
    Salisbury Steak
    Three-Cheese Stuffed Shells
    Turkey Divan
    Veal Marsala
LE MENU, LIGHT-STYLE
        ENTRÉES
    Cheese Tortellini
    Chicken Dijon
    Chicken Enchiladas
    Chicken à la King
    Express Chicken
    Glazed Turkey

Herb-Roasted Chicken
Lasagna with Meat Sauce
Spaghetti with Meat Sauce
Swedish Meatballs
Traditional Turkey
Vegetable Lasagna
LEAN CUISINE
    Beef & Pork Cannelloni with
        Mornay Sauce*
    Beefsteak Ranchero
    Breast of Chicken in Herb
        Cream Sauce*
    Breast of Chicken Marsala
        with Vegetables
    Breast of Chicken Parmesan
    Cheese Cannelloni with
        Tomato Sauce*
    Chicken Chow Mein with
        Rice
    Chicken Oriental
    Filet of Fish Divan
    Filet of Fish Florentine*
    Filet of Fish Jardiniere with
        Souffled Potatoes*
    French Bread Pizza,
        Mexican Style
    Glazed Chicken with
        Vegetable Rice
    Lasagna with Meat & Sauce
    Linguini with Clam Sauce
    Meatball Stew*
    Oriental Beef with
        Vegetables & Rice
    Rigatoni Bake with Meat
        Sauce & Cheese*
    Salisbury Steak with Italian-
        Style Sauce & Vegetables

Lean Cuisine (cont.)
Salisbury Steak*
Shrimp & Chicken
  Cantonese with Noodles
Sliced Turkey Breast in
  Mushroom Sauce
Spaghetti with Beef &
  Mushroom Sauce
Stuffed Cabbage with Meat in
  Tomato Sauce
Szechuan Beef with Noodles
  & Vegetables*
Tuna Lasagna with Spinach
  Noodles & Vegetables*
Turkey Dijon*
turkey loaf/homemade
Veal Primavera*
Vegetable & Pasta Mornay
  with Ham*
Zucchini Lasagna
LEAN POCKETS
  Beef & Broccoli
  Chicken Parmesan
  Chicken Supreme
  Pizza Deluxe*
LOUIS RICH
  turkey nuggets, prepared
  turkey patties, prepared
  turkey pie, frozen
  turkey pot pie
  turkey sticks
LUNCH BUCKET, LIGHT
  BALANCE,
  MICROWAVABLE
  Beef America
  Beef & Pasta Bordeaux
  Chicken Cacciatore
  Chicken Fiesta

Pasta & Garden Vegetables
Mushroom Stroganoff
MICRO MAGIC, FROZEN
  SANDWICHES
Cheeseburger
Chicken*
Hamburger
MORTON
  Beans & Franks Dinner*
  Beef Meat Pie Dinner
  Fish Dinner
  Ham Dinner
  Meatloaf Dinner
  Salisbury Steak Dinner
  Sliced Beef Dinner
  Spaghetti & Meatball Dinner
  Turkey Dinner
  Turkey Pot Pie
  Veal Parmigiana Dinner
HORMEL, NEW TRADITIONS
  SANDWICHES
Bacon Cheeseburger
Cheeseburger
Chicken*
Fish Filet
PITARIA, PITA STUFFS
  Gyros
  Ham 'N Swiss*
  Pizza*
  Taco*
SCHWAN'S
  turkey breast, frozen
  turkey pie, frozen
  turkey roll, frozen
  turkey sticks, homemade
  turkey pot pies and meat
    pies, frozen
  turkey pot pie

SCHWAN'S, HOME DELIVERY
Bagel Dogs
Ball Tip Steaks
BBQ Beef
BBQ Beef Brisket
BBQ Ribs
Beef Casserole
Beef Lasagna*
Beef Patties
Beef Patty Melt
Beef Teriyaki
Beef Tortellini
Big Sam Steaks
Breaded Beef Steak Fingers
Cheese Tortellini
Chicken à l'Orange
Chicken Casserole
Chicken Oriental
Chopped Beef Steak
Club Croissant Sandwich
Cross Cut Tenderloin Steak
Floured Cubed Beef Steak
Grandma's Chicken Casserole
Haugin's Pride Dinner Steaks
Jumbo Beef Ravioli
Macaroni & Cheese
Pizza Patties
Ranchero Sandwich*
Ribeye Steak
Roast Beef & Swiss Croissant
Round Cheese Ravioli*
Shrimp Oriental
Sirloin Filet Of Beef
Strip Steak, Lean & Fat
Strip Steak, Lean Only
Sweet & Sour Chicken Bag
Sweet & Sour Chicken Plate*

Vegetable Lasagna
STOUFFER'S
Bar B Que Style Chicken
Beef Chop Suey with Rice
Beef Fajitas*
Beef Pie
Beef Short Ribs in Gravy
Beef Stroganoff with Parsley
    Noodles
Beef Teriyaki in Sauce with
    Rice & Vegetables
Cashew Chicken in Sauce
    with Rice*
Chicken à la King with
    Rice
Chicken Divan
Chicken Fajitas
Creamed Chicken
Creamed Chopped Beef
Escalloped Chicken &
    Noodles
Green Pepper Steak with
    Rice
Ham & Asparagus Bake
Homestyle Chicken &
    Noodles
Lasagna*
Lobster Newburg
Macaroni & Beef with
    Tomatoes*
Macaroni & Cheese
meat pies, frozen
Roast Beef Hash
Salisbury Steak in Gravy
Southern-fried Chicken
Spaghetti with Meat Sauce
Spaghetti with Meatballs*

Stouffer's (cont.)

Stuffed Green Peppers with
  Beef in Tomato Sauce
Swedish Meatballs in Gravy
  with Parsley Noodles
Tortellini, Cheese, in Alfredo
  Sauce
Tortellini, Cheese, with
  Tomato sauce
Tortellini, Cheese, with
  Vinaigrette Dressing
Tortellini, Veal, in Alfredo
  Sauce
Tuna Noodle Casserole*
Turkey Casserole with Gravy
  & Dressing
Turkey Tetrazzini
turkey pot pies, frozen
Vegetable Lasagna
Welsh Rarebit
STOUFFER'S RIGHT COURSE
Barbeque Chicken
Beef Dijon with Pasta &
  Vegetables
Beef Ragout with Rice Pilaf
Broiled Chicken Tenderloins
  with Vegetables & Rice
Broiled Chicken
  Tenderloins in BBQ
  Sauce
Chicken Italiano with
  Fettucine & Vegetables
Chicken Tenderloins in
  Peanut Sauce with
  Linguini & Vegetables
Fiesta Beef with Corn Pasta
Homestyle Pot Roast
Sesame Chicken

Sliced Turkey in a Mild
  Curry Sauce with Rice
  Pilaf
Shrimp Primavera
Vegetarian Chili
SWANSON, CHICKEN DUET
  GOURMET NUGGETS
Ham & Cheese
Mexican Style
Pizza Style
Salisbury Steak
Spinach & Herb
SWANSON, BUDGET
  DINNERS
Beans & Franks*
Fried Chicken
Macaroni & Beef*
Macaroni & Cheese*
Spaghetti & Meatballs*
SWANSON, 3 COMPARTMENT
  DINNERS
Beans & Franks
Fried Chicken Platter
Macaroni & Beef*
Macaroni & Cheese*
Noodles & Chicken*
Spaghetti & Meatballs*
SWANSON, 4 COMPARTMENT
  DINNERS
Beef
Beef in Barbecue Sauce
Chicken in Barbecue Sauce
Chicken Nuggets
Chopped Sirloin Beef
Fish 'N Chips*
Fish Nuggets
Fried Chicken, BBQ Flavored*
Fried Chicken, White Meat

Swanson, 4 Compartment Dinners (cont.)
- Fried Chicken, Dark Meat
- Loin of Pork*
- Meatloaf
- Salisbury Steak
- **Sweet 'n Sour Chicken**
- **Swiss Steak**
- **Turkey**
- Veal Parmigiana
- Western Style

SWANSON, CHICKEN DIET
ENTRÉES
- Creamy Broccoli
- Creamy Green Bean
- Saucy Tomato
- Savory Wild Rice

SWANSON, HOMESTYLE
RECIPE
- Cheese Ravioli*
- Chicken & Noodles*
- Chicken Cacciatore
- Fish 'N Chips
- Fish 'N Fries
- Fried Chicken
- Lasagna with Meat Sauce*
- Macaroni & Cheese
- Salisbury Steak
- Scalloped Potatoes & Ham
- Sirloin Tips in Burgundy
  Sauce*
- Spaghetti with Italian-Style
  Meatballs*
- Swedish Meatballs
- Tuna Noodle Casserole
- Turkey with Dressing &
  Potatoes
- Veal Parmigiana*

SWANSON, HUNGRY MAN
DINNERS
- Boneless Chicken*
- Chopped Beef Steak
- Fried Chicken, White Meat
- Fried Chicken, Dark Meat
- Salisbury Steak
- **Sliced Beef**
- **Turkey**
- Veal Parmigiana*

TYSON, GOURMET ENTRÉES
- Beef Champignon*
- **Chicken & Beef Luau**
- Lasagna*
- Pasta Trio*
- **Pepper Steak**
- Salisbury Supreme
- Short Ribs

TYSON, LOONEY TUNES
- Bugs Bunny Chicken
  Chunks*
- **Daffy Duck Spaghetti &
  Meatballs**
- Road Runner Chicken
  Sandwich*
- Speedy Gonzales Beef
  Enchilada*
- Sylvester Fish Sandwich*
- **Tweety Macaroni & Cheese**
- Yosemite Sam BBQ Glazed
  Chicken
- **Wile E. Coyote Hamburger
  Pizza**

ULTRA SLIM FAST
- **Chicken & Vegetables**
- **Chicken Fettuccine**
- **Mesquite Chicken**

Ultra Slim Fast (cont.)
- **Pasta Primavera**
- **Roasted Chicken with Mushrooms**
- **Shrimp Marinara**
- **Shrimp Creole**
- **Spaghetti with Beef & Mushrooms**
- **Turkey Medallions**

WEIGHT WATCHERS
- Baked Cheese Ravioli*
- Beef Salisbury Steak Romania
- **Beef Sirloin Tips & Mushrooms in Wine Sauce**
- Beef Steak, Chopped
- Breaded Chicken Cordon Bleu
- **Broccoli & Cheese Baked Potato**
- Cheese Manicotti*

- **Chicken Divan Baked Potato**
- Chicken Patty Parmigiana
- **Fillet of Fish Au Gratin**
- Garden Lasagna*
- **Imperial Chicken**
- Italian Cheese Lasagna*
- **Lasagna with Meat Sauce**
- **London Broil in Mushroom Sauce**
- Oven-Fried Fish*
- Pasta Primavera*
- **Pasta Rigati**
- **Seafood Linguini**
- Southern Fried Chicken Patty
- **Spaghetti with Meat Sauce**
- **Stuffed Sole with Newburg Sauce**
- **Sweet 'N Sour Chicken Tenders**
- Turkey, stuffed breast*

APPENDIX 8: ENTRÉES, CANNED
···

It is difficult to make generalized statements about canned entrées. Most contain too much fat.

Remember that canning can increase the fat-forming potential of pasta when the pasta looses its firmness and becomes pasty.

BEANS
- **baked with pork**
- **baked, Boston**
- baked, with franks

BEEF STEW
- **Bounty**

- Chef Boyardee
- Dinty Moore
- **Dinty Moore Micro-Cup**
- Estee
- Featherweight
- Heinz*

Beef Stew (cont.)
    Libby's
    Nalley's
    Wolfscant, cup*
  Beef-A-Roni
  CHICKEN ENTRÉES
    Chef Boyardee, chicken stew*
    Heinz, chicken stew*
    International Lites, Chicken Fiesta
    Rice-A-Roni, Chicken & Rice

Savoy Classics, Chicken & Rice
corned beef
corned beef, lean
corned beef hash
herring
lasagna
macaroni
noodle dishes, canned
pasta, all canned
ravioli, Chef Boyardee
ravioli, Franco American
tamales, canned, all*

APPENDIX 9: ENTRÉES, FROZEN AND REFRIGERATED

...

Frequently, chicken products have a greater fat content than do the equivalent fresh-cooked products. Therefore, don't assume that white-meat products are low in fat.

Fish entrées tend to be high in fat because many are battered and fried. As a general rule you should avoid all such products unless less than 30 percent of their calories come from fat (39 percent after you cure the Starvation Response, as part of a cheating meal).

CHICKEN ENTRÉES
  KRAFT
    Chicken egg noodles*
    Chicken Applause, BBQ
    Chicken Applause, cheese
    Chicken Applause, mushroom
  LEAN CUISINE
    Chicken Cacciatore*
    Chicken Marsala

SCHWAN'S
BBQ Wings
breaded chicken
breast fillet, unbreaded
breast patties
breast strips
breast with asparagus
chicken Kiev
Cordon Bleu
diced chicken meat*
Drummies

Schwan's (cont.)
    hot wings
    Marco Polo, chicken parts*
    Nuggets
SWANSON
    chicken dipsters
    Drumlets
    fried breast
    fried chicken, whole
    Nibbles
    Nuggets
    thighs and drumsticks
    chicken stew*
TASTY BIRD
    breaded breast quarters
    breast fillet
    breast strip
    breast tenderloins
    chicken Delites
    chicken nuggets
    Hi-Pro chicken patties
    leg quarters
TYSON
    boneless breast chunks
    boneless breast fillets
    boneless breast patties
    boneless Chic 'n Cheddar
    boneless Chic 'n Chunks
    boneless diced meat*
    Boneless Thick & Crispy
      Patties
    butter garlic chicken*
    Dijon chicken
    Gourmet Selections, à
      l'orange
    Gourmet Selections, Chicken
      Luau*

Gourmet Selections, Dijon
Gourmet Selections,
    Francais*
Gourmet Selections, Kiev
Gourmet Selections, Lasagna*
Gourmet Selections, Marsala*
Gourmet Selections,
    Mesquite
Gourmet Selections, Picatta
Italian chicken
lemon pepper chicken
Marinated Chicken Breast,
    BBQ
Marinated Chicken Breast,
    butter dill
microwave breast sandwich*
microwave chicken corn
    dogs
microwave chunks
microwave Mini sandwich
microwave nuggets
microwave Tenders
roasted chicken
savory chicken
wings
WEAVER
    battered-dipped breasts
    battered-dipped thighs and
      drumsticks
    battered-dipped wings
    breast fillet
    breast patties
    Cheese Rondelet
    Chicken Au Gratin
    Chicken Nuggets
    Crisp Mini Drums
    Crispy Fried, assorted

Weaver (cont.)
> Crispy Fried, breasts
> Crispy Fried, thighs and
>   drumsticks
> Crispy Fried, wings
> croquettes
> Herb 'N Spice
> Homestyle Roundels
> Spicy Herb Fried Chicken
> Tenders
> Zesty Wings
> WEIGHT WATCHERS
>   Chicken à la King*
>   Cordon Bleu
>   **Imperial Chicken**
> CHINESE EGG ROLLS
>   Chun King, chicken*
>   Chun King, meat and
>   shrimp*
>   Chun King, pork*
>   Chun King, shrimp*
>   Jeno's Snacks, chicken*
>   Jeno's Snacks, meat and
>   shrimp
>   Jeno's Snacks, shrimp and
>   cheese*
>   Worthington Foods*
> eggplant parmigiana
> enchilada, beef, Hormel*
> Fish Entrées
>   BLOCK
>   **cod**
>   fish nuggets
>   fish portions
>   fish sticks
>   fishburger
>   **flounder**

> **ocean catfish**
> sole
> whiting
> Frionor, fish sticks
> GORTON'S
>   fish Florentine*
>   Lite, fish entree, battered
>   fish entrée, battered
>   fish sticks
> Lean Cuisine, fish entrée,
>   Florentine*
> MRS. PAUL'S
>   Crispy Crunchy, fish entrée,
>   battered
>   Light, fillets in butter*
>   **Light, fish Divan**
>   **Light, fish entrée, Dijon**
>   Light, fish entrée, Florentine*
>   fish entrée, battered
>   fish entrée, cakes*
>   fish sticks*
>   shrimp, battered or breaded
>   **shrimp, cooked**
>   shrimp, fried
>   shrimp, garlic butter*
> VAN DE KAMP
>   fish entrée, battered
>   fish entrée, cakes
>   fish sticks
>   **Wakefield, fish gems**
> lasagna, frozen*
> lasagna, diet, frozen*
> MEXICAN ENTRÉES, FROZEN
>   Banquet Family Entrée,
>   enchilada, beef, chili gravy,
>   **Budget Gourmet Slim Selects**
>   **Enchilada, Chicken Suiza**

EL CHARRITO BURRITO
  Beef & Bean*
  Beef, Grande*
  Beef, Green Chili*
  Beef, Jalapeno*
  Beef, Red Chili
  Beef, Red Chili Grande*
  Beef, Red Hot*
HEALTHY CHOICE
  burrito, bean & cheese*
  burrito, beef, Burrito
    Grande*
  burrito, cheese
  burrito, chili, hot
  enchilada, cheese*
  fettuccine Alfredo
  tamales
  Le Menu Lite enchilada,
    chicken
LEAN CUISINE
  enchilada, beef and bean*
  enchilada, chicken
  Vegetable & Tofu
OLD EL PASO
  burrito, beef & bean, hot*
  burrito, beef & bean,
    medium*
  burrito, beef & bean, mild*
  enchilada, beef
  enchilada, cheese*
  enchilada, chicken with sour
    cream
  enchilada, chicken
  tamales
PATIO
  burrito, Beef & Bean Green
    Chili*

burrito, Beef & Bean Red
    Chili*
burrito, beef & bean
burrito, Red Hot Burritos*
burrito, cheese*
burrito, chicken and rice*
burrito, chicken*
burrito, chicken, spicy*
burrito, chili, green*
burrito, chili, red*
Red Hot burrito, chili*
Schwan's burrito, beef &
  bean
Schwan's tamales*
Stouffer's enchilada, cheese
Stouffer's enchilada, chicken
VAN DE KAMP
  enchilada, beef*
  enchilada, cheese
  enchilada, cheese ranchero*
  enchilada, chicken suiza*
  enchilada, chicken*
  enchilada, shredded beef*
WEIGHT WATCHERS
  fajita, beef*
  fajita, chicken
  burrito, beef*
  enchilada, beef ranchero*
  enchilada, cheese ranchero*
  enchilada, chicken suiza*
TURKEY ENTRÉES
  Banquet, supreme microwave,
    turkey pot pie
  Banquet, turkey Dijon,
    frozen*
  Lean Cuisine, turkey loaf,
    homemade*

Turkey Entrées (cont.)
    Louis Rich, turkey nuggets,
      prepared
    Louis Rich, turkey patties,
      prepared
    **Louis Rich, turkey pot
    pie, frozen**

Louis Rich, turkey sticks
Morton, turkey pot pie
Stouffer's, turkey pot pies and
    meat pies/frozen
Swanson, turkey pot pie
**Weight Watchers, turkey,
    stuffed breast***

APPENDIX 10: FISH

...

Many of the most popular fish are high in fat, including crab, mussels, pompano, roughy, and some salmons.

abalone*
alewife (herring)*
anchovy
anchovy, canned
bass, black
bass, freshwater
bass, striped
bluefish*
butterfish
carp
carp, fried
carp, roe
carp, smoked*
catfish
caviar
chub
clams, breaded and fried
clams, canned
clams, steamed
cocktail sauce
cod
cod, frozen, raw

CRAB
    crab salad
    deviled
    Dungeness
    imitation
    king
    soft shell, fried
crayfish
cuttlefish
dock
dogfish
eel
flounder
gefilte fish, in broth
grouper
haddock
haddock, breaded and fried
halibut, raw
halibut, smoked
herring
herring, kippered
lobster*

mackerel
monkfish
mussels
octopus
oyster, breaded and fried
oyster*
perch, breaded and fried
perch, fresh water
perch, ocean
pike
pompano
rockfish
roughy
sable fish
SALMON
   Atlantic
   blueback, canned
   chinook
   chum*
   chum, canned*
   coho*
   fish farm

pink, canned*
smoked lox
sockeye
sardines
scallops
scallops, breaded and
   fried
scrod
sea bass
sea trout*
shad
shark*
sheepshead
shrimp
shrimp, canned
smelt
snapper
sole
sturgeon
swordfish
tuna, canned in oil
tuna, canned in water

APPENDIX 11: FRUIT, FRESH

...

Avoid dried fruits because the process of drying concentrates the sugar. Soaking does not help.

Bananas induce one-third more blood sugar than does table sugar. However, if you eat bananas that are not totally ripe, there is some suggestion that the induced blood sugar will be much lower.

apple
apricot, dried
apricot, fresh
banana

blackberry
blueberry
boysenberry
cantaloupe

215

casaba melon
cherries
dates
figs, dried
figs, fresh
grape
grapefruit
honeydew melon
kiwifruit
lemon
lime
mandarin orange

mango
nectarine
orange
orange juice
papaya
peaches
pears
pineapple
plums
prunes
raisins
watermelon,

APPENDIX 12: FRUIT, CANNED

...

Canned fruits are Good Calories as long as they are not overcooked or packaged in syrup. Many baby foods are processed into a paste that may be acceptable for babies but are Bad Calories for adults.

apple butter
applesauce, natural
  (unsweetened)
applesauce, sweetened
apricot, natural
  (unsweetened)
apricot, sweetened
blackberry, in syrup
blackberry, in water
blueberry, in water
blueberry, sweetened
cherries, in water
cherries, maraschino,
  unsweetened
cherries, in syrup
figs, in syrup

figs, in water
fruit cocktail, in syrup
fruit cocktail, in water
fruit salad, in syrup
fruit salad, in water
jam and jelly, sweetened
jam and jelly, unsweetened
mandarin orange, in syrup
mandarin orange, in water
peaches, sweetened
peaches, unsweetened
pears, sweetened
pears, unsweetened
plums, sweetened
plums, unsweetened
prunes

APPENDIX 13: FRUIT, FROZEN

•••

Avoid any frozen fruit packaged in syrup.

raspberry, in syrup

raspberry, in water

rhubarb

rhubarb, sweetened

blackberry, in syrup

blackberry, in water

blueberry, in water

blueberry, sweetened

cherries, in water

cherries, in syrup

APPENDIX 14: LEGUMES

•••

Legumes are probably the best food for people on the Good Calorie Diet. They often have less than half the blood sugar-producing potential of table sugar. By adding them to a meal, you can drastically reduce that meal's fat-forming potential.

Combining 1 unit of legumes to 2½ units of grain (rice or corn) produces a perfect protein that supplies all the body's needs. If you are trying to maximize your weight loss by avoiding meat products, this combination is a great substitute.

adzuki beans, boiled

adzuki beans, canned

adzuki beans

beans, baked, canned

black bean soup

black-eyed peas

butter beans

chickpeas, canned

chickpeas, dried

chili beans

dal, lentils

garbanzo beans

great northern beans

green peas, dried

green peas, frozen

kidney beans, canned

kidney beans, dried

lentils, green canned

lentils, green dried

lima beans

moth beans

mung bean sprouts

navy beans

peanuts

peanut butter

peas, dried

peas, frozen

pinto beans, canned

pinto beans, dried

soybeans, canned

soybeans, dried

white beans, haricot, dried

APPENDIX 15: MEAT

···

These listings are based on the most commonly sold grades of meat. The higher grades of meat are also the highest in fat, which enhances their taste. However, it is possible to raise animals so they produce less fat. You may be able to find more kinds of cuts of beef and other meats at specialty stores.

Do not confuse "health food" meats with low-fat products. Health food stores often feature meats that may not contain as many chemicals as regular products, but contain just as much fat.

BEEF
  blade
  brisket, lean
  chuck, no fat
  club steak, lean*
  corned beef
  flank, lean
  ground, lean
  kidneys
  liver*
  porterhouse, no fat
  rib eye
  rib roast
  ribs
  round, bottom, no fat*
  round, eye, no fat*
  round, full cut, no fat*
  round, tip, no fat*
  round, top, no fat
  rump roast, no fat*
  sirloin, lean*
  T-bone
  tenderloin
  tongue
  top loin
  horse meat

HOT DOGS
  beef
  chicken
  turkey
KIDNEYS
  beef
  lamb
  pork
  veal
LAMB
  chops
  foreshank
  ground
  kidneys
  leg, roast
  liver
  loin
  ribs
  shank
  shoulder
  sirloin
LIVER
  beef
  lamb
  pork
  veal

PORK
  all except those listed
  arm, lean roasted
  ham, extra lean
  heart
  kidney
  lean tenderloin
  liver
  loin
  ribs
  tenderloin, roasted, lean
  rabbit wild
  rabbit, domestic
VEAL
  breast
  chop

chop, lean only*
chuck
cutlet
cutlet, lean only
heart*
kidneys
liver
loin
ribs
round
rump
sweetbreads
tongue*

APPENDIX 16: MEAT, LUNCHEON
•••

ARMOUR, TURKEY SELECTS
  barbecued turkey, packaged
  golden star, raw links or
    patties
  turkey bacon
  turkey bologna
  turkey breakfast strips
  turkey ham
BUTTERBALL
turkey breast, all*
  turkey ham, all
  chicken
  smoked turkey
  turkey
Butterball, turkey, deli, no salt*
Butterball, Fresh 'n Easy
  turkey slices, cooked
BUTTERBALL, SLICE 'N SERVE
  TURKEY

barbecued seasoned, breast of
  turkey
hickory smoked, breast of
  turkey
oven prepared, smoked
oven prepared, turkey
  breast with broth
oven roasted, breast of
  turkey
turkey ham
turkey pastrami*
Danola, ham 98 percent fat
  free
ECKRICH
  Corned Beef Slender
  Gourmet Loaf*
  Ham Cooked Lite*
  Slender Beef
  Turkey Breast, Lite

Eckrich (cont.)
    Turkey Breast, Lite smoked*
Hebrew National Bologna Deli
    Beef*
HILLSHIRE FARMS DELI
    SELECT
    Cajun ham
    corned beef
    cured beef
    honey ham
    pastrami
    smoked beef
    smoked chicken breast
    smoked turkey breast
    smoked ham
    turkey breast
HORMEL LIGHT & LEAN
    barbecued ham*
    Canadian bacon
    cooked ham*
    glazed ham*
    peppered ham*
    smoked ham*
    turkey breast*
Hormel Luxury Loaf
Hormel, turkey breast, all*
GENERIC
    bologna
    bratwurst
    bockwurst
    corned beef
    corned beef, lean
    frankfurter
    frankfurter, light and lean
    ham, extra lean*
    kielbasa
    knockwurst
    liverwurst

LOUIS RICH
    chicken breast*
    chicken breast, smoked*
TURKEY BREAST*
    turkey breast, fat free
    turkey ham
    turkey, smoked*
LOUIS RICH, FULLY COOKED
    TURKEY
    barbecued turkey
    hickory smoked turkey
    turkey ham with water
    added
New England brand sausage*
OSCAR MEYER
    barbecue loaf, fat free*
    chicken breast, 97 percent
    fat free
    corned beef, 98 percent fat
    free*
    ham baked, 97 percent fat
    free
    ham boiled, 95 percent fat
    free
    ham honey loaf, 95 percent
    fat free
    ham honey, 95 percent fat
    free*
    ham, lower salt, 95 percent
    fat free*
    Luxury Loaf, 95 percent fat
    free
    pastrami, 97 percent fat
    free*
    smoked beef, 97 percent fat
    free*
    turkey, smoked, 98 percent
    fat free

SWIFT PREMIUM, HAM*
TURKEY, GENERIC
    turkey, canned and boned
       with broth*
    turkey frankfurter
    turkey pastrami*
    turkey patties, battered and
       fried

light turkey roll
turkey salami
turkey sausage
WEAVER
    chicken breast
    turkey breast, all*
    turkey ham*

APPENDIX 17: MEAT SUBSTITUTES

•••

Very few meat substitutes are Good Calories. Manufacturers add fats in an attempt to make them taste more like meat.

LA LOMA
    baconlike bits
    Big Franks
    Bologna Roll
    Bologna Slices
    Chicken Nuggets
    Chicken Patties
    Chicken Roll*
    Chicken Slices*
    Chicken Supreme
    Corn Dogs*
    Dinner Cuts
    Fried Chicken
    Griddle Steaks*
    Linketts
    Little Links
    Nuteena Luncheon Loaf
    Ocean Fillets
    Ocean Platter
    Olive Loaf
    Olive Loaf Slices
    Patty Mix
    Proteena Nut Loaf
    Rediburger

    Roast Beef Roll*
    Roast Beef Slices*
    Salami Roll*
    Salami Slices*
    Sandwich Spread
    Savory Meatball
    Sizzle Burger
    Sizzle Franks
    Spicy Chicken
    Stew Pack
    Swiss Steak
    Tastee Cuts
    Tender Bits*
    Tender Rounds
    Turkey Roll*
    Turkey Slices*
    Vege Beans
    Vege Scallops
    Vege-Burger mix
    Vegeburger
    Vegelona
    Vegetein Beef*
    Vegetein Chicken*
    Vegetein Chorizo*

La Loma (*cont.*)
    Vegetein Taco Mix*
    Wheat Fries
MORNINGSTAR FARMS
    Breakfast Links
    Breakfast Strips
    Country Breakfast, Cinnamon
       French Toast & Patties*
    Country Breakfast,
       Scramblers, Links, & Hash
       Browns
    Country Breakfast,
       Scramblers, Links, &
       Pancakes
    Country Crisp Patties
    Grillers
    Homestyle Country Crisps
    Scramblers
    Zesty Country Crisps
WORTHINGTON
    Chili
    chili
    Choplets
    Country Stew
    Non Meat Balls
    Prime Steaks
    Protose*
    Saucettes
    Savory Slices
    Super Links
    Turkee Slices
    Vega Links
    Vegetable Skallops
    Vegetable Steaks
    Vegetarian Burger
    Vegetarian Burger, no salt*

WORTHINGTON, FROZEN
    Beef Pie*
    Beef Style Roll
    Bolono
    Chic-ketts roll*
    Chicken Stiks
    Chicken, diced
    Chicken, roll
    Chicken, slices
    Corned Beef
    Crispy Chili
    Dinner Roast
    Dixie Dogs
    Egg Rolls*
    Fillets
    Fripats
    Harvest Bake Lentil Loaf
    Leanies
    Natural Touch Dinner Entree
    Okra Patties
    Prosage
    Salami
    Smoked Beef
    Smoked Turkey
    Stakelets
    Tofu Garden Patties*
    Tuno Roll
    Wham
WORTHINGTON, NATURAL
    TOUCH MIX
    Dry Loaf*
    Spicy Chili
    Stroganoff
    Taco

APPENDIX 18: NUTS

...

Nuts are popular with health food advocates, but are very high in fat. Soaking does not help.

acorn
acorn flour
almond butter
almond powder, defatted*
almond powder, normal
almond
Brazil nut
butternut
cashew
cashew butter
chestnut
coconut milk

coconut water
coconut, sweetened
coconut, unsweetened
coconut, whole
filbert
macadamia
peanut
peanut, dry roasted
pecans
pine nuts
pistachio
walnut

APPENDIX 19: PASTA AND PASTA SAUCES

...

Do not overcook.

clam sauce, red
clam sauce, white
Hamburger Helper, all
**macaroni, white, boiled 5
minutes**
noodle dishes
noodles, egg
**spaghetti, brown, boiled 15
minutes**

spaghetti, protein enriched
spaghetti, white, boiled 15
minutes
**spaghetti, white, boiled 5
minutes**
**star pasta, white, boiled 5
minutes**

APPENDIX 20: PASTA, FROZEN

...

fettuccine Alfredo, Stouffer's
fettuccine Alfredo, Weight
    Watchers*
fettuccine primavera, Green
    Giant*
fettuccine primavera, Green
    Giant Microwave

fettuccine with broccoli,
    Budget Gourmet*
fettuccine with meat sauce,
    Dining Lite*

APPENDIX 21: PIZZA, FROZEN

...

In contrast to fast-food pizzas, many of the pizzas highlighted here have a fat content of less than 30 percent. They make excellent meals.

Celentano, Nine Slice
Celentano, Thick Crust
Celeste, all
CHEF BOY-AR-DEE
    pepperoni
    plain
    sausage
Fox, all
Jeno's, all
JOHN'S
    sausage
    cheese*
    deluxe sausage
LEAN CUISINE
    French Bread, cheese
    French Bread, deluxe*
    French Bread, pepperoni*
    French Bread, sausage*
Lean Pockets, pepperoni
Micro Magic, all
Mr. P's Pizza, all

PAPPALO'S
    92 percent fat-free cheese
    92 percent fat-free
        pepperoni*
    92 percent fat-free sausage
    cheese*
    combination
    pepperoni
    sausage
PAPPALO'S, PAN PIZZA
    combination
    hamburger*
    pepperoni*
    pan pizza, sausage
PAPPALO'S, THIN CRUST
    combination*
    hamburger*
    pepperoni*
    sausage*
Pepperidge Farm Croissant, all

PILLSBURY, MICROWAVE
  cheese*
  combination
  French bread, cheese*
  French bread, pepperoni
  French bread, sausage and
    pepperoni
  French bread, sausage*
  pepperoni
  sausage
Red Baron, Deep Dish, all
Red Baron, Deep Dish,
  Microwave, all
STOUFFER'S FRENCH BREAD
  Canadian bacon*
  cheese*
  deluxe
  double cheese
  hamburger
  pepperoni
  pepperoni and mushroom
  sausage
  sausage and mushroom
  sausage and pepperoni
  vegetable
TOMBSTONE
  93% fat-free, sausage
  93% fat-free, sausage &
    pepperoni
  93% fat-free, supreme
  93% fat-free, vegetable
  Canadian style*
  cheese and hamburger
  cheese and pepperoni
  cheese and sausage*
  cheese*
  combination sausage*
  real pepperoni

sausage and mushroom*
sausage deluxe*
smoked sausage*
Totino's, Classic Deluxe, all
TOTINO'S, LEANER MEATS
  Canadian bacon*
  combination
  hamburger*
  pepperoni*
  sausage
TOTINO'S, MICROWAVE
  cheese
  pepperoni*
  sausage
  sausage and pepperoni
TOTINO'S, PAN PIZZA
  three-cheese*
  pepperoni*
  sausage*
Totino's, Party Pizza, all
TOTINO'S, PIZZA SLICES
  combination*
  pepperoni
  sausage
TOTINO'S, TEMPTIN'
    TOPPINS
  bacon
  Canadian bacon*
  cheese
  hamburger
  Mexican style
  pepperoni
  sausage
  sausage and pepperoni
  vegetable*
WEIGHT WATCHERS
  cheese
  deluxe combination

225

Weight Watchers (cont.)
    French bread, cheese*
    French bread, deluxe*
    French bread, pepperoni*
    pepperoni
    sausage

ZAP, FRENCH BREAD
cheese
deluxe*
pepperoni*

APPENDIX 22: POULTRY

...

The Good Calorie Diet is like any other diet when it comes to poultry. Choose low-fat portions. Skin-free breasts, white meat, and skin-free drumsticks are the best choices.

Always separate protein-rich foods, especially ones high in saturated fat (e.g., chicken), from starchy carbohydrates. When possible, eat protein at lunch and eat other foods two hours before or after it.

CAPON
    skinned, dark meat
    skinned, white meat
    whole
CHICKEN
    back, no skin
    breast with skin*
    breast, no skin
    breast, smoked*
    canned, Swanson, chunk
        white or white and dark*
    chicken frankfurter
    chicken roll, light luncheon
        meat
    chicken salad
CHICKEN SPREAD
    Hormel, chunk dark meat,
        canned
    Hormel, chunk light meat,
        canned
    Hormel, whole, with broth,
        canned

liver, canned
    Underwood, chunky canned
    dark meat, no skin
    drumstick with skin
    drumstick, no skin*
    fried
    leg, no skin
    roasting, whole roasted*
    stewing, whole
    thigh, no skin
    thigh, with skin
    white luncheon meat*
    white meat, no skin
    wing, no skin*
    wing, with skin
DUCK
    domesticated
    liver*
    wild, meat only*
GOOSE
    guinea hen, meat only (no
        skin)

guinea hen, whole*
pheasant
quail, breast
quail, whole
TURKEY
   ARMOUR, TURKEY
     SELECTS
     breast roast*
     breast slices
     breast tenderloins
     turkey strips*
     back meat only*
     breast, fillet, without skin
     breast, half, without skin*
     breast, slices, without skin
     breast, cooked*
     dark meat without skin*
     dark meat with skin
     drumsticks

drumsticks without skin*
giblets, simmered
gizzard, simmered
heart, simmered
light meat without skin
light meat with skin*
liver, simmered
meat and skin, dark and
    light, no giblets or neck
meat only, light and dark
thighs without skin
thighs with skin
whole turkey
wing drumettes
wing drumettes without
   skin*
wings
wings without skin

APPENDIX 23: RICE DISHES

...

HAIN, 3 GRAIN SIDE DISHES
   Chicken Meatless Style
   Herb
   Rice Almondine*
   Rice Oriental 3 Grain*
LIPTON, RICE & SAUCE
   Beef
   Broccoli & Cheddar*
   Chicken
   Herb & Butter
   Long Grain & Wild
   Mushroom
   Pilaf*
   Spanish
MINUTE MICROWAVE, ALL
rice

polished, boiled 5 minutes
brown
instant, boiled 1 minute
instant, boiled 6 minutes
parboiled, boiled 15
   minutes
parboiled, boiled 5 minutes
polished, boiled 10–25
   minutes
RICE-A-RONI
   almond chicken and wild
     rice
   beef
   broccoli au gratin
   cauliflower au gratin*
   chicken

Rice-A-Roni (cont.)
- **chicken and broccoli**
- **chicken and broccoli Dijon**
- chicken and mushrooms*
- **chicken and vegetables**
- **chicken Florentine**
- **creamy parmesan and herbs**
- fried rice with almonds*
- **garden pilaf**
- green bean salad Almondine
- **herb and butter**

- **long grain and wild**
- Oriental stir-fry*
- **rice pilaf**
- **risotto**
- **Spanish**
- spring vegetables and cheese*
- Stroganoff*
- **wild rice pilaf**
- yellow*
- zesty cheddar

APPENDIX 24: RICE DISHES, FROZEN

•••

BIRD'S EYE INTERNATIONAL
- **French style**
- **Italian style**
- **Spanish style**

Country Inn, all

GENERIC
- **asparagus**
- **asparagus pilaf**
- broccoli and cheese
- broccoli in butter
- **broccoli in water**
- brussels sprouts and cheese
- brussels sprouts in butter
- **brussels sprouts in water**

GREEN GIANT
- Italian Blend in Cheese*
- **Rice Jubilee***
- **Rice Medley**
- **Rice Pilaf**
- Rice with Herb Butter*
- Rice 'n Broccoli in Cheese*
- **White and Wild Rice**

KRAFT
- **3 Cheese**
- **Cheddar and Chicken**
- **Cheddar Broccoli**
- **Cheddar Pilaf**

APPENDIX 25: SNACKS

•••

BREAKFAST BARS
- Carnation Slender
- Health Valley
- Kellogg's Nutri-Grain
- Quaker Granola Bar

candy

cheese snacks
- Cheetos
- Cheetos Lite Cheese Flavored
- Cheetos Puffs
- Eagle Cheese Crunch
- Health Valley Cheddar Light

cheese snacks (cont.)
    Planter's Cheez Balls
    Planter's Cheez Curls
    Wise Cheese Doodles
chocolate, all
corn chips
crisp breads
granola bars
potato chips, all
pretzels
rice cakes

TORTILLA CHIPS
Arizona, traditional rounds
Arizona, traditional
Doritos, all
Mi Ranchito, all
Azteca, corn
El Charrito
Old El Paso, baked

APPENDIX 26: SOUP, CANNED

...

bean, Grandma Brown's
bean, bacon and ham,
    Campbell's Microwave
bean, black, Health Valley
bean, ham, Campbell's
    Chunky
bean, ham, Campbell's Home
    Cooking
bean, ham, Hormel Micro-
    Cup
beef, Campbell's Chunky
beef, Progresso*
beef barley, Progresso
beef broth, all
beef minestrone, Progresso
beef noodle, Progresso
beef Vegetable, Campbell's
    Home Cooking
beef Vegetable, Hormel Micro
    Cup
beef Vegetable, Lipton Hearty
    Ones
beef Vegetable, Progresso

berry fruit, Great
    Impressions
blueberry fruit, Great
    Impressions
borscht, all
cherry fruit, Great
    Impressions
chicken, Campbell's Chunky
chicken, Progresso
chicken barley, Progresso
chicken broth, Campbell's*
chicken broth, College Inn
chicken broth, Hain
chicken broth, Health Valley
chicken broth, Progresso
chicken broth, Swanson
chicken corn chowder,
    Campbell's Chunky
chicken gumbo, Campbell's
chicken minestrone,
    Campbell's*
chicken minestrone,
    Progresso

chicken mushroom creamy,
  Campbell's
chicken noodle, all
chicken vegetable, Campbell's
  Chunky*

chicken vegetable, Campbell's
  Low Sodium
chicken vegetable, Progresso

APPENDIX 27: SUGARS

...

fructose
glucose
honey
lactose

maltose
molasses
sucrose (table sugar)

APPENDIX 28: VEGETABLES, FRESH

...

acorn squash
alfalfa sprouts
aloe vera juice
artichoke
arugula
asparagus
avocado
avocado dip
bamboo shoots
bean sprouts
beet greens
beets
broccoli
brussels sprouts
butternut squash
cabbage
cabbage, coleslaw
carrot
cauliflower
celery
coleslaw

collards
corn, sweet
cranberry
cucumber
dandelion greens
eggplant
endive
green beans
Jerusalem artichoke
kale
leek
lettuce
mushroom
mustard greens
okra
olives
onions
parsnip
peas
peppers, sweet, green and
  red

POTATO
  peeled, sliced, and
    microwaved
  instant
  mashed
  russet, baked
  white, boiled, new

radish
rhubarb
spinach
squash
sweet potato
tomato
yam

APPENDIX 29: VEGETABLES, CANNED

...

Canned vegetables are Good Calories as long as they are not overcooked. Many baby foods are processed into a paste that may be acceptable for babies but are Bad Calories for adults.

artichoke hearts, marinated
asparagus
baby food
bamboo shoots ,
bean dip
bean salad
bean sprouts
beans
beets
black-eyed peas
butter beans
butter beans, with pork*
Chinese vegetables
collards
corn
cranberry
cranberry sauce
cucumber, pickled

green beans
kale
kidney beans
lima beans
mushroom
mustard greens
okra
olives
onions
peas
pickles
pinto beans, canned
potato
refried beans
refried beans, low fat
sauerkraut
tomato paste

APPENDIX 30: VEGETABLES, FROZEN

•••

Bird's Eye
BIRD'S EYE, MIXED
VEGETABLES IN ONION
SAUCE, FROZEN
Vegetables in authentic
oriental sauce*
**baby carrots, peas, and
pearl onions**
broccoli, carrots, and pasta
with lightly seasoned
sauce*
**broccoli, carrots, and water
chestnuts**
**broccoli, cauliflower, and
carrots**
broccoli, cauliflower, and
carrots in cheese sauce
**broccoli, corn, and red
peppers**
**broccoli, green beans, pearl
onions, and red peppers**
**broccoli, red peppers,
bamboo shoots, and
straw mushrooms**
**brussels sprouts,
cauliflower, and carrots**
carrots and pasta*
**carrots, peas, and pearl
onions**
cauliflower and carrots
cauliflower, baby carrots, and
snow peas
Chinese style, international
recipe
Chinese style, stir-fry

chow mein style,
international recipe
corn, green beans, and pasta
curls
corn, green beans, and pasta
curls with light cream
sauce, frozen
Custom Cuisine vegetables in
creamy Stroganoff*
Custom Cuisine, creamy
mushroom
Custom Cuisine, vegetables
with herb sauce
French green beans, toasted
almond*
green peas and pearl onions
Italian style, International
Recipe
**Japanese stir-fry,
International Recipe**
Japanese style, International
Recipe
Mandarin style, International
Recipe
mixed vegetables, regular
New England style,
International Recipe
pasta primavera style,
International Recipe*
peas and carrots
peas and onions
rice and green peas
San Francisco style,
International Recipe

BUDGET GOURMET, SIDE
   DISHES
Nacho Potatoes
New England Recipe
   Vegetables
New Orleans Potatoes in Sour
   Cream Sauce
Oriental Rice & Vegetables
Pasta Alfredo with Broccoli*
Peas & Cauliflower in Cream
   Sauce*
**Peas & Water Chestnuts
   Oriental**
Rice Pilaf with Green Beans*
Spinach Au Gratin*
**Spring Vegetables in Cheese
   Sauce**
Sweet Corn in Butter Sauce
Three Cheese Potatoes
Ziti in Marinara Sauce*
Del Monte, sweet corn, pinto
   beans, and red bell pepper
   in a savory sauce
FRESHLIKE
   **broccoli, pasta, and carrots
      in cheese sauce**
   California blend
   **Chuck Wagon blend, Italian
      style**
   **corn, Italian green beans,
      and red peppers in butter
      sauce**
   Midwestern blend
   mixed vegetables
   **mixed vegetables in butter
      sauce, frozen**
   Oriental blend

**peas, carrots, and onions in
   cheese sauce**
Scandinavian blend
vegetables for soup
vegetables for stew
winter blend
Wisconsin blend
GREEN GIANT
   **broccoli and cauliflower in
      creamy Italian cheese
      sauce, one serving***
   **broccoli, cauliflower, and
      carrots in cheese sauce**
   **broccoli, cauliflower, and
      carrots with butter sauce,
      frozen**
   **broccoli, cauliflower, and
      carrots, one serving**
   **broccoli, peas, and carrots,
      one serving**
   **Microwavable/Pantry
      Express, corn, green
      beans, carrots, and pasta**
   **Microwavable/Pantry
      Express, green beans,
      potatoes, and
      mushrooms***
   **Harvest, fresh-mixed
      vegetables**
   Ore-Ida, custom cuisine
      vegetable medley, breaded,
      frozen
   Ore-Ida, stew vegetables
PICTSWEET
   **broccoli, carrots, and water
      chestnuts**
   broccoli and cauliflower

Pictsweet (cont.)

broccoli, French beans, onions, and red peppers
carrots and water chestnuts
Express, Microwave
mixed vegetables
peas, pearl onions, and mushrooms
squash, onions, and peppers
succotash
Vegetables, Belgian
Vegetables, California
Vegetables, Cantonese
Vegetables Del Sol
Vegetables for Stir-fry
vegetables for stir-fry, prepared as directed
Vegetables Grande
Vegetables Italian
Vegetables Japanese
Vegetables Milano
Vegetables New England
Vegetables Oriental
Vegetables Parisian
Vegetables Romano
Vegetables Swiss
Vegetables Western

STOKELY SINGLES
broccoli, carrots, and water chestnuts
broccoli and cauliflower*
broccoli, cauliflower, and carrots in cheese sauce*
broccoli, cauliflower, and carrots*
sweet corn
VALLEY COMBINATION
American Style
Broccoli Fanfare
Broccoli-Cauliflower Medley
Broccoli-Cauliflower Supreme
Broccoli, Carrot Fanfare
Cauliflower-Green Bean Festival
Corn-Broccoli Bounty
Italian Style without sauce
Italian Style with sauce
Japanese Style
Le Sueur Style
Mexican Style
Sweet Pea and Cauliflower Medley

Chapter 1

1. F. X. Pi-Sunyer, *Nutrition* 7: 292–94 (1991).

Chapter 2

1. J. S. Sweeney, *Arch. Internal Med.* 40: 818–30 (1927).
2. H. P. Himsworth, *Clin. Sci.* 2: 67–94 (1935).
3. *Nutrition Reviews* 49: 364–66 (1991).
4. K. J. Achenson et al., *Am J. Clin. Nutr.* 48: 240–47 (1988).
5. D. M. Mott et al., *Metab. Clin. Exp.* 35: 160–65 (1986); L. Tappy et al., *Diabetes Care* 14: 1180–88 (1991); J. F. Caro et al., *Diabetes Metab. Rev.* 5: 665(1989); and J. P. Felber et al., *Diabetes* 36: 1341–50 (1987).
6. R. Schmid et al., *J. Clin. Endocrinol. Metab.* 68: 1106–10 (1989); and P. Damsbo et al., *Diabetologia* 34: 239–45 (1991).
7. F. X. Pi-Sunyer, *Nutrition* 7: 292–94 (1991).
8. P. Martin et al., *Metabolism* 36: 1154–64 (1988); J. P. Flatt, *Ann. NY Acad. Sci.* 499: 104–23 (1987); K. J. Achenson et al., *Am. J. Clin.* 48: 240–47 (1988); and S. J. Bhathena et al., *European J. Clin. Nutr.* 42: 465–72 (1988).
9. K. J. Achenson et al., *Am. J. Clin. Nutr.* 48: 240–47 (1988).
10. T. J. Yost and R. E. Eckel, *J. Clin. Endocrinol. Metab.* 67: 259–64 (1988).
11. Ibid.
12. R. S. Schwartz and J. D. Brunzell, "Recent Advances in Obesity Research: III" (1981).
13. N. B. Ruderman, *Am. J. Clin. Nutr.* 34: 1617–21 (1988); S. Lillioja et al., *J. Clin. Endocrinol. Metab.* 73: 866–76 (1991); J. V. Neel, *Am. J. Hum. Genet.* 14: 353–62 (1962); G. Reaven, *Diabetes* 37: 1595–1607 (1988); and J. F. Caro, *J. Clin. Endocrinol. Metab.* 73: 691–9 (1991).
14. J. S. Romijn et al., *Metabolism* 39: 525–30 (1990); R. Schmid et al., *J. Clin. Endocrinol. Metab.* 68: 1106 (1989); A. Franssila-Kallunki et al., *Metabolism* 40: 689–94 (1991); G. C. Cook, *Metabolism* 17: 1073–83 (1968); G. C. Cook, *Nature* 215: 1295–96 (1976); W. P. T. James and H. G. Coore, *Am. J. Clin. Nutr.* 23: 386–89 (1970); and J.-P. Felber, *Int. J. Obesity* 16: 937–52 (1992).
15. D. Porte and S. C. Woods, *Diabetologia* 20: 274–80 (1981).
16. I. J. Stein et al., *Endocrinology* 113: 299–301 (1983); and J. Rodin et al., *Metabolism* 34: 826–31 (1985).
17. S. J. Bhathena et al., *Proc. Soc. Exp. Biol. Med.* 181: 71–77 (1986); R. Schmid et al., *J. Clin. Endocrinol. Metabol.* 68: 1106 (1989); Y. B. Lombardo et al., *Horm. Metab. Res.* 25: 69–76 (1983); and N. Geary, *Neuroscience Behav. Rev.* 14: 323–38 (1990).
18. R. P. S. Kwok and A. V. Juorio, *Neuroendocrinol.* 45: 267–73 (1987); R. J. Wurtman and J. J. Wurtman, *Appetite* 7 (Suppl.): 88–103 (1986); D. V. M. Ahsley et al., *Am. J. Clin. Nutr.* 42: 1240–45 (1985); S. Paykfl

et al., *Br. J. Psychiat.* 123: 501–7 (1973); and I. Blum et al., *Am. J. Clin. Nutr.* 57: 486–89 (1993).

19. E. K. Hamalainen et al., *J. Steroid Biochem.* 20: 459–64 (1984); and B. R. Goldin and S. L. Gorbach, *Am. J. Clin. Nutr.* 48: 787–90 (1988).
20. G. M. Reaven, *Diabetes* 37: 1595–1607 (1988).

Chapter 3

1. H. C. Burkett and H. C. Trowell, *Western Diseases: Their Emergence and Prevention* (1981).
2. L. H. Storlin et al., *Am. J. Phsyiol.* 251: E576–E583 (1986).
3. B. A. Swinburn et al., *J. Clin. Endocrinol. Metabol.* 73: 156–65 (1991); and J. A. Marshall et al., *Am. J. Epidemiol.* 134: 590–603 (1991).
4. A. Astrup and A. Raben, *Eur. J. Clin. Nutr.* 46: 611–20 (1992); and D. H. Ekwyn et al., *Am J. Clin Nutr.* 32: 1597–1611 (1979).
5. J. E. Blundell and V. J. Bruley in *Progress in Obesity Research*, eds. Oomura, Y. et al. London: John Libbey, 453–57 (1990).
6. M. C. Gulliford et al., *Am J. Clin. Nutr.* 50: 773–77 (1989); E. Gatti et al., *Eur. J. Clin. Nutr.* 46: 161–66 (1991); and G. Collier et al., *Diabetologia* 26: 50–54 (1984).
7. C. R. Sitori et al., *Am. J. Clin. Nutr.* 44: 635–42 (1986).
8. E. Gatti et al., *Eur. J. Clin. Nutr.* 46: 161–66 (1991).
9. P. J. H. Jones et al., *Metabolism* 37: 145–51 (1988).
10. P. J. H. Jones et al., *Metabolism* 41: 396–401 (1992); L. Forsgren, *Arch. Kemi* 30: 355–60 (1968); and J. B. Watkins et al., *Gastroenterol.* 82: 911–17 (1982); and P. J. H. Jones et al., *Am. J. Clin. Nutr.* 42: 769–77 (1985).
11. S. W. Mercer and P. Trayhurn, *J. Nutr.* 117: 2147–53 (1987); and P. J. H. Jones et al., *Metabolism* 41: 396–401 (1992).
12. P. J. H. Jones et al., *Metabolism* 41: 396–401 (1992).
13. K. Hermansen et al., *Diabetic Medicine* 9: 739–43 (1992); and T. M. S. Wolever et al., *J. Clin. Nutr. Gastroenterol.* 3: 85–88 (1988).
14. J. D. Brand et al., *Am. J. Clin. Nutr.* 42: 1192–96 (1985).
15. J. Holm et al., *Eur. J. Clin. Nutr.* 46: 629–40 (1992).
16. G. R. Herxberg and M. Rogerson, *J. Nutr.* 118: 1061–67 (1988).
17. H. L. Higgins, *Am. J. Physiol.* 41: 258–65 (1916).
18. G. R. Herxberg and M. Rogerson, *J. Nutr.* 118: 1061–67 (1988).
19. J. Hallfrisch et al., *J. Nutr.* 113: 1819–26 (1983); S. Resier et al., *Am. J. Clin. Nutr.* 45: 580–87 (1987); and A. W. Thorburn et al., *Am. J. Clin. Nutr.* 49: 1155–63 (1989).
20. J. Hallfrisch et al., *Am. J. Clin. Nutr.* 37: 740–48 (1983); and J. Hallfrisch et al., *J. Nutr.* 113: 1819–26 (1983).
21. J. Hallfrisch et al., *J. Nutr.* 113: 1819–26 (1983).
22. Ibid.
23. J. V. Selby et al., *Am J. Epidemiol.* 125: 979–88 (1987); D. T. Fowman, *Ann. Clin. Lab. Sci.* 18: 181–89 (1988); and M. J. Gerald et al., *Diabetes* 26: 780–85 (1977).

24. Lancet (October 30, 1965).
25. P. Felig, et al., *JAMA* 242: 1591 (1979); O. Pederson, *New England J. Med.* 302: 886–92 (1980); and D. M. Klatchko et al., *Diabetes* 21: 89–100 (1972).
26. D. L. Costill et al., *J. Appl. Physiol: Respirat. Environ. Exercise Physiol.* 43: 695–99 (1977); G. K. Grimditch et al., *Am. J. Clin. Nutr.* 48: 38–43 (1988); J. E. Donnelly et al., *Am. J. Clinc. Nutr.* 54: 56–61 (1991); R. J. Harvel et al., *J. Appl. Phsyiol.* 23: 90–99 (1967); and C. Foster et al., *Med. Sci. Sports* 11: 1–5 (1979).
27. C. Connell, *Associated Press* (July 30, 1993).
28. J. C. Cohen and R. Hickman, *J. Clin. Endocrinol. Metab.* 64: 960–63 (1987).

Chapter 4

1. D. J. A. Jenkins et al., *Diabetes Care* 11: 149–59 (1988).
2. D. J. A. Jenkins et al., *BMJ* 297: 958–60 (1988).
3. R. N. Podel and W. Proctor, *The G-Index Diet.* New York: Warner Books (1993).
4. L. J. D. O'Donell et al., *BMJ* 298: 1616–17 (1989).
5. P. R. Ellis et al., *Br. J. Nutr.* 46: 267–76 (1981).
6. D. J. Scholfield et al., *Am. J. Clin. Nutr.* 46: 955–61 (1987).
7. Quoted in B. Lehamn, *Marin Independent Journal* D1 (September 13, 1993).
8. H. Liljeberg et al., *Eur. J. Clin. Nutr.* 46: 561–75 (1992).
9. T. M. S. Wolever et al., *Diabetes Care* 9: 401–4 (1986).

Chapter 5

1. J. E. Nester et al., *Diabetes Care* 11: 755–60 (1988).
2. D. J. A. Jenkins et al., *Am. J. Clin. Nutr.* 35: 1339–46 (1982).
3. A. S. Levine et al., *Am J. Clin. Nutr.* 50: 1303–7 (1989); and J. E. Blundell et al., *Int. J. Obesity* 11 (Suppl. 1): 9–25 (1987).
4. T. M. S. Wolever et al., *Am. J. Clin. Nutr.* 48: 1041–47 (1988).
5. J. Bertelsen et al., *Diabetes Care* 16: 4–7 (1993).
6. R. Schmid et al., *J. Clin. Endocrinol. Metab.* 68: 1106 (1989); G. B. Forbes, *Am J. Clin. Nutr.* 52: 224–27 (1990); J. C. Floyd et al., *J. Clin. Invest.* 45: 1476–86 (1966); D. Estrich et al., *Diabetes,* 16: 232–37 (1967); D. Rabinowitz et al., *Lancet* 2: 454–57 (1967); G. A. Spiller et al., *Am J. Clin. Nutr.* 46: 474–80 (1987); R. Schmid et al., *J. Clin. Endocrinol. Metab.* 68: 1106–10 (1989); and P. J. Crowe and G. T. Royle, *J. Nutr.* 118: 1240–44 (1988).
7. M. C. Gullford et al., *Am. J. Clin. Nutr.* 50: 773–77 (1989).
8. O. Rasmussen et al., *Metabolism* 42: 214–17 (1993).
9. W. C. Rose, *J. Biol. Chem.* 217: 997–1004 (1955).
10. J. M. Whitaker, *Reversing Diabetes.* New York: Warner Books (1987).

11. A. De Burgos et al., *Eur. J. Clin. Nutr.* 46: 803–8 (1992); R. A. DeFronzo, *Metabolism* 37: 105–8 (1988); and J. Kersteer et al., *Metabolism* 40: 707–13 (1991).

12. C. J. Schorah et al., *Internat. J. Vit. Res.* 58: 312–18 (1988).

13. E. Altenburger, *Klinische Wochenschrift* 15: 1129–31 (1936).

14. C. G. King, *J. Biol. Chem.* 116: 489–92 (1936); S. Banerjee, *J. Biol. Chem.* 168: 207–11 (1947); and S. Banners, *Nature* 152: 152 (1943).

15. J. Kersteer et al., *Metabolism* 40: 707–13 (1991).

16. O. Geddik and S. Akalin, *Diabetolgica* 29: 142–45 (1986).

17. G. Paolisso et al., *Am. J. Clin. Nutr.* 57: 650–56 (1993).

18. J. Durlach et al., *Magnesium* 2: 192–224 (1983); and G. Paolisso et al., *Diabetes Care* 12: 265–69 (1989).

19. R. Baltzan et al., *J. Clin. Invest.* 41: 108–14 (1962); P. J. Kesterns et al., *Metabolism* 12: 941–50 (1963); and R. A. DeFronzo et al., *Am. J. Physiol.* 238: E421–E427 (1980).

20. D. Rabinowitz and K. L. Zierler, *J. Clin. Invest.* 41: 2173–81 (1962); and R. A. DeFronzo, *Metabolism* 37: 105–8 (1988).

21. National Academy of Sciences, National Research Council, *Recommended Dietary Allowances* (9th ed.). Washington, DC: National Academy Press (1980); L. M. Klevay et al., *JAMA* 241: 1916–18 (1979); and J. M. Holden et al., *J. Am. Dietetic Assoc.* 79: 23–28 (1979).

22. S. J. Bhathena et al., *Eur. J. Clin. Nutr.* 42: 465–72 (1988).

23. P. J. Charley et al., *Biochem. Biophysc. Acta* 69: 313–21 (1963); M. Fields et al., *Am. J. Clin. Nutr.* 39: 289–95 (1984); M. Fields et al., *J. Nutr.* 113: 1335–45 (1983); S. Reiser et al., *Am. J. Clin. Nutr.* 38: 214–22 (1983); and S. Reiser et al., *Am. J. Clin. Nutr.* 42: 242–51 (1985).

24. R. A. Anderson and A. S. Kozlovsky, *Am. J. Clin. Nutr.* 41: 1177–83 (1985).

25. R. A. Anderson et al., *Am. J. Clin. Nutr.* 51: 864–68 (1990); W. Mertz, *Physiol. Rev.* 49: 163–239 (1969); and R. A. Anderson, *Clin. Physiol. Biochem.* 4: 31–41 (1986).

26. L. L. Hopkins et al., *Am. J. Clin. Nutr.* 21: 203–11 (1968); R. A. Levine et al., *Metabolism* 17: 114–25 (1968); L. L. Hopkins and M. G. Price, *Nutrition Congress* 2:40 (1968); W. H. Glinsmann and W. Mertz, *Metabolism* 15: 510–15 (1966); E. Glaser and G. Halpern, *Biochem. Z.* 207: 377–83 (1929); W. Mertz, in *Present Knowledge in Nutrition* 365–72 (1976); R. A. Anderson, *Metabolism* 36: 351–55 (1987); R. A. Anderson et al., *Am. J. Clin. Nutr.* 54: 909–16 (1991); R. W. Truman and R. J. Doisy, in *Trace Elements Metabol. in Animals*—2, J. W. Hoekstra, 678 (1974); and A. S. Abraham et al., *Metabolism* 41: 768–71 (1992).

27. R. G. Lefavi et al., *Inter J. Sports Nutr.* 2: 111–22 (1992); R. J. Moore and K. E. Friedl, *Nat. Strength Cond. Assoc. J.* 14: 47–51 (1992); P. M. Clarkson, *Inter J. Sports Nutr.* 1: 289–93 (1991); R. G. Lefavi, *Inter. J. Sports Nutr.* 3: 120–21 (1993); M. A. Hallmark et al., *Med. Sci. in Sports & Exercise* 25: S101 (1993); S. Clancey et al., *Med. Sci. in Sports & Exercise* 25: S194 (1993); C. J. Seal, *Ann. Nutr. Metbol.* 32: 186–91 (1988); D. L. Hasten et al. (conference abstract) S. E. Regional

Chapter, Am. College of Sports Med. (1991); J. A. Fernadez-Pol and G. S. Johnson, *Cancer Res.* 37: 4276–79 (1977); and K. R. Etzel et al., *Nutr. Res.* 8: 1391–1401 (1988).

28. M. Urberg and M. B. Zemel, *Metabolism* 36: 896–99 (1987); R. W. Squires et al., *Mayo Clin. Proc.* 67: 855–60 (1992); R. Lefavi et al., *FASEB J.* 5: A1645 (1991); and M. Urberg et al., *J. Family Practice* 27: 603–6 (1988).
29. J. E. Nester et al., *Diabetes Care* 11: 755–60 (1988).

Chapter 6

1. B. Linde et al., *Am. J. Physiol.* 256: E12–E18 (1989).
2. E. Hagstrom-Toft et al., *J. Clin. Endocrinol. Metabol.* 76: 392–98 (1993).
3. C. R. Kahn et al., *Endocrinol.* 10: 1054, 1066 (1978); and R. H. Rao et al., *Metabolism* 40: 1292–97 (1991).
4. R. H. Rao et al., *Metabolism* 40: 1292–97 (1991); W. P. T. James and H. G. Coore, *Am. J. Clin. Nutr.* 23: 386–89 (1970); G. C. Cook, *Metabolism* 17: 1073–83 (1968); and G. C. Cook, *Nature* 215: 1295–96 (1976).

Chapter 7

1. T. M. S. Wolever, *Metabolism* 39: 947–51 (1990).
2. J. A. Jenkins et al., *Am. J. Clin. Nutr.* 42: 604–17 (1985).
3. B. A. Swinburn et al., *J. Clin. Endocrinol. Metab.* 73: 156–65 (1991).
4. A. Walter et al., *Exerpta Medica*: 434–44 (1981).
5. W. E. Connor and S. L. Connor, *Med. Clin. N. Am.* 66: 485–518 (1982).
6. T. M. S. Wolever et al., *Diabetic Medicine* 9: 451–58 (1992).
7. A. M. Fontvielle et al., *Diabetic Medicine* 9: 444–50 (1992).
8. J. E. Blundell et al., *Int. J. Obesity* 11: (Suppl. 1): 9–25 (1987).
9. J. C. Brand et al., *Appetite* 18: 129–41 (1992).
10. P. Leathwood and P. Pollet, *Appetite* 10: 1–10 (1988).
11. J. Stevens et al., *Am. J. Clin. Nutr.* 46: 812–17 (1987).
12. A. S. Levine et al., *Am J. Clin. Nutr.* 50: 1303–7 (1989).
13. G. M. Ward et al., *Eur. J. Clin. Invest.* 12: 93–96 (1982); D. Porte and S. C. Woods, *Diabetologia* 20: 274–80 (1981); I. J. Stein et al., *Endocrinol.* 113: 299–301 (1983); J. Rodin et al., *Metabolism* 34: 826–31 (1985); S. J. Bhathena et al., *Proc. Soc. Exp. Biol. Med.* 181: 71–77 (1986); R. Schmid et al., *J. Clin. Endocrinol. Metabol.* 68: 1106 (1989); Y. B. Lombardo et al., *Horm. Metab. Res.* 25: 69–76 (1983); and N. Geary, *Neuroscience Behav. Rev.* 14: 323–338 (1990).
14. K. J. Achenson et al., *Am. J. Clin. Nutr.* 45: 78–85 (1987); Y.-J. Hannele et al., *Diabetes* 39: 157–67 (1990); G. D. Foster et al., *Am. J. Clin. Nutr.* 51: 167–72 (1990); and T. A. Wadden et al., *JAMA* 264: 707–11 (1980).

15. R. A. Mathieson et al., *Metabolism* 35: 394–99 (1986); and S. W. Spaulding et al., *J. Clin. Endocrinol. Metabol.* 46: 197–200 (1976).
16. M. F. Saad et al., *New Eng. J. Med.* 319: 1500–6 (1988).
17. J. C. Brand et al., *Am. J. Clin. Nutr.* 51: 416–20 (1990).
18. W. C. Knowler et al., *Am. J. Clin. Nutr.* 53: 1543S–51S (1991).
19. A. W. Thornburn et al., *Am. J. Clin. Nutr.* 46: 282–85 (1987).
20. Ibid.
21. B. A. Swinburn et al., *J. Clin. Endocrinol. Metab.* 73: 156–65 (1991).
22. J. C. Brand et al., *Diabetes Care* 14: 95–101 (1991).
23. D. J. A. Jenkins et al., *Am. J. Clin. Nutr.* 48: 248–54 (1988); and A. M. Fontevielle et al., *Diabetes Nutr. Metab.* 1: 139–44 (1988).
24. J. C. Brand et al., *Diabetes Care* 14: 95–101 (1991).
25. R. K. Bernstein, *Diabetes, Type II.* Englewood Cliffs, NJ: Prentice Hall (1990).
26. F. Grande et al., *J. Nutr.* 86: 313–17 (1965).
27. J. W. Anderson et al., *Am. J. Clin. Nutr.* 51: 1013–19 (1990).
28. R. Doll and R. Peto, *J. Nat. Cancer Inst.* 66: 1191–1308 (1981); and *Cancer Rates and Risks.* Washington, DC: National Cancer Institute (1985).
29. S. Graham et al., *J. Nat. Cancer. Inst.* 70: 687–92 (1983); and National Research Council, *Diet, Nutrition, and Cancer.* Washington DC: National Academy Press (1982).
30. A. S. Turstwell, *Eur. J. Clin. Nutr.* 46: (Suppl. 2): S91–S101 (1992).
31. D. E. Thomas et al., *Int. J. Sports Med.* 12: 180–86 (1991).

INDEX

Alcohol, 42, 56, 66, 242
Amino acids, 50
Animal fat, 32, 34
Animal products, 77
Appetite control, 22–23, 53, 90
Atherosclerosis, 31
Artificial sweeteners, 55
Avocados, 34

Bad Calorie foods:
  avoidance of, 30
  characteristics of, 51–52
  estrogen and, 24
  list of, by category, 192–234
  overview, 52–57
Bakery items, Good Calorie/ Bad Calorie list, 192–93
Bananas, 36, 38, 54, 242
Bean and pumpkin stew, 137
Bean dip, 67
Beef:
  Good Calorie/Bad Calorie list, 218
  hamburgers, 68
Beer, 56, 73, 193–94
Beverages:
  Good Calorie/Bad Calorie list, 193–94
Binges, see Food binges/ cravings
Birth control pills, 24, 75
Black-eyed pea salad, 123
Borscht, 128–29
Breads:
  Bad Calorie characteristics, 242

glycemic index of, 186
Good Calorie/Bad Calorie list, 192–93
Good Calorie characteristics, 241
pumpernickel, 46–47
rye, 46
unbuttered, 8
wheat, 52, 68
whole grain, 47
Breakfast food:
  cereals
    Bad Calorie characteristics, 54, 242
    glycemic index of, 187
    Good Calorie/Bad Calorie list, 194–95
    Good Calorie characteristics, 50, 241
Broccoli with lemon vinaigrette, 152
Burritos, 50
Butter, 32, 51
Butternut squash puree, 157

Cake, 52, 242
Calcium, 74
Candy, 34, 42
Canola oil, 34
Cantaloupe soup, 129
Capon, 226
Carbohydrates:
  conversion to blood sugar, 36
  fat-forming ability, 6–7
  overcooked, 36, 57
  unsaturated fats and, 32
Carrots, 50–52, 54, 242

Cereal grains, glycemic index of, 187
Cheese:
  Good Calorie/Bad Calorie list, 196–97
Chicken:
  and beet salad, 142
  Good Calorie/Bad Calorie list, 226
  Good Calorie characteristics of, 48, 241
  Good Calorie chicken salad, 144
  marinated chicken breasts, 144–45
  Mexican chicken fajitas, 147
  saturated fat in, 35, 71
  spicy chicken salad, 146
  spread, 226
Chicken noodle soup, 39
Chickpea flour "quiche," 139
Chili:
  Good Calorie/Bad Calorie list, 195–96
  Turkey Chili Diablo, 145
Chinese food:
  Good Calories in, 62
  restaurant tips for, 163–65
  rice, 36, 53
Cholesterol, 31, 73–74
Chromium, 73–74
Cigarette smoking, 43
Coconut oil, 34
Coffee, decaffeinated, 48
Condiments, 196
Cookies, 52, 242
Cooking oils, 34

Copper, 73, 74
Corn, 53, 242
Corn oil, 32–34, 51, 57
Corn syrup, 39, 42
Cottage cheese:
  Good Calorie/Bad Calorie
    list, 197
  nonfat, 48
  toasts, 152–53
Cranberry-ginger-orange
  relish, 153–54
Creamy winter squash soup,
  127
Cuban black bean soup, 125
Cucumber salad, 122

Dairy products:
  glycemic index of, 190
  Good Calorie/Bad Calorie
    list, 196–97
  low-fat, 48, 242
  saturated fats in, 34–35
  starches combined with, 68
Dates, 54
Desserts, glycemic index of,
  188
Diabetes, 71, 90, 92, 96
Dips:
  bean, 67
  dill-yogurt, 154
  horseradish, 156
  pinto bean, 155
  tzatziki: Greek cucumber-
    yogurt, 154
Dressings and sauces:
  avoidance of, 169
  black bean sauce, 149
  dill sauce, 142–43
  green sauce, 143
  high-fat dressing, 55–57
  lemon-mustard sauce, 148
  lemon vinaigrette, 152
  olive oil dressing, 56
  oriental dressing, 122
  shiitake mushroom sauce,
    138
  vinegar-herb dressing, 122
  yellow bell-pepper sauce,
    153
Drinks, see Beverages
Duck, 226

Eggplant-tomato stew, 136
Entrees, Good Calorie/Bad
    Calorie list:
  canned, 209–10
  frozen and refrigerated,
    210–14
Enzymes, 20, 24
Estrogen, 14, 23–24, 75
Ethnic foods, glycemic index
    of, 189. See also specific
    types of ethnic foods
Exercise:
  Bad Calories and, 43–44
  drinks, 97
  excessive, 3
  types of, 43–44
  weight loss and, 83

Fast foods:
  Bad Calorie characteristics,
    55, 242
  restaurant tips for, 166–
    69
Fat, 2, 14–15, 31, 91
Fat cells, 20
Fat formation, avoidance
    factors, 72
Fatty foods, see High-fat foods
Fish:
  bass, 48
  clams, 48
  cod, 48
  crab, 48
  flounder, 48
    with lemon-mustard
      sauce, 148
  Good Calorie/Bad Calorie
    list, 214–15
  Good Calorie
    characteristics, 48–49,
      241
  grilled, 70
  haddock, 48
  halibut, 48
    grilled with green sauce,
      143
  lobster, 73
  mussels, New Orleans
    fettucine with, 143–44
  oysters, 73
  perch, 48

salmon
  and black bean sauce,
    149
  unsaturated fat in, 49
sashimi, 175
scallops, 48
scrod, 48
sea bass, grilled, with dill
  sauce, 142–43
shrimp, 48, 73
  with lemon and ginger,
    148–49
  with tomatoes, 146–47
snapper, 48
starches combined with, 53,
  68
sushi, 175
trout, 48
tuna, canned, 48, 68
Food binges/cravings, 13, 20,
  39, 71, 73, 78, 90
French/continental-style food,
  169–70
French fries, 34, 53
Frozen dinners/entrees:
  Good Calorie/Bad Calorie
    list, 197–209
  Good Calorie
    characteristics, 49,
      242
Fructose, 39–42, 55, 73, 242
Fruit:
  baked tomatoes, 149–50
  dried, 49, 54, 242
  glycemic index of, 189–90
  Good Calorie/Bad Calorie
    list, 215–17
  Good Calorie
    characteristics, 49, 242
  overly ripe, 36–37, 49
  as snack, 67
Fruit drinks, 38, 56
Fruit ice ("granita"), 159
Fruit juice, 56, 242

Gazpacho, 131
Genetic inheritance,
    impact of,
    14-15, 60
Glucagon, 22, 68
Glucocorticoid, 83

Glycemic index:
  of common foods
    breads, 186
    breakfast cereals, 187
    cereal grains, 187
    dairy products, 190
    desserts, 188
    ethnic foods/meals, 189
    fruit, 189–90
    legumes, 188–89
    pasta, 186
    rice and rice products, 187
    root vegetables, 188
    snack foods, 190
    sugars, 190
  defined, 7, 9
  saturated fats, 33
  unsaturated fats, 33
  weight loss and, 8
Glycogen, 18, 22, 73
Good Calorie chicken salad,
    144
Good Calorie Diet:
  benefits of, 92, 96–97
  cookbook sources for, 118–
    20
  overview, 241
  recipes, 121–59
  two-stage program, 30, 58.
    See also Starvation
    Response
Good Calorie foods:
  characteristics of, 3, 10, 46–
    51
  list of, by category, 192–
    234 '
Goose, 226–27
"Granita" (fruit ice), 159
Grilled halibut with green
    sauce, 143
Grilled sea bass with dill
    sauce, 142–43

HDL triglycerides, 88–89
High-fat foods:
  avoidance of, 31–32
  Bad Calorie characteristics,
    57, 242
Hormones:
  effect of, 13–14, 65
  glycogen, 18, 22, 73

Horseradish and beet puree,
    156
Horseradish dip, 156
Hot dogs, 218
Hyperglycemia, 7
Hypoglycemia, 7–8, 96

Ice cream:
  Good Calorie/Bad Calorie
    list, 197
  nonfat, 48
Indian dal (lentil) soup, 126–
    27
Indian food, Good Calories in,
    62
Insulin, 22, 24, 39, 54, 74
Insulin resistance:
  anabolic steroids and, 44
  artificial sweeteners and, 55
  chromium and, 74
  defined, 22
  exercise, effect on, 43
  fructose and, 39
  Starvation Response and, 24
Italian food:
  Good Calories in, 62
  restaurant tips for, 170–74

Jam:
  avoidance of, 42
  sugar-free strawberry, 158
Japanese food:
  Good Calories in, 62
  restaurant tips for, 175–77
Jasmine rice and split peas, 150

Kidney beans, 39
Kidneys, 218

Lactose intolerance, 48
Lamb, 218
Legumes:
  canned, 39, 50
  glycemic index of, 188–89
  Good Calorie/Bad Calorie
    list, 217
  Good Calorie
    characteristics, 49–50,
    242
  vegetable proteins
    combined with, 71

Lentils:
  canned, 39
  glycemic index, 50
  lentil-stuffed zucchini,
    140
  stew with garlic and ginger,
    137
Linguini with shiitake
    mushroom sauce, 138
Lipids, 24
Lipoprotein lipase activity, 20,
    24
Liver:
  chromium and, 73
  Good Calorie/Bad Calorie
    list, 218
Low-density lipoproteins
    (LDLs), 96
Low-fat diets, 31–32
Luncheon meats, 219–21

Magnesium, 73, 74
Margarine, 33, 51
Marinated chicken breasts,
    144–45
Marinated green tomato salad,
    121
Meal planning:
  and animal products, 111–
    17
  dinner, 66–67
  Good Calorie meals before
    Bad Calorie meals, 76–
    78
  lunch, 65–66, 77
  parties, 77–78
  sample menus, 101–17
  vegetarian, 103–11
Meat:
  Bad Calorie characteristics,
    55, 242
  Good Calorie/Bad Calorie
    list
    luncheon meat, 219–21
    overview, 218–19
    substitutes, 221–22
  saturated fats in, 34–35
  starches combined with, 68
Mexican food:
  burritos, 50
  chicken fajitas, 147

Mexican food (*continued*)
  Good Calorie
    characteristics, 50, 62
  restaurant tips for, 177–79
Middle Eastern chickpea-
  cabbage soup, 128
Milk, nonfat, 48
Mineral supplements, 72–74
Minestrone, 39
Miso soup with scallions and
  seaweed, 131
Mung bean–tomato stew, 134–
  35
Mushrooms, 73

New Orleans fettucine with
  mussels, 143–44
Nuts:
  glycemic index, 54
  Good Calorie/Bad Calorie
    list, 223
  saturated fat in, 34

Oatmeal:
  instant, 36, 48, 54
  slow-cooked, 48, 54, 242
Olive oil, 32, 34, 51–53, 56–
  57
Orange-glazed turkey breast,
  147–48
Oriental dressing, 122
Oriental sweet potato stew,
  135–36
Osteoporosis, 71
Overcooked foods, 36, 53, 57,
  242

Palm oil, 34
Pasta:
  canned, 39, 54
  glycemic index of, 8, 186
  Good Calorie/Bad Calorie
    list, 223–24
  Good Calorie
    characteristics, 47–48,
    68, 242
  linguini with shiitake
    mushroom sauce, 138
  New Orleans fettucine with
    mussels, 143–44
  overcooked, 36

pasta fagioli, 141–42
pasta primavera, 141
Pastries, 52, 242
Peanut oil, 34
Pinto bean dip, 155
Pizza:
  frozen, 224–25
  Good Calorie/Bad Calorie
    list, 224–25
  Good Calorie
    characteristics, 49, 68,
    242
  restaurant tips for, 168,
    171
Popcorn, 57, 242
Pork, 219
Potassium, 73, 74
Potatoes:
  Bad Calorie characteristics,
    52–53, 242
  baked, 8
  blood sugar and, 50
  Good Calorie/Bad Calorie
    list, 231
  mashed, 52
  overcooked, 36, 57
Poultry:
  Good Calorie/Bad Calorie
    list, 226–27
  starches combined with, 53,
    68
Processed foods:
  avoidance of, 38
  Bad Calorie characteristics,
    57, 242
  saturated fats in, 34
Protein:
  intake limitations, 55
  at lunch, 66, 77
  starches combined with, 34,
    47–48, 53, 68–70
Psyllium, 50

Raisins, 54
Red and green salad, 122
Red bean pistou, 132
Red meat, *see* Meat
Rice:
  Bad Calorie characteristics,
    242
  glycemic index of, 187

Good Calorie/Bad Calorie
  list, 227–28
  instant, 53
  jasmine and split peas, 150
  overcooked, 36, 53, 56, 164
  pilaf, 157–58
  saffron, 158
Rice cakes, 8, 53, 242
Rice drinks, 53, 242
Rice pilaf, 157–58

Safflower oil, 34
Saffron rice, 158
Salad dressing, *see* Dressings
  and sauces
Salads:
  black-eyed pea, 123
  chicken and beet, 142
  cucumber, 122
  Good Calorie chicken, 144
  high-fat salad dressing and,
    55–56, 242
  marinated green tomato, 121
  protein combined with, 70
  red and green, 122
  spicy chicken, 145
  three-bean, 121
  wild rice, 123
Salmon and black bean sauce,
  149
Sandwiches, 70
Saturated fats:
  avoidance of, 32–36
  intake limitations, 55
Seafood, *see* Fish
Serotonin, 22, 71
Sesame oil, 34
Shrimps with lemon and
  ginger, 148–49
Shrimps with tomatoes, 146–47
Side dishes:
  baked tomatoes, 149–50
  cottage cheese toasts, 152–53
  cranberry-ginger-orange
    relish, 153–54
  dill-yogurt dip, 154
  fresh broccoli with lemon
    vinaigrette, 152
  fruit ice ("granita"), 159
  Good Calorie vegetable
    medley, 151–52

Side dishes (*continued*)
  horseradish and beet puree, 156
  horseradish dip, 156
  jasmine rice and split peas, 150
  pinto bean dip, 155
  puree of butternut squash, 157
  rice pilaf, 157–58
  saffron rice, 158
  savory baked yams, 156
  stewed tomatoes and okra, 155
  sugar-free strawberry jam, 158
  tzatziki: Greek cucumber-yogurt dip, 154
  white beans and garlic puree, 151
  yellow bell-pepper sauce, 153
Snacks:
  frequency of, 59
  glycemic index of, 190
  Good Calorie/Bad Calorie list, 228–29
  late-night, 13–14, 66, 75
Soft drinks, 48, 56, 242
Soups:
  basic vegetable stock, No. 1, 124
  basic vegetable stock, No. 2, 124–25
  borscht, 128–29
  canned, 54, 229–30
  canned pasta in, 39
  cantaloupe, 129
  creamy winter squash, 127
  Cuban black bean, 125
  gazpacho, 131
  Good Calorie/Bad Calorie list, 229–30
  Indian dal (lentil), 126–27
  Middle Eastern chickpea-cabbage, 128
  miso with scallions and seaweed, 131
  overcooked carbohydrates in, 36
  red bean pistou, 132

  spinach and garlic, 133
  spring asparagus, 130
  tomato-herb, 126
  Turkish cucumber-yogurt, 133
  vegetable medley, 134
Soybean oil, 34
Soybeans, 50
Soy drinks, 194
Spicy chicken salad, 146
Spinach and garlic soup, 133
Spring asparagus soup, 130
Starches, 34, 39, 47–48, 53, 68–70
Starvation Response:
  blood sugar conversion, 18
  caloric restriction and, 15, 67
  curing, 70
  Good Calories and, 88–90
  metabolism and, 2
  stress and, 83–84
  symptoms of, 11–14, 75
  triggering foods, 72, 241
  in women, 23–24
Stews:
  bean and pumpkin, 137
  eggplant-tomato, 136
  lentil with garlic and ginger, 137
  mung bean–tomato, 134–35
  oriental sweet potato, 135–36
  overcooked carbohydrates in, 36
Sugar:
  glycemic index of, 190
  Good Calorie/Bad Calorie list, 230
Sunflower oil, 34
Sweet potatoes, 53
  oriental sweet potato stew, 135–36
  see also Yams

Tea, 48
Three-bean salad, 121
Tofu, 55, 242

Tomatoes:
  baked, 149–50
  stewed, and okra, 155
Tomato-herb soup, 126
Triglycerides, 18–19, 24, 39, 68, 73–74. *See also* HDL triglycerides
Turkey:
  Good Calorie/Bad Calorie list, 227
  orange-glazed turkey breast, 147–48
  saturated fat in, 35, 71
  turkey chili diablo, 145
Turkish cucumber-yogurt soup, 133
Tzatziki: Greek cucumber-yogurt dip, 154

Unsaturated fats, 32–36

Veal, 219
Vegetable oils, 34
Vegetables:
  Broccoli with lemon vinaigrette, 152
  Good Calorie/Bad Calorie list
    canned, 231
    fresh, 230–31
    frozen, 232–34
  Good Calorie characteristics, 50–51, 242
  Good Calorie medley, 151–52
  overcooked, 36
  protein combined with, 70
  roasted, 140
  root, glycemic index of, 188
  soup stock, 124–25
  winter puree, 138–39
Vegetarian food:
  sample menus, 103–11
  recipes, 134–42
Vinegar-herb dressing, 122
Vitamins:
  deficiencies, 72–73
  recommended supplements, 74

Index

Weight loss:
    failure of, 75, 80–87
    fat-burning process and,
      2
    hormonal flows and, 14
    rate of, 3

Wheat flour, 46–47
White beans and garlic puree,
    151
Wild rice salad, 123
Winter vegetable puree, 138–
    39

Yams, 53
    savory baked, 156
Yeast, brewer's, 73
Yellow bell-pepper sauce, 153

Zinc, 74

THE GOOD CALORIE DIET: AN OVERVIEW

TRIGGERS OF THE STARVATION RESPONSE
Foods high in fat
Saturated fats; substitute unsaturated fats
Overcooked carbohydrates
Overly ripe fruit
Processed foods
Canned starches & legumes
Fructose
Alcohol before a meal
Smoking before a meal
Bad Calories before and during exercise

THE RULES EVERYONE MUST INITIALLY FOLLOW
1. Eat primarily Good Calories.
2. Combine Good and Bad Calories to make a four to one ratio.
3. Eat Good Calorie breakfasts.
4. Eat the most fattening food for lunch, not dinner.
5. Eat Good Calorie snacks.
6. Don't miss a meal.
7. Avoid combining excessive amounts of animal protein with starches and ripe fruit.
8. Avoid excessive amounts of animal products while overcoming the Starvation Response.
9. Avoid the Starvation Response triggers.
10. Avoid vitamin and mineral deficiencies.

RULES TO FOLLOW AFTER OVERCOMING THE STARVATION RESPONSE
11. Eat Good Calories preceding and following Bad Calorie meals.
12. Find your personal limits of freedom.

GOOD CALORIES

BREAD: Rye bread with no wheat flour or whole grain bread made from whole, unmilled, wheat kernels.

BREAKFAST CEREALS: Most are Bad Calories; however, Kellogg's Heartwise and Fiberwise cereals, Extra All Bran and General Mills's Fiber One are Good Calories.

CHICKEN TURKEY: Skinless low-fat meats, except wings and thighs. Do not combine with starches.

DRINKS: Decaffeinated and without fructose or corn syrup sweeteners.

FISH: High in good unsaturated fats: striped bass, clams, cod, crab, haddock, halibut, perch, northern pike, salmon (Atlantic, Coho, pink), scallops, shrimp, sea bass, snapper, trout, tuna, whitefish, and whiting. Avoid fish with saturated fats: abalone, catfish, gefilte fish, lobster, mussels, oyster, pompano, roughy, sablefish, salmon (Chinook, Chum), sea trout, sturgeon, and swordfish.

FROZEN DINNERS & ENTREES: Good Calories predominate among these brands: Armour Classics, Armour Dinner Classics Light, Banquet Gourmet Light & Healthy, Budget Gourmet Slim Selects, Healthy Choice, Kraft Eating Right, Lean Cuisine, Le Menu Healthy, Le Menu Light Style, Stouffer's Right Course, Tyson Loony Tunes, Ultra Slim Fast, Weight Watchers. Avoid high fat or starch.

FRUIT: Avoid dried fruits, fruits packaged in syrup, and overly ripe fruit.

LEGUMES (BEANS): Combining legumes (peas and beans) with other foods is extremely beneficial.

LOW-FAT DAIRY PRODUCTS

OATMEAL: Slow-cooked oatmeal only.

PASTA: Serve with limited amounts of animal protein.

PIZZA: Make sure that less than 30% of the calories come from fat, typically a thin-crust pizza with slightly less than a single portion of cheese and no meat toppings. Avoid deep-dish pizzas.

VEGETABLES: Avoid carrots and potatoes.

VEGETARIAN CHILI

BAD CALORIES

ALCOHOL: includes beer.

BREAKFAST CEREALS

BREADS, COOKIES, CAKES, & PASTRIES: Even "diet" products are bad.

CANNED & DEHYDRATED SOUPS

CANNED PASTA

CARROTS

CORN: Avoid corn chips, taco shells and fresh corn.

DRIED FRUIT

FAST FOOD: Resist french fries and sandwiches.

FRUCTOSE SWEETENER

HIGH-FAT FOODS

INSTANT & OVERCOOKED RICE

INSTANT OR PROCESSED FOODS

OVERCOOKED FOODS

POPCORN

POTATOES: Yams and sweet potatoes are Good Calorie alternatives.

RED MEAT: Eat protein early in the day. Separate from the next meal by several hours. Avoid successive meals that feature protein. Eat only low-fat meats.

RICE CAKES & DRINKS

RIPE BANANAS

SALADS WITH HIGH-FAT SALAD DRESSING

SUGARED SOFT DRINKS JUICES

TOFU